This book is to be returned on or before
the last date stamped below.

HUANAINEN, M.

A STUDY ON THE ORIGINS OF MENTAL RETARDATION

Clinics in Developmental Medicine No. 51

A Study on the Origins of Mental Retardation

by

MATTI IIVANAINEN

1974

Spastics International Medical Publications

LONDON : William Heinemann Medical Books Ltd.

PHILADELPHIA : J. B. Lippincott Co.

DED

ISBN 0 433 16300 3

Printed in England at THE LAVENHAM PRESS LTD., Lavenham, Suffolk

Contents

Preface

Until recently, more attention has been paid to the classification and placement of patients suffering from mental retardation than to their comprehensive clinical study. There have been somewhat random genetic, chromosomal and biochemical studies of series of mentally handicapped patients in institutions and in the community; unfortunately many of these have not been related to detailed clinical assessments. It is still too common, in hospitals for the mentally retarded, to find that clinical documentation of patients is scanty, even when reports from psychologists, social workers, therapists, and nurses may be relatively profuse.

The apparent lack of interest in the neurological aspects of their patients shown by many psychiatrists may be due, in part, to the fact that they lack expertise in neurological assessment, and do not fully appreciate what can be learnt by modern techniques of electroencephalographic and neuroradiological investigation. The paucity of reliable recent neurological, neuroradiological and neuropathological studies is indicated by Dr. Iivanainen in his 'Review of the Literature' in this monograph. The criteria for inclusion of patients in some of the selected series studied are inadequately described; in others reports of histories or clinical findings (especially neurological investigations) have been found wanting.

Dr. Iivanainen is fully aware of the importance of environmental factors in causing and exacerbating the effects of mental retardation. He discusses, at least by implication, the concept of 'sub-cultural mental retardation'. However, in this work he is predominantly concerned to demonstrate that careful history taking and examination, with further neurological and especially neuroradiological investigations, may define causes of severe mental retardation.

Dr. Iivanainen is careful to point out that his series of 338 patients subjected to detailed investigation is a selected one. It comprises predominantly patients with severe degrees of mental defect in the Rinnekoti Institution. He says that he sets out to answer two questions: '(1) In what ways do the clinical findings correlate with the aetiology of the mental retardation? (2) Of what value are neuroradiological methods in the aetiological diagnosis of mental retardation?' His meticulous clinical studies, supplemented by beautiful air encephalograms, electroencephalographic and other investigations, go a long way to providing the answers to his questions. He agrees with Hagne (1962) 'that it should be possible to make a fairly accurate aetiological diagnosis in about 90 per cent of patients suffering from mental retardation—at least in selected groups'. Dr. Iivanainen's work justifies his claim that 'the same care should be taken in investigating and prescribing treatment for the mentally retarded as is taken with patients of normal intelligence'.

Dr. Iivanainen's dedicated work makes a considerable advance in our understanding of the causes of severe mental retardation. It is to be hoped that other doctors will be stimulated by it to undertake similar studies of differently selected patients in their care.

T. T. S. Ingram

ACKNOWLEDGEMENTS

My teacher in neurosciences, Professor Erkki Kivalo, Head of the Department of Neurology, University of Helsinki, gave me the opportunity to use modern neurological techniques in the study of the aetiology of mental retardation. The idea was to perform neurological examinations on mentally retarded patients according to the same principles as would be applied in the examination of patients of normal intelligence. I am extremely grateful to Professor Kivalo for his far-sightedness in encouraging the use of neuroscientific methods in the field of developmental neurology and especially in the aetiological study of mental retardation.

Dr. Risto Collan performed the majority of the general anaesthesias in connection with this study, and has helped to show that in skilful hands neuroradiological methods are not dangerous, even for the mentally retarded.

The cytogenetic examinations were performed by Ulla Gripenberg, Ph.D., and Karin Hongell, B.Sc., the neuropathological examinations by Dr. Matti Haltia, and the psychological examinations by Harriet Lindgren, M.A. The statistical analyses were made by Pekka Sarvala, M.A., in the computer centre, University of Helsinki.

The heads and staff of other institutions for the mentally retarded and of a number of hospitals in Finland have helped me in connection with the present work. Numerous persons from the University of Helsinki have given criticism and advice in the preparation of the manuscript, in particular Dr. Märta Donner, Dr. Viljo Halonen, Dr. Jorma Palo, Dr. Mauro Roukkula and Dr. Anna-Maija Seppäläinen. Dr. Martin C. O. Bax revised the English. Thanks to all of you.

This study was supported by the National Pensions Institute of Finland, the National Welfare Association for the Mentally Deficient in Finland (Kehitysvammaliitto r.y.), Oy Medica Ab, Co Nyegarrd Ab, and the North Savo Fund of the Finnish Cultural Foundation, which I gratefully acknowledge.

I dedicate this book to the patients and their families. Their helpful and co-operative attitude has made easier the task of shedding light on the aetiology of mental retardation. It is only in such an atmosphere of co-operation that researchers in the field of mental retardation can expect to achieve their goal, which in the short term must be to establish which methods of treatment and rehabilitation will be of most benefit to the patients and indirectly their families, and, in the long-term, the prevention of mental retardation.

Matti Iivanainen

Introduction

A precise and early knowledge of the cause(s) and clinical manifestations of a disease is a basic requirement if prevention and/or effective treatment are to be instituted. This applies equally to mental retardation as to other diseases.

Traditionally, mentally retarded patients were classified into various groups according to their external physical characteristics. Hippocrates and Galen knew the forms of mental retardation associated with certain cranial deformities such as anencephaly and hydrocephalus. However, until comparatively recently, medical science was unable to explain the aetiology of inborn defects, or to suggest any remedy, and thus the door was left open for superstitious speculations and platitudes. In 1603 Paracelsus described among other things cretinism, and wondered why God allowed such defective children to be born (see Øster 1968).

It was during the 19th century that medical workers first began to differentiate between the various forms of mental retardation on a less superficial level. Little (1861) described a neurological syndrome due to brain lesion following birth injury and characterised by convulsions, spasticity and mental retardation. Shortly afterwards, mongolism or Down's syndrome (Langdon Down 1866) and tuberous sclerosis (Bourneville 1880) were also recognised and described.

The 20th century saw the advent of neuroradiological (Dandy 1918, Moniz 1927) and neurophysiological (Berger 1929) methods, which provided considerably better tools for neurological diagnostics. When biochemical (Følling 1934) and cytogenetical (Lejeune *et al.* 1959) investigations were initiated, the basic elements were present for more dynamic research in the field of mental retardation. However, even though detailed research into neurological symptoms has been carried out for more than ten years in patients of normal intelligence, it does not appear to have been extensively applied to cases of mental retardation.

Although, ultimately, information about the aetiology of mental retardation may come from autopsy findings, such studies do not benefit existing patients. On the other hand, the findings of pneumoencephalography combined with other neuroradiological methods correlate closely with those of autopsy, and so make investigation possible during life. Such studies early in life may open up new possibilities for treatment and rehabilitation; in addition, they may throw more light on the aetiology than autopsies in older patients in whom changes relating to age may obscure the basic pathology.

The fact that the aetiological diagnosis of mental retardation in a great number of patients is unspecified and very often unknown is *per se* an indication that the most careful investigation is required in order to elucidate the aetiology of mental retardation at the earliest possible age.

The present monograph describes the results of an investigation into the aetiology of mental retardation in a large number of patients, using current neuroradiological and other methods. It also contains an evaluation of these methods. It is hoped that the results will arouse interest in this type of research, and encourage other clinical research workers to investigate larger populations of mentally retarded people than has hitherto been the case.

CHAPTER 1

Review of the Literature

Classifications of the Degree of Mental Retardation

Several classifications of the degree of mental retardation exist (Gelof 1963). They are all based on the intellectual abilities and social behaviour of the patient, as measured by psychological tests.

The classification of mental retardation into 'mild' and 'severe' forms is traditional, and is useful in daily practice (Penrose 1963*b*).

The old classification of the World Health Organization (WHO) (1948) consisted of four classes: border-line (IQ 70 to 89), feeble-minded (IQ 50 to 69), imbecile (IQ 20 to 49) and idiot (IQ < 20). The feeble-minded are those who, though unsuitable for normal elementary schooling, may later be fairly independent and able to live without constant care, if their learning, education and vocational training are looked after. Imbeciles may be able to perform some simple tasks and do well with the aid of other people in a sheltered environment, but are unable to live independently under any circumstances. Idiots need continuous care in everything, including the performance of daily living functions.

This tripartite classification (the border-line cases not being considered as mentally-retarded) was revised by dividing the group classified as imbeciles into two sub-groups, and by slightly modifying the IQ limits of the various classes (Heber 1959). In this modified classification, the categories 'high-grade imbeciles' and 'feeble-minded' (or simpleton morons or 'debiles') can be considered to be equivalent to the old 'mild' form, while the idiots and low-grade imbeciles correspond to the old 'severe' cases of mental retardation.

The present WHO classification of the degree of mental retardation is the same as Heber's classification. It was recommended by the WHO in 1968 and is as follows:

border-line (IQ about 68 to 85)
mild (IQ 52 to 67)
moderate (IQ 36 to 51)
severe (IQ 20 to 35)
profound (IQ < 20) and
unspecified.

Partly because of testing difficulties, there is a great deal of overlapping between the various groups in this somewhat artificial system of classification. The characteristics of each class are not therefore specific.

Classifications of the Causes of Mental Retardation

Various classifications of the causes of mental retardation have been suggested. Traditionally, mentally retarded patients were separated into two categories, according to when the brain was thought to have been affected. The first group comprised patients with a 'congenital' form, with its origin before birth, and the second comprised patients with an 'acquired' form, of postnatal origin. However, this classification is unsatisfactory, because (1) it cannot be assumed that a disease, just because it manifests itself postnatally, does not have a prenatal origin, (2) 'congenital' confuses hereditary cases with those in which the prenatal environment has proved unfavourable to the fetus, and (3) injuries which occur during birth are difficult to ascribe to either class.

Another, more usual classification separates mentally retarded cases in which the origin is in the germ cells from those in which the origin is environmental. Typical hereditary causes are common genes (multiple additive genes, sex chromosome aberrations) in 'mild' cases, and rare specific genes (autosomal aberrations) in 'severe' cases. Typical environmental causes are deprivation in 'mild' cases, and prenatal maternal influence (such as toxoplasmosis infections) in 'severe' cases. The traditional terms 'endogenous' and 'exogenous' and the terms 'primary' and 'secondary' introduced by Tredgold (1908) have been widely used to define the two groups of causes in this system of classification.

The system of classification suggested by Yannet (1945, 1956), which is basically a more detailed development of the two systems described above, involves four main aetiological categories of mental retardation: 'prenatal', 'perinatal', 'postnatal', and 'genetic'. In the present study, Yannet's ideas are modified by using the following five categories:

(1) prenatal,
(2) perinatal,
(3) postnatal,
(4) multiple aetiological timepoints, and
(5) unknown aetiological timepoint.

This system of classification is called Yannet's classification throughout this volume.

According to Yannet, genetic and prenatal factors together are responsible for about 90 per cent of all cases of mental retardation, while three per cent are due to perinatal and seven per cent to postnatal factors. However, according to Lelong and Satgé (1962), about one third of cerebral lesions in childhood are due to prenatal (including genetic) disorders, one third to birth injuries, and one third to postnatal factors. The results of other investigations fall somewhere between these two extremes (Penrose 1938, Halperin 1945, Malamud 1954, Pitt and Roboz 1965, Covernton 1967, Freytag and Lindenberg 1967). The differences are essentially attributable to variations in the selection of material and in the methods of investigation used. A basic flaw of all such investigations is that true figures for the incidences of different forms of mental retardation in the whole population are almost impossible to assess, because the majority of very severe cases (e.g. those lost in spontaneous abortions) and also of very mild cases (e.g. those who are living unrecognised in society) are not investigated.

Another approach towards the problem of how to classify the clinical manifestations of mental retardation was the extension of the 'endogenous/exogenous' system of classification by subdividing these two categories into various sub-groups (Larsen 1931, Penrose 1938, Halperin 1945, Thomas 1957).

2

When considering all these different systems of classification, it must be remembered, as Wildenskov (1934) and Penrose (1938) pointed out, that both genetic and environmental factors can combine to produce the end result of mental deficiency. The abnormal organism may elicit abnormal responses from the environment, and these themselves may lead to further deviation from normal development. It may well be impossible to separate these two strands, even at birth, and by the time a child reaches the age of seven or eight years it is often impossible to say to what extent retardation could have been ameliorated if adverse environmental factors had not been operative.

Heber's system of classification divides mental retardation into eight categories, 36 (Heber 1959) or 39 (Heber 1961) sub-categories, and several sub-groups. This classification differs from Yannet's classification in that it lays more emphasis on the presumed cause of the retardation and less on the actual timing of the insult. The eight main categories are as follows:

I   Infection
II   Intoxication
III   Trauma or physical agent
IV   Disorder of metabolism, growth or nutrition
V   New growths
VI   Unknown prenatal influence
VII   Unknown or uncertain cause, with the structural reactions manifest
VIII Uncertain or presumed psychological cause, with the functional reaction alone manifest

According to Benda (1960), there is an association between the degree of mental retardation and its aetiology. Only about 20 per cent of cases of mild retardation (IQ 50 to 75) are attributable to exogenous factors (pre-, peri- and postnatal developmental disturbances and childhood diseases), whereas 80 per cent are caused by endogenous factors (minor variations and hereditary factors, in equal proportions). On the other hand, amongst cases of severe retardation (IQ less than 50), the relative incidence of different aetiological forms in Benda's study was as follows: prenatal developmental disorders—40 per cent; birth injuries—25 per cent; infections—15 per cent; and metabolic and degenerative diseases, neoplasms and unknown psychoses —20 per cent. Benda's aetiological classification of 175 cases of severe mental retardation into nine categories is set out in Table I.

Slight modifications to Heber's system of classification were made by Pitt and Roboz (1965) and Roboz and Pitt (1968a). One sub-category (toxaemia of pregnancy) was omitted, while five new sub-categories (oxygen intoxication—retrolental fibroplasia in category II; dwarfism, chromosomal abnormalities and hereditary syndromes in category VI; epilepsy in category VII) and some new criteria for classification were introduced. A new category called 'encephalopathy due to more than one probable cause' was added as category IX.

The aetiological classification of mental retardation presented in the 8th revision of the International Classification of Diseases was a modification of Heber's classification and was recommended by the World Health Organization in 1968.

TABLE I

Aetiological classification of mental retardation of 175 autopsy cases from the Walter E. Fernald
State School between 1947 and 1957 (Benda 1960)

Aetiological category	No. of cases	Per cent
Malformations	49	28
Encephalomalacia	39	22
Oligocephaly	29	17
Down's syndrome	21	12
Disorders of metabolism	10	6
Infections	9	5
Neoplasms	6	3
Heredo-degenerative diseases	2	1
Unclassified	10	6
TOTAL	175	100

The ten main categories of this classification are as follows:

(.0) Infections and Intoxications
(.1) Trauma or physical agents
(.2) Disorders of metabolism, growth or nutrition
(.3) Gross brain disease (postnatal)
(.4) Diseases and conditions due to unknown prenatal influence
(.5) Chromosomal abnormalities
(.6) Prematurity
(.7) Major psychiatric disorder
(.8) Psycho-social (environmental) deprivation
(.9) Other and unspecified

In the past few years, attempts have been made to standardize both the medical classification of mental retardation based on aetiological and pathogenetic criteria, and also the classification based on behavioural and psychological criteria. Thus, the results of different investigations can be expected to become more comparable than has previously been the case, as well as being more useful for preventive and therapeutic purposes.

Previous Studies on the Aetiology of Mental Retardation, Using Other Than Neuroradiological Techniques

Sociological Studies

Unfavourable environmental conditions are known to affect a child's development, and, both directly and indirectly, to cause mental retardation (see Category 8 of the WHO's classification). Generally, there are many more mildly retarded children in the lower than in the higher social classes, and, although cases of severe retardation are much more evenly distributed, it seems that these too may occur more frequently in the lower social classes (Birch et al. 1970). Economic, medical and biological factors probably combine to produce this pattern (Penrose 1963b). The influence of social class upon the intellectual development of a child may distort the assessment of his intelligence level. It would, therefore, be wiser to compare the test scores of children within the same social class rather than to compare them with the scores of the general population. This would serve the dual purpose of uncovering mental retardation where it exists, and of preventing deficiencies of the developmental environment from being confused with deficiencies of native ability (Jedrysek *et al.* 1968). Thus, the examination of social classes may reveal important facts about the aetiology of mental retardation.

Mental retardation as a whole poses very striking *social* problems (O'Connor and Tizard 1956, Stein and Susser 1963). Very full discussions of these problems have recently been presented (*e.g.* by Tizard 1970).

Studies Based on Clinical History and Physical and Psychiatric Examinations

The traditional approach towards the examination of the mentally subnormal child is that described by, for example, Paine and Oppé (1966). Family history, including information about previous miscarriages, is elicited. A careful account is obtained of the relevant pregnancy and the ensuing delivery. A medical development history is also taken, after which the child is given a full physical, psychiatric and psychological examination. The care with which these procedures have been carried out has varied considerably, and the present study suggests that history-taking and examination should be carried out much more carefully in future. Zappella (1964) emphasised the value of a full neurological examination of handicapped children. The characteristics of many syndromes associated with mental retardation were reviewed by Carter (1965, 1966).

O'Gorman (1967) drew attention to the relationship between psychological and/ or psychiatric disorders and mental retardation. The identification of a particular disorder may make it possible to initiate treatment, the outcome of which is so successful that opinions about the patient's intellectual status have to be radically altered. Thus, some autistic children prove to have almost intact intellectual function. Sometimes, too, surprising improvement may follow the control of seizures (Blaw and Torres 1967). In such instances the term pseudo-retardation may be used.

An erroneous diagnosis of mental retardation may cause irreparable harm to the future of the child and his family (Huntley 1967). Visual disorders, hearing defects, speech disorders, and severe cerebral palsy have all lead to such misdiagnosis. All physical disease affects intellectual functioning, and the combined effects of, for example, chronic disease, malnutrition and hospitalisation may have both short- and long-term consequences for intellectual status.

Biochemical, Microbiological and Serological Studies

A number of screening tests are now available which make it possible to detect metabolic disorders in the mentally retarded. Rather than discuss all these tests in detail, I propose merely to list the more important ones. Firstly, there are certain routine haematological tests—*e.g.* sedimentation rate, leucocytes, vacuoles in leucocytes (Bagh and Hortling 1946), and the complement fixation test of Wassermann or the flocculation test of Kahn or VDRL (for the detection of syphilis).

Routine urine tests include the determination of protein, glucose, cells and other sediment, and the measurement of the specific gravity. Thereafter it is usual to perform a chromatographic analysis of sugars and aminoacids in the urine and/or serum, and, in some particular cases, certain serological tests such as the Dye and complement fixation test (if there is a suspicion of toxoplasmosis) and the determination of antibody titres against measles virus (in cases of suspected or subacute sclerosing panencephalitis); in addition, *Treponema pallidum* immobilisation (TPI) and Reiter's test may be indicated if there is a suspicion of neuro-syphilis.

Determination of the glucose concentrations in urine and/or serum is useful in the diagnosis of some carbohydrate disorders, such as neonatal hypoglycaemia, and some forms of glycogen storage disease (Eastman and Jancar 1968). Proteinuria is a sign of renal affection, for instance in Lowe's syndrome (Lamy *et al.* 1962). The identification of specific micro-organisms by means of isolation is indicated in cases of suspected primary infectious disorders of the central nervous system (Carter 1965, Brain and Walton 1969).

Tests on cerebrospinal fluid are also performed. In addition to the above-mentioned serological reactions for syphilis, the following tests are in general use: inspection of the CSF, cell count, determination of protein and glucose concentrations, colloidal gold test, and electrophoretic fractioning of proteins (Brain and Walton 1969).

Bickel (1968) reports that the following screening tests are in routine use: two-dimensional paper chromatography for aminoaciduria, phenolic acid and indolic acids; one dimensional paper chromatography for melituria; microbiological inhibition test for phenylalanine, leucine, histidine and galactose; cyanide nitroprusside test for homocystinuria. Certain haematological tests are used in selected cases: sugar, calcium, phosphorus, sodium, bilirubin, ammonia (NH_3), electrophoresis and bicarbonate (HCO_3); there may also be indications for tests for mucopolysaccharides and for sulphatides in the urine and for pyridoxine trials in cases of infantile convulsions.

Various neurochemical techniques may help with the further elucidation of metabolic disorders (Lajtha 1972).

Neurophysiological Studies
Several electroencephalographic studies on mentally retarded patients have been published (Gibbs and Gibbs 1965). In addition to being useful in cases of epilepsy, EEG can also be used to elucidate the localisation, and sometimes the quality and severity, of a cerebral affection. The *degree* of mental retardation has been observed in some cases to be associated with the type of EEG recording, in that abnormal EEGs are more common among the severely than the mildly retarded. Furthermore, cases with a combination of epilepsy and mental retardation are more likely to show EEG abnormalities than cases of epilepsy alone. Even when there is no known evidence of an organic lesion, mental retardation is associated with a fairly high incidence of EEG abnormalities. On the other hand, some severely retarded patients are known to have EEGs without any definitely pathological findings.

More or less characteristic and distinctive EEG features are recorded in some conditions associated with mental retardation, for example (i) in certain infectious diseases like sclerosing sub-acute panencephalitis (Cobb and Hill 1950), (ii) in metabolic disorders like cretinism (Nieman 1961), Spielmeyer-Vogt's disease (Angrisani *et al.* 1961), Lowe's oculo-cerebro-renal syndrome (Illig *et al.* 1963), and phenylketonuria (Stadler 1961), and (iii) in certain syndromes such as 'childhood epileptic encephalopathy with diffuse slow spike-waves' or 'Lennox Syndrome' (Gastaut *et al.* 1966). Of all the different aetiologies of mental retardation without epilepsy, the highest incidence of abnormal EEGs occurs in cases produced by encephalitis, and the next highest amongst those with brain damage sustained before birth or in the neonatal period (Gibbs *et al.* 1960). Until recently, very few abnormal findings were reported in investigations of Down's syndrome (Beley *et al.* 1959, Hirai and Izawa 1964). However, some recent studies have reported clearly pathological EEG recordings in a majority of cases with Down's syndrome (Seppäläinen and Kivalo 1967).

The patient's age is known to affect the type of EEG activity recorded. Hypsarrhythmia is seen only in young children; it gradually disappears with increasing age, and does not often occur without epilepsy. On the other hand, mentally retarded persons without epilepsy have a minimum of EEG abnormalities in infancy and early childhood. It is thought that rhythmic voltage production is relatively undeveloped in the neonatal and immediate post-natal period, and various forms of normal and abnormal activity are not fully expressed.

The EEG abnormalities that have been commonly reported among unclassified samples of mentally retarded patients belong to types which correlate with epilepsy and organic brain damage. In other words, the EEG abnormalities associated with mental retardation are not specific. An exception may be extreme spindles, which, according to Gibbs and Gibbs (1962), seem to correlate specifically with mental retardation and not with epilepsy or cerebral palsy. On the other hand, extreme spindles are known to be associated with several conditions (*e.g.* head trauma) without mental retardation (Chatrian *et al.* 1963).

Mentally retarded patients with few seizures have often been observed to exhibit photosensitivity in EEG recordings. According to Hedenström and Schorsch (1966), about one third of photosensitive epileptics are mentally retarded.

Some minor findings on EEG occur more frequently in cases of mental retardation without epilepsy or cerebral palsy than in normal persons. Such findings are: slow waves (*i.e.* frequencies below 8 per second) and fast waves (*i.e.* frequencies above 11.5 per second); low voltage waking activity (except in retarded children below 10 years of age); and absence of sleep spindles. Also, sub-clinical epilepsy, diagnosed on the basis of EEG findings, has been noted to be more common than clinical epilepsy among mentally retarded patients. One reason for this may be that some clinical epileptic manifestations, such as attacks of headache, dizziness, disordered sensation, visceral and vegetative disturbances, or loss of emotional control, are not easily identified in mentally retarded patients, and so often pass unnoticed (Gibbs *et al.* 1960).

From the neurophysiological point of view, it seems possible that one type of mental retardation is associated with processes underlying epilepsy, one with processes causing spastic forms of cerebral palsy, and one with processes commonly producing athetoid and non-spastic forms of cerebral palsy. The first two types correlate closely with EEG abnormalities which indicate cortical involvement. The third might be assumed to be related to basal ganglion lesions, which, like deep-lying disorders in general, are relatively non-evident in the waking EEG, and appear mainly in sleep recordings (Gibbs and Gibbs 1965).

The results of the investigations reported by Gibbs *et al.* (1960) and Gibbs and Gibbs (1965) are of interest, but are not comparable with those of this study, because the other examinations carried out in the present series, especially those affecting the aetiological diagnosis, are quite different.

Electromyographic recordings and the examination of motor nerve conduction velocity can assist in the diagnosis of neuromuscular disorders associated with mental retardation, *e.g.* myotonic dystrophia (Walton 1970), or progressive encephalopathies with involvement of peripheral nerves, *e.g.* leucodystrophy (Hagberg *et al.* 1969). The examination of evoked potentials to an auditory stimulus, with the aid of an electroencephalograph and a computer, can be useful for making an objective determination of hearing ability (Rose and Rittmanic 1968, Seppäläinen 1969). At the same time, because deafness is known to be associated with some cerebral disorders, this technique may prove helpful in the diagnosis of the aetiology of mental retardation; it is also a useful aid in the differential diagnosis of pseudo-retardation due to a hearing defect.

Cytogenetic Studies

The karyotypic analysis is made on cultured cells taken from various tissues (*e.g.* blood, skin, bone marrow), with the aid of photomicroscopy and photographic reproduction. The analysis of nuclear sex is most frequently made on oral mucosa cells, obtained by buccal smears (see Bartalos and Baramki 1967).

Cytogenetics found a practical application in developmental medicine in 1959, when Lejeune *et al.* found an extra chromosome in group G of a patient with Down's syndrome. Subsequently, several other syndromes associated with chromosome aberration and mental retardation were detected. These disorders were found both in autosomes and in sex chromosomes. A remarkably large number of chromosome aberrations have been described in association with spontaneous abortions (Carr 1965, Szulman 1965). A review of a total of 254 cases of spontaneous abortion studied by various authors showed that 71 (27.9 per cent) of them had had some sort of chromosome aberration (Bartalos and Baramki 1967). This is over sixty times the incidence of chromosome abnormalities at birth. These cases represent the most severe forms of developmental disorder, in as much as they are already lethal during the fetal or embryonal period.

The best-studied of all mentally retarded patients are those who are institutionalised. The incidence of chromosomal aberrations amongst these patients varies between 8 and 17 per hundred, of which all but about 10 per cent are cases of Down's syndrome (Roboz and Pitt 1969a and b, Iivanainen *et al.* 1970b, Jacobsen and Dupont 1971).

Generally speaking, little attention has been paid to the neurological manifestations and, in particular, to the neuropathological findings in patients with chromosome aberrations. Some typical findings, such as a low alpha frequency on the EEG in men with an excess of X chromosomes (Hambert and Frey 1964), aggressive behaviour in men with an extra Y chromosome (Berg and Smith 1971), and anomalies of the cerebellum in trisomy cases (Terplan *et al.* 1966, Polani 1967), have been identified. In principle, it would seem that a variety of neurological deficits may be particularly associated with brain dysfunction in these patients with particular chromosomal aberrations, but careful neuroradiological studies are still needed.

Dermatoglyphic Studies

Dermatoglyphic studies are concerned with the determination of a patient's dermatoglyphic pattern, *i.e.* the patterns formed by the dermal ridges and flexion creases on the palms and soles. A monograph on human dermatoglyphics written by Cummins and Midlo in 1943 is still considered a useful guide in this field.

A number of different techniques, involving the use of a variety of procedures and materials (*e.g.* with or without ink, using smokey or glossy paper), have been employed to record dermatoglyphic patterns (Uchida and Soltan 1963).

Flexion creases on the palm and sole are more easily observed than the dermal ridges. The most usual abnormal flexion crease pattern is a simian crease, which is formed by the fusion of the two distal palmar creases. A simian crease is frequently seen in cases of Down's syndrome; so too is a marked crease on the sole between the first and second toes (Penrose 1963a). Several other characteristic dermatoglyphic patterns have been described in association with particular cytogenetic disorders (see Bartalos and Baramki 1967).

Dermatoglyphic patterns are influenced by a variety of factors, including both the patient's genotype and the intra-uterine conditions during embryogenesis and early fetal life. Since different patterns have different origins, analysis of the dermatoglyphic pattern can give useful information in a patient with a developmental disorder. For instance, in patients with chromosome aberrations dermatoglyphic information can be used in sorting out which chromosome is involved (Penrose 1963a). By using a method of pattern classification based on topological ideas, which defines all loops and tri-radii, many of the peculiarities which characterise any given clinical syndrome can be simultaneously appreciated. Moreover, by means of pattern dictionaries, the number of times whole palmar or plantar pattern types occur in different clinical conditions can be compared (Penrose and Loesch 1971).

Neuropathological Studies

Neuropathological studies have contributed the most reliable information about the aetiology of mental retardation, despite the great variety of ways in which different workers have classified their findings. Meyer (1949) found gross anatomical changes in about two thirds of a group of 385 mentally retarded children, excluding those with Down's syndrome. Of these gross changes, vascular lesions accounted for 40 per cent. The other main groups of pathological findings were as follows: pure developmental disorders, developmental disorders combined with vascular lesions, the sequelae of meningitis, and miscellaneous findings. Malamud (1954) showed malformations in 74

9

per cent, destructive processes in 22 per cent, metabolic disorders in 2 per cent, and neoplasms in 2 per cent of 543 mentally retarded patients at autopsy. Benda (1960) used nine categories, which were partly based on the degree of mental retardation. Crome (1960), on the basis of morphological findings obtained at autopsy from the brains of 282 mentally retarded patients, mostly of low grade, divided them into two groups: 32 per cent were classified as having recognised syndromes with characteristic clinical and pathological disease patterns, and 68 per cent could not be so classified. Most cases showed gross and obvious neural abnormalities. Of the unclassified cases, only eight showed no morphological changes. Christensen *et al.* (1964) reported the brain findings of 175 mentally retarded institutionalised patients. According to brain weight, the series was almost equally divided into those with micrencephaly and those with normal brains. The other main observations were as follows: cortical changes in 82 per cent, pachy- and microgyria in 19 per cent, mongolism in 11 per cent, intracranial calcifications in 7 per cent, and intracranial tumours in 6 per cent. Freytag and Lindenberg (1967) divided the neuropathological findings from 359 cases into sixteen sub-classes. They found that 83 per cent had morphological disorders accounting for the clinical deficits. Malformations and circulatory lesions were the most frequent alterations. Fifty per cent of the lesions were already present at birth, another 16 per cent were related to the birth process, and 24 per cent occurred after birth from various endogenous and exogenous causes. In the remaining 10 per cent, it was not possible to determine whether the lesions were of perinatal or postnatal origin.

Neuropathological, and particularly microscopic, examinations have consistently revealed that the brains of a great majority of institutionalised mentally retarded patients are in some way affected, and that a remarkably large number of cases have primary cerebral maldevelopment suggesting a prenatal origin (Meyer 1949, Malamud 1954, Bredmose and Christensen 1955, Benda 1960, Crome, 1960, Yakovlev 1960, Gross and Kaltenbäck 1962, Christensen *et al*, 1964, Gross *et al*. 1964, Malamud *et al*. 1964, Palo *et al*. 1966, Freytag and Lindenberg 1967). In a number of studies, however, the correlation between clinical and neuropathological findings has not been discussed. It is important to recognise that there have been few studies of non-institutionalised patients.

When the results of neuropathological studies are compared with those of clinical studies, discrepancies may be observed as regards the presence of pathological findings and their interpretation as being causal. Clinical studies reveal proportionally less cases of prenatal origin, and less examples of vascular lesions or of general pathological findings, than do pathological studies (*e.g.* Halperin 1945, Meyer 1949, Malamud 1954, Pitt and Roboz 1965, Freytag and Lindenberg 1967, Dupont and Dreyer 1968). This discrepancy is understandable when we remember that mentally retarded persons are very rarely studied by all available methods. Since in many cases the aetiology only becomes apparent when a particular type of investigation is carried out, a failure to use all available diagnostic methods often results in the aetiology of mental retardation remaining obscure in life. In particular, it is important that neuroradiological investigations should not be omitted. For example, a number of cases of cerebrovascular lesions are diagnosed during life only by cerebral angiography (Isler 1971).

Previous Neuroradiological Studies on the Aetiology of Mental Retardation
Skull X-Ray Studies

Growth mechanisms of the brain are known to have an effect on cranial size, shape, texture and symmetry (Spitzer and Quilliam 1958, Dorst 1964, Campbell 1966). Thus, in the initial period of development, the noxious agents which affect the brain may disturb growth and change the dimensions of the skull. Such changes (*e.g.* hemiatrophy) have been found, for instance, in cases of epilepsy (Miribel *et al.* 1963).

Certain skull changes correlate closely with conditions particularly associated with mental retardation. For example, a high incidence of metopic sutures and congenital defects of the paranasal sinuses, facial structures and teeth had been found in cases of Down's syndrome, and disorders of the cranial vault are frequent in microcephalics (Spitzer and Quilliam 1958). The pathogenesis of primary craniosynostosis is thought to be a disorder of the membranous bones of the skull and their anlage (Laitinen 1956). The typical appearance of the vault in oxycephaly has been observed to be related to a primary deformity at the base of the skull (Schmidt 1966).

McLean and Manfredi (1962) found skull x-rays helpful in supporting the aetiological diagnosis in cases of mental retardation, particularly when there were abnormal cerebral calcifications such as in Sturge-Weber syndrome, toxoplasmosis, tuberous sclerosis or subdural haematoma.

The classification of the findings of a routine plain skull x-ray can be made on an anatomical (*e.g.* Spitzer and Quilliam 1958) and/or an aetiological (*e.g.* Epstein and Epstein 1967) basis. In the last mentioned and currently used method of classification, six categories of abnormalities are described: (1) asymptomatic surface anomalies; (2) congenital and hereditary cranial deformities; (3) neoplasms, localised and generalised; (4) traumatic defects; (5) changes in the skull overlying intracranial lesions; and (6) inflammations. However, Epstein and Epstein do not give a separate description of the findings in mentally retarded cases.

Echoencephalography

Echoencephalography was introduced into medical diagnostics by Leksell (1955/1956). This technique can reveal the displacement of cerebral mid-line structures caused by expansive, atrophic or other processes (Jeppsson 1961), the thickness of cerebral substance (*e.g.* in infantile hydrocephalus), or an extra cavity in the brain (Sjögren 1965). Some physiological phenomena should be taken into consideration in the interpretation of the results. For instance, the reflecting surfaces between the brain and the cerebrospinal fluid are known to vary, depending on the age of the child. In children below 18 months, echo from the brain does not appear to arise at the brain/CSF junction (Emery 1967).

Good agreement between the findings of pneumoencephalography and echoencephalography with regard to ventricular size has been reported (West 1967, Sjögren *et al.* 1968).

Echoencephalography is a valuable supplement to other neuroradiological examinations, and has been quite extensively applied in paediatric and neurological clinics. However, it is used in these clinics for examining individual cases, and has not yet been systematically applied to large numbers of mentally retarded children.

11

Cerebral Angiography

Cerebral angiography was developed by Moniz in 1927. Since then, it has gradually become an important technique in the investigation of neurological anomalies in patients of normal intelligence, but it is still not usually applied to the mentally retarded.

Brandt *et al.* (1961) performed cerebral angiography on 24 children with cerebral palsy, and, on the basis of their findings, reached the following conclusions concerning its diagnostic value in this disease. They reported that the course of the arterial trunks can provide some evidence as to whether or not there is ventricular dilatation, and that a shift may indicate atrophy of the affected hemisphere. Occasionally, an indication of a vascular abnormality may be found which would have remained undiagnosed by pneumoencephalography. Brandt *et al.* (1961) recommended that cerebral angiography should be preferred to pneumoencephalography in patients with cerebral palsy under three circumstances: (1) in cases of hemiplegia, especially those with recurrent acute symptoms and exacerbations; (2) in cases complicated by focal epileptic manifestations; and (3) in persons in whom the symptoms of cerebral palsy have only appeared relatively recently, who may not have completely recovered from their acute disease, and in whom there exists a suspicion of overlooked pathology or complicating bleeding. They concluded, however, that cerebral angiography offers little more information than pneumoencephalography in the stationary stage of the disease.

The findings of cerebral angiography in cases of acute hemiplegia due to cerebrovascular disorders during childhood have also published (Till and Hoare 1962, Isler 1971). Isler, whose primary concern was not with mental retardation, included only 33 mentally retarded patients (IQ less than 85) in his 82 detailed case reports (Isler, personal communication).

The indications and contra-indications for cerebral angiography are basically the same in mentally retarded patients as they are in patients of normal intelligence. As with other patients, refusal of the parents or guardians may be an absolute contra-indication. But if permission is not withheld, cerebral angiography may often be indicated in the mentally retarded, especially if they suffer from focal epilepsy, show asymmetrical or unilateral neurological defects, manifest focal EEG changes, or suffer from subarachnoid haemorrhages (see Table II, page 17).

Generally, however, cerebral angiography has not been regarded as valuable in institutions for the mentally retarded, and cannot be performed there. Also, in paediatric clinics the indications for cerebral angiography in severely mentally retarded children are not considered as important as they are in children who are mentally normal or slightly retarded. Thus, the majority of cerebrovascular disorders are not diagnosed in mentally retarded patients during life.

Pneumoencephalography

Since the time of Dandy (1918) remarkable progress has been made in the field of pneumoencephalography. The earliest studies are now only of historical value, because certain structures of the brain, such as the temporal horns, infratentorial space and cisternal system, could not at that time be filled with gas (Bruijn 1959).

Nowadays, pneumoencephalography is considered to be a useful supplementary tool in the investigation of patients with neurological symptoms, and is in routine use in neurological departments everywhere.

The indications for pneumoencephalography in the study of mental retardation have been discussed by several authors. Basically they are the same as they would be in the study of neurological patients of normal intelligence. The indications suggested by Vesterdal *et al.* (1954) were as follows: (1) focal changes in the EEG; (2) suspicion of a brain tumour; (3) epilepsy, when a thorough examination has not been carried out before; (4) sequelae of cranial lesions; (5) sequelae of intracranial haemorrhage; and (6) cases in which an attempt to chart the brain lesion is desirable. At the same time, these authors stressed that the indications for pneumoencephalography are practically never absolute, but only relative. Hagberg *et al.* (1959) agreed with this.

Spitz *et al.* (1962) suggested certain criteria for the use of pneumoencephalography in the differential diagnosis of mental retardation. Their view was that this technique is indicated when the symptoms of both encephalopathy and psychiatric impairment have persisted: (1) after a minimum of nine months' residence in an environment of therapeutically oriented group-living; (2) where the patient's medical history (including family movies when available) and the observed response to special education techniques are suggestive, but not confirmatory, of encephalopathy; and (3) where psychological, neurological and electroencephalographical studies have failed to establish a likely diagnosis.

According to Gaal (1963) the indications for pneumoencephalography are: (1) hereditary mental retardation; (2) postnatal meningitis; (3) perinatal lesions (including Little's disease); (4) sequelae after encephalitis; and (5) epilepsy. This, however, is a far from complete list of the currently recognised indications for pneumoencephalography in the diagnostic study of mental retardation.

Other possible indications are malformations or abnormalities discovered on physical examination, chromosome karyotyping or microscopical examination of the skin. The most important contra-indications are increased intracranial pressure and, of course, refusal of permission by parents or guardians.

The first pneumoencephalographic studies were frequently associated with potentially serious complications (Mader 1923, Dannenbaum 1926, Eley and Vogt 1932, Smith and Crothers 1950, Anderson 1951, Casamajor *et al.* 1951, Schuleman 1953, Charash and Dunning 1956). However, anaesthetic techniques have greatly improved in recent years, and there has been a consequent reduction in the frequency and severity of these complications. In fact, recent investigations performed with the modern fractional technique have unanimously shown that complications associated with pneumoencephalography are very much less of a danger than was once believed, and have confirmed the value and safety of this method (Brandt *et al.* 1955, Robertson 1957, Hagberg *et al.* 1959, Melchior 1961, Spitz *et al.* 1962, Iivanainen *et al.* 1970a). Thus it would appear that the alleged 'dangerousness' of pneumoencephalography (Casamajor *et al.* 1949, Charash and Dunning 1956) was probably attributable to defective technique, and that the method *per se* was not at fault.

Although pneumoencephalography is not regarded as a routine method of investigation in the study of mentally retarded patients, its use is well documented in the literature. In early studies (*i.e.* those performed with the non-fractional technique), the findings were scanty and insignificant (Levinson 1947, Casamajor *et al.* 1949, Anderson 1951, Charash and Dunning 1956). On the other hand, studies done with the more modern fractional technique have shown more positive results in mentally retarded patients (Malamud and Garoutte 1954, Salomonsen *et al.* 1957, Hagberg *et al.* 1959, Melchior 1961, Spitz *et al.* 1962, Bruijn 1963, Gaal 1963, Dyggve and Melchior 1964, Brett and Hoare 1969).

Some of the most significant studies are discussed briefly below. Mäurer (1939) reported on about 400 cases examined over a period of five years. He suggested that, since no clear changes could be found in most cases of congenital mild mental retardation, mental retardation with marked pneumoencephalographic findings is more likely to be exogenous.

The largest material of mentally retarded patients studied with pneumoencephalography was published by Levinson (1947), who examined over 800 patients. This author tried to estimate the prognosis on the basis of the pneumoencephalographic findings. An absence of air in the subarachnoid space, especially if it was on one side only, was likely to be due to arachnoiditis. Ventricular dilatation was present in every case of cortical atrophy, and displacement of the ventricles usually indicated a brain tumour or abscess. Occasionally the pneumoencephalogram was normal. However, Levinson did not present any details of the material, and made only four pictures in each examination.

Anderson (1951) published a report of the pneumoencephalographic findings in 400 children, including 228 who were mentally retarded. He considered that, on its own, this method is of little value in the investigation of mental retardation. Nevertheless, the pneumoencephalographic findings were pathological in about 64 per cent of his 228 mentally retarded cases.

Malamud and Garoutte (1954) published the results of pneumoencephalography and post-mortem studies performed on 30 mentally retarded and/or cerebral palsied patients. Twenty were considered to have cerebral malformations. In seven of these pneumoencephalography revealed incomplete gas filling of the frontal cerebral cortex. Ventricular dilatation was general. Occipital flattening of the skull was considered to correlate with small malformed occipital lobes of the brain.

A close correlation between pneumoencephalographic and autopsy findings has been found by Melchior (1961) and other authors (*e.g.* Kruse and Schaetz 1935, Weintraub 1953, Malamud and Garoutte 1954).

Charash and Dunning (1956) found a poor correlation between the pneumoencephalographic findings and the degree of mental retardation in 106 patients. However, because they used different indications and techniques, their results cannot be compared with those of this study.

Melchior (1961) and Dyggve and Melchior (1964) did find a close correlation between the size of the cerebral ventricular system and the degree of mental retardation. However, certain cases of severe retardation, a number of which belonged to their category of infantile autism or schizophrenia, had normal or only slightly abnormal pneumoencephalograms. These authors also reported that a considerable enlargement of the third ventricle was connected with a severe degree of mental retardation.

Cortical abnormalities at pneumoencephalography were of some minor importance. No serious abnormalities of Evans' ratio, of the width of the third ventricle, or of the amount of gas around the hemispheres could be found in the cases with a good social prognosis. No serious complications appeared in any of Dyggve and Melchior's (1964) series of 197 cases. Thus they concluded that pneumoencephalography is safe, and should be recommended in almost all cases of mental retardation, in order to evaluate the degree of anatomical cerebral damage and exclude surgically amenable disorders.

McLean and Manfredi (1962) reported a series of 139 cases of mental retardation (IQ less than 70), in 75 (54 per cent) of which the pneumoencephalograms appeared to be normal. In all but two cases (a case of agenesis of the corpus callosum and a case of hydranencephaly), the only abnormality was 'cerebral atrophy.' The technique and indications employed, and the criteria for assessing ventricular dilatation, were not described.

Gaal (1963) reported that the pneumoencephalographic findings were pathological in 90 per cent of his series of 232 mentally retarded patients. He divided the patients with pathological findings into four groups. Patients in the first group had unilateral rounding or lateral displacement of the angle between the caudate nucleus and corpus callosum (as seen in the antero-posterior view), often in association with localised dilatation of the parietal subarachnoid space, but only slight, if any, enlargement of the other CSF spaces (e.g. the third ventricle). The second group consisted of cases with nearly symmetrical dilatation of the lateral ventricles, combined with dilatation of the third ventricle. (In severe cases, a general dilatation of the subarachnoid space, with meningeal adhesions, was also noted). Gaal's third group comprised patients with asymmetrical dilatation of the lateral ventricles, combined with dilatation of the third ventricle, and, in severe cases, a slight movement of midline structures towards the larger lateral ventricle. In this group the subarachnoid findings were variable. The fourth was a miscellaneous group of cases with pneumo-encephalographic findings typical of all the other three groups.

In addition, Gaal (1963) paid great attention to those pneumoencephalographic findings which were associated with particular conditions. For example, in microcephaly caused by birth injury, extreme 'hydrocephalus' was a frequent finding, while in congenital microcephaly the ventricles tended to be of normal size. Gaal contended that pneumoencephalography is not at all dangerous in the study of children with mental disorders, and that it is not only of diagnostic and prognostic, but also of therapeutic, use. He did not describe the pneumoencephalographic findings or his technique in detail, nor did he include any aetiological classification. Furthermore, he did not provide any information concerning the clinical findings or the degree of mental retardation suffered by his patients.

The report of Brett and Hoare (1969) described the pneumoencephalographic findings in 176 mentally retarded patients. Cerebral atrophy was found in 60 per cent, and was most common in the cases of retardation and epilepsy. No surgically treatable lesions were found. The pneumoencephalographic findings were somewhat similar in the groups of patients with mental retardation, epilepsy and cerebral palsy, an observation made by several previous authors (Vesterdal *et al.* 1954, Salomonsen *et al.*

1957, Hagberg *et al.* 1959). The report of Brett and Hoare included no account of cortical, temporal or infratentorial pneumoencephalographic findings, nor were the clinical findings described in detail. All the patients were very selected, in that children with a suspicion of any form of gross lesion and/or postnatal head injury, or with no record of head circumference measurements at the time of the investigation, were excluded. Thus, any comparison with other studies is difficult. This criticism is also true of many of the other studies discussed, which often failed to state where the patients came from, and what criteria were used to select them for pneumoencephalography.

The conflicting conclusions drawn from the studies discussed above are not perhaps surprising. Consistently close correlations between the degree of cerebral loss and the degree of mental retardation should not be expected, since rare cases occur in which quite a severe loss of cerebral tissue leaves a child unretarded (Lorber and Zachary 1968). As techniques improve, however, one hopes that pneumoencephalographic studies will provide more information about the underlying pathological and disease processes which cause mental retardation.

Brain Scanning with Radioisotopes

Brain scanning with radioisotopes was developed for diagnostic use in the 1950's. Indicator agents such as γ-radiators J^{131} serum albumin (Di Chiro 1961b), Hg^{203} neohydrin (Blau and Bender 1962), or Tc^{99m} pertechnetate (Mc Afee *et al.* 1964) introduced into the blood show a tendency to accumulate in an affected area of the brain, *e.g.* in cases of neoplasm, haematoma or infarct. Radioactive radiation from this local area is recorded by means of an extracranial detector, usually by a commercial scanner equipped with a photographic recorder. The method is painless and reasonably risk-free, and, like echoencephalography, acts as a valuable supplement to other neuroradiological investigations. Brain scanning is of greatest value in the diagnosis of neoplasms (see DeLang and Wagner 1969).

Very few investigations of mentally retarded patients using this method have been published.

CHAPTER 2

The Present Study: Aims, Material and Methods

Aims

Prompted by the belief that successful treatment and prophylaxis in cases of mental retardation depend on an understanding of the aetiology and clinical signs, the present study is a detailed investigation into the aetiology of mental retardation, using, where relevant, all the diagnostic techniques described in the previous chapter. In particular, this report is concerned with the findings in those cases in which it was felt there were indications for neurological studies, and sets out to answer two specific questions.

(1) In what ways do the clinical findings correlate with the aetiology of the mental retardation?

(2) Of what value are neuroradiological methods in the aetiological diagnosis of mental retardation?

Material: Patients

One thousand mentally retarded patients admitted consecutively to the Rinnekoti Institution for the Mentally Retarded during the 23 years prior to 31st December 1966 constituted the basic material. Of these, all 880 who were still alive on 31st December 1966 were subjected to further physical, cytogenetical, electroencephalographical and echoencephalographical examinations. On the basis of these examinations, the indications and contra-indications for pneumoencephalography and/or cerebral angiography in each case were assessed, and 368 patients were selected for further neuro-radiological investigations. The cases selected were those in which it was felt that there were positive indications for cerebral angiography (Table II) or pneumoencephalography (Table III). Focal epilepsy was the most important indication for cerebral angiography, while epilepsy plus cerebral palsy was present in more than half

TABLE II

Indications for cerebral angiography

Indication	No. of cases	Per cent
Focal epilepsy	49	54
Insufficient gas filling at pneumoencephalography	10	11
Displacement of cerebral structure	8	9
Hemiplegia due to unknown origin	7	8
Focal EEG abnormality alone	6	7
Primary subarachnoid haemorrhage	1	1
Miscellaneous	9	10
TOTAL	90	100

TABLE III

Indications for pneumoencephalography

Indication	No. of cases	Per cent
Epilepsy with or without cerebral palsy	199	60
Malformations	56	17
Cerebral palsy	39	12
EEG abnormality alone	11	3
Large head	8	2
Miscellaneous	21	6
TOTAL	334*	100

*Four cases had cerebral angiography but not pneumoencephalography.

the cases selected for pneumoencephalography. In fact, in only four cases who were submitted to cerebral angiography was it felt that pneumoencephalography was not indicated. Patients who died after 31st December 1966 were included only if before they died they had been examined with pneumoencephalography and/or cerebral angiography.

In fact, not all the patients originally selected for pneumoencephalography and/or cerebral angiography are included in this report. A written enquiry was sent to the parents and guardians of each of the 368 selected, asking for permission to perform neuradiological examinations under general anaesthesia. A positive answer was obtained in 338 cases (92 per cent). The remaining 30 patients are being investigated with the 512 who were alive on 31 December 1966, but who were not selected for this study.

The collection of data relating to the 120 dead and 542 living patients who were not investigated by neuroradiological methods is continuing, and a preliminary report of the findings is presented in Tables XLIV to XLVI. Comparison between these findings and those relating to the present study indicate the significant differences between the two groups of patients.

Because of the criteria used for selection, the final series of patients selected for this study is not typical of the general institutionalised patient population. In particular, it includes more cases of epilepsy and cerebral palsy, and less of Down's syndrome.

Age and Sex Distribution

Of the 338 patients who were finally included, 197 (58 per cent) were males, and 141 were females. Their ages at the time of the neuroradiological examinations ranged from one to 49 years, with a mean of 17 years. The mean year of birth was 1952. This mean was used for the selection of control groups in connection with some of the findings. For example, children born in the general population in 1952 were chosen for the comparison of birthweights. One hundred and seventy-nine patients were over 15 years of age. Details of the age and sex distribution in this series are presented in Table IV.

TABLE IV

Age and sex distribution of the patients

Age in years	Males No.	Females No.	Total No.	Per cent
5 or less	6	7	13	4
6-10	41	22	63	19
11-15	52	31	83	25
16-20	38	33	71	21
21-25	32	24	56	17
26-30	21	17	38	11
More than 30	7	7	14	4
TOTAL	197	141	338	100

Degree of Mental Retardation

More than half the patients (59 per cent) were profoundly retarded, according to the system of classification recommended by the World Health Organization (WHO) in 1968 (see page 1). Details of the classification of the patients according to the degree of mental retardation are set out in Table V. This distribution is based on the results of psychological tests (207 testings with the Terman-Merrill-Lehtovaara test, 107 with the Cattel test, 57 with the KTK performance test, 34 with the Goodenough test, 29 with the Vineland test, 20 with the Columbia test, 8 with the WAIS test, 8 with the Raven test, and 3 with the Bender test), performed before the present investigations were begun by several psychologists, and controlled in connection with this study by the senior psychologist (Mrs. Harriet Lindgren) of the Rinnekoti Institution for the Mentally Retarded.

Not only was there a high percentage of severely mentally retarded patients in this series, but the majority of the rest were at least moderately retarded. In fact, 93 per cent of the whole series had IQs of less than 50. The mean degree of mental retardation in the series as measured by tests of intelligence is greater than that in many similar studies (*e.g.* Hagne 1962, Dyggve and Melchior 1964, Pitt and Roboz 1965, Covernton 1967, Dupont and Dreyer 1968). Furthermore, although there are more

TABLE V

Degree of mental retardation

Degree of mental retardation	No. of cases	Per cent
Borderline (IQ about 68 to 85)	3	1
Mild (IQ about 52 to 67)	18	5
Moderate (IQ about 36 to 51)	50	15
Severe (IQ about 20 to 35)	67	20
Profound (IQ less than 20)	199	59
Unspecified	1	0
TOTAL	338	100

mild retardates amongst the 662 patients not selected for this study, the whole population of mental retardates at the Rinnekoti Institution would appear to be more severely retarded than most other institutionalised populations which have been studied. This reflects the great shortage of facilities provided for mentally handicapped people in Finland at the time of this study. Around 1966, there were day care facilities for perhaps only 700 individuals. Consequently, only severely handicapped patients were accepted. The patients in this study were drawn from a population of about four and a half million, and represent the most severely retarded patients surviving in such a population over a period of approximately twenty years.

At the time this investigation was begun, 310 of the patients were living in institutions for the mentally retarded, 15 were at home, 7 were in family wards, 5 were in mental hospitals, and 1 was in a communal home. The majority of patients were from the southern parts of Finland.

Methods
History
Available sources were used to collect historical information about the patients. The medical records at the Rinnekoti were scanned, and any additional records from other hospitals were traced and inspected. This information was supplemented in most cases by interviewing the parents or guardians, and, where this was not possible, by sending out questionnaires for the relatives to fill in. All these data were eventually sorted and compressed into a number of items for analysis with a computer (see Appendix Table IV). When dealing with some items, it was difficult to assess the accuracy of the reports. This was particularly the case with the developmental histories, because parents' memories concerning the performance of their children are notoriously inaccurate. However, with severely handicapped patients, parents' memories are likely to be more accurate, as they will remember the significant delays which alerted and alarmed them.

Physical Examination
Every patient was examined personally by the author, using a standardised form of examination developed by the Department of Neurology, University of Helsinki. The examinations never took less than one hour and often took very much longer. Additional data were usually available from observations made by the author during the three years he had been at the Rinnekoti. All the information collected was sifted and summarised for computer analysis. The items selected for computer analysis are listed in Appendix Table IV, from which it can be seen that some of the data were compressed in the form of diagnoses. Reliability studies were not carried out in respect of these diagnoses. However, all patients were examined without reference to their medical records, and it was only after a clinical diagnosis had been made that this was compared with any previous diagnosis. In general, there was agreement between the examining doctor's assessment and the previous assessment. Children in whom the findings at clinical examination presented difficulties were seen with a colleague.

Certain physical abilities such as hearing and vision are particularly difficult to test in mentally retarded patients. Thus, only a crude assessment of visual acuity was made, although confrontation perimetry was carried out routinely. Hearing ability had usually been assessed previously, but clinical tests were always performed by the author, and evoked potentials were used in difficult cases (see page 22). Most of the patients in this series had no speech. Information concerning the children's speech and language development was provided by a speech therapist from the Rinnekoti.

Inspection of the eye ground in severely handicapped children can be very difficult, but it was usually successfully performed on the children in this sample by playing with them and seeking their co-operation. Where necessary, mild sedation was administered. In addition, the eye grounds of all the patients were re-examined personally by the author when they were anaesthetised for neuroradiological examination. Cases in which interpretation of the findings was difficult were referred to the consultant ophthalmologist at the Rinnekoti.

Sensory examination of mentally retarded patients also presents difficulties, as few can co-operate during testing of response to light and touch or testing of positional sense. One is forced to observe response to pin-prick, and make a clinical judgement about whether they feel less stimulating sensations. Deep sensation is often impossible to estimate.

Some patients were examined in their own homes with the help of their parents, and this in fact proved to be the easiest method of examination. However, any child who was seen at home was of course admitted to the Institution for about a week, so that pneumoencephalography and, if necessary, further physical examinations could be carried out.

Where it was considered appropriate, the standard neurological examination of the Department of Neurology, University of Helsinki, was freely supplemented with other neurological techniques. Thus, the assessment of cerebral palsied children included testing for responses such as the Moro response, asymmetric tonic neck reflex, and the placing response. Some details of the results of these neurological tests will be included in a report on the neurological findings in the whole series of 880 patients. All physical data, such as measurements of height, weight and head circumference, were personally collected by the author and not, simply transcribed from existing records.

Information concerning each child's functional abilities (*e.g.* dressing, feeding, toiletting) was obtained from the nursing staff, though, where possible, this information was re-checked by the author. Thus, an opportunity was taken at the time of the physical examination to re-assess the patient's skill at dressing and undressing, and at meal-times to confirm the nurses' reports concerning his feeding skills. Close personal contact between the children and the nursing staff make it likely that information provided by the latter was reliable. However, it should be borne in mind that information provided by nurses concerning their patients' functional abilities may not always be accurate. Faced with large numbers of severely handicapped children to care for, they may not realise that a particular child is capable, albeit slowly, of dressing himself and participating in feeding activities.

A detailed report on the clinical neurological findings both in the present series and in the patients not investigated in connection with the present study is in preparation.

Cerebrospinal fluid (CSF) samples were obtained through lumbar puncture made in connection with pneumoencephalography in 334 cases. The tests performed on the CSF included cell count, glucose concentration (colour reaction with O-toluidine), protein concentration (folin phenol reagent), colloidal reaction (Mastix test), electrophoretic fractioning of proteins (cellulase acetate method), cytological investigation (Millipore technique and Papanicolau staining), immunological syphilitic reactions (the complement fixation test of Wassermann, the flocculation test of Kahn). In 305 cases, amino acid and carbohydrate concentrations were studied on frozen samples (prepared layers).

Laboratory Studies

Serum calcium, phosphorus, potassium and alkaline phosphate concentrations were determined in 53 cases of convulsions, and a glucose loading test was performed in a further five cases of convulsions.

Other laboratory studies performed on a number of patients in this series have been reported elsewhere (Palo 1966, 1967).

Electroencephalography

Three hundred and twenty patients were subjected to EEG, and 585 recordings were made (482 waking, 93 asleep/awake, and 10 sleep recordings). The remaining 18 cases could not be studied because of restlessness. Chloral hydrate or pentobarbital sodium ('Nembutal') was administered beforehand to anxious patients.

Auditory Evoked Potentials

Auditory evoked potentials were determined in 63 cases of suspected deafness by means of an electroencephalograph and a computer.

Electromyograms and motor nerve conduction velocity were recorded in three cases of muscular disease, with the aid of a 3-channel electromyograph (DISA 14 A 30).

Chromosome Karyotyping

All patients with one or more major or two or more minor malformations were submitted to chromosomal analysis. It was thought that chromosome aberrations were the most likely common cause of malformations affecting such varied organs as the skin, eyes, ears, nose, mouth, tongue, teeth, chin, heart, genitals, hands, feet and brain. The final selection was approved by the cytogeneticist.

Chromosome karyotyping was performed on peripheral venous blood samples from 123 cases of malformations, by culturing lymphocytes and using an air-drying method (Moorhead et al. 1960). The karyotypes were determined from a skin biopsy in four cases of suspected mosaicism. Tests to determine the presence of sex chromatin were performed in 15 cases of gonadal infantilism, using cell samples taken from the mucous membrane of the inner wall of the cheek. The preparation was stained by the Feulgen method.

The nomenclature used was that recommended by the Chicago Conference (1966).

Skull X-ray Examination

Skull x-ray examination was performed in 331 cases. Four pictures were taken, *i.e.* one antero-posterior view, one half-axial view, one lateral view, and one special picture, with small diaphragm, of the sella turcica in lateral view. The film focus distance was 90 mm. The skull table of Lysholm and an Elema Schönander x-ray system were used throughout the neuroradiological examinations.

The volume of the sella turcica was determined from the skull x-rays in 323 cases, according to the method described by Di Chiro and Nelson (1962), and the cranial volume in 286 cases, using Gordon's (1966) modification of the method of MacKinnon *et al.* (1956).

Echoencephalography

Echoencephalography was performed by means of an 'A' scanner with a polaroid camera electroencephalograph (USM 1, system Krautkrämer) in 70 cases suspected of having macroventriculy, a cerebral mass shift, or an extra cavity.

Cerebral Angiography

Cerebral angiography (53 left and 50 right carotid, and 2 left vertebral angiograms) was performed in 90 patients under general anaesthesia. Details of the anaesthetic procedure used have been described in a previous publication (Iivanainen *et al.* 1970a). A percutaneous puncture was made of a carotid and/or vertebral artery, using a salt solution of metritsoe acid (Isopaque Cerebral[R]) as an x-ray contrast medium. A dose of 8 ml was injected manually into the common carotid artery, 6 ml into the internal carotid artery and 4 ml into the vertebral artery. Two lateral series were taken, each of three pictures, for the visualisation of the arterial, capillary and venous phases. In order that a stereoscopic effect might be achieved, the x-ray pictures in the two lateral series were taken at an angle of six degrees to each other. A direct and half-axial series, each of two pictures, were taken in antero-posterior projection. A picture of the neck was taken in order to visualise the cervical part of the carotid artery, and to check the location of the needle in the lumen of the carotid artery. An antero-posterior picture taken during compression of the contralateral carotid artery was also included in the investigation. In cases of subdural haematoma and arterial aneurysm, special oblique angle pictures were taken (Abrams 1961). The cassettes containing the x-ray films were changed manually.

A mild handicap was the lack of apparatus for performing serial angiography. An effort was made to compensate for this lack by taking several consecutive stereoscopic pictures, using a manual timer. For this reason, contrast medium (Isopaque Cerebral[R]) had to be injected many times into the same patient. However, in no case did any serious complications arise in connection with cerebral angiography.

The neuroradiological procedures employed at the Rinnekoti are standardised, considered reliable, and in widespread use, so it was not considered necessary to carry out any new control investigations in connection with the present study. This was true not only for cerebral angiography, but also for pneumoencephalography and skull x-ray examination (Lindgren 1954, Abrams 1961, Diethelm and Strnad 1963, Decker and Backmund 1970).

The great majority of the patients examined neuroradiologically were examined by the author himself (*i.e.* 323 of the 334 submitted to pneumoencephalography, and 86 of the 90 submitted to angiography), so the results should be more uniform and of more future value than if this had not been the case. Even in the twelve cases where the neuroradiological examinations were performed elsewhere, the x-ray pictures were re-examined by the author.

Pneumoencephalography

Pneumoencephalography was performed according to the fractional method (Lindgren 1954) in 334 of the 338 cases. As with cerebral angiography, the method and procedure employed were standardised and in common use, so control investigations were not considered necessary. Only six cases were examined without general anaesthesia. The same gas mixture that the patient was breathing (*i.e.* a mixture of anaesthetic gases) was used as contrast gas, and was injected into the spinal subarachnoid space via lumbar puncture.

The following supratentorial ventricular measurements were made from the pneumoencephalograms: the width of both cellae mediae (the width of the bodies of both lateral ventricles), the lengths of the 'nucleus caudatus septum lines' (see Engeset and Skraastad 1964)—that is the heights of the lateral ventricles (Nielsen *et al.* 1966*a*) —and the widths of the frontal horns, of the temporal horns, of the occipital horns and of the third ventricle (Fig. 1). Also measured were the widths of the supratentorial cortical sulci in the frontal, parietal, temporal and occipital areas, and, in the infra-

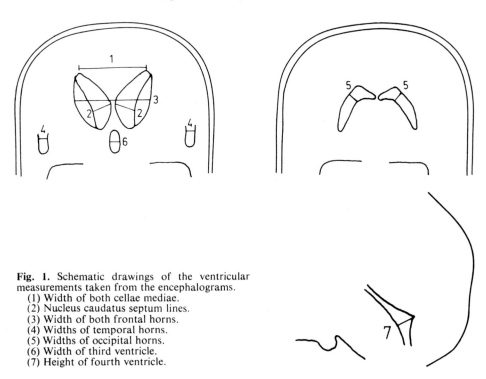

Fig. 1. Schematic drawings of the ventricular measurements taken from the encephalograms.
 (1) Width of both cellae mediae.
 (2) Nucleus caudatus septum lines.
 (3) Width of both frontal horns.
 (4) Widths of temporal horns.
 (5) Widths of occipital horns.
 (6) Width of third ventricle.
 (7) Height of fourth ventricle.

tentorial space, the width of the fourth ventricle (Fig. 1) and the widths of the cerebellar sulci.

The sizes of the ventricles, as assessed from the pneumoencephalograms, were classified according to the method outlined by Evans (1942) and modified by Melchior (1961) in cases aged 20 years or less, and according to the method of Nielsen *et al.* (1966*a*) in cases over 20 years of age. The techniques used for measuring the widths of the frontal and temporal horns (Engeset and Skraastad 1964), the height of the fourth ventricle (Salomonsen *et al.* 1957), and the widths of the supratentorial cortical sulci (Nielsen *et al.* 1966*b*), have all been described elsewhere.

The size of the cerebral ventricles at different ages in normal patients is known from autopsy studies (Knudsen 1958) and pneumoencephalography (Di Chiro 1961*a*, Lodin 1968). The present findings were interpreted with reference to these changes with age. Since the data obtained at autopsy are known to correspond with those obtained at pneumoencephalography (Weintraub 1953, Malamud and Garoutte 1954, Melchior 1961), there are no indications for control pneumoencephalograms on normal living patients.

Brain Scanning with a Radioisotope

Five patients in whom brain tumour was suspected on the basis of the angiographic and pneumoencephalographic findings were examined by means of brain scanning with a radioisotope. The examination was performed under the same pre-medication and general anaesthesia as cerebral angiography. Only one of the five patients did not need general anaesthesia. Technetium 99m pertechnetate served as an indicator agent, and was injected intravenously in quantities proportional to the body weight of the patient. The antero-posterior and lateral scans were registered by means of a Pigler scanner equipped with a photographic (black and white and colour) and x-ray recorder.

Macroscopic and Microscopic Neuropathological Examinations

A macroscopic investigation of the central nervous system was performed at autopsy in all the ten patients who died. A microscopic examination of the brain was performed *post mortem* in four cases in which the aetiological diagnosis of mental retardation was unclear and in one case of cerebral neoplasm; a microscopic examination of the brain was also carried out during life (brain biopsy at operation) in two cases of cerebral tumour. Histological examination was carried out on a skin biopsy in five cases of skin disorder, and on a muscle biopsy in three cases of muscular disease.

Statistical Analysis

The data were processed automatically at the Computing Centre of the University of Helsinki. The correlations between the various findings and the aetiology of mental retardation were investigated by means of library programmes. The primary number of different variables was 320. The variables of clinical history and physical examination are listed in Appendix Table IV.

The χ^2 test and Student's 't' test were utilized to determine statistically significant correlations.

25

CHAPTER 3

Results

Clinical History

Social Class

Social class was assessed and classified according to the criteria laid down by Rauhala (1966). This author proposed two systems of classification, one of nine and the other of three points, both of which are similar to those commonly used in other countries.

Compared with the general population (see Rauhala 1966), a slightly higher proportion of the parents of the patients in this series belonged to the lower social classes. This difference was statistically significant (Table VI).

TABLE VI

Social class distribution

Social Class	Present series		General population†	
	No. of cases	*Per cent*	*No. of cases*	*Per cent*
I	30	8·9	139	10·8
II	178	52·6*	759	58·7
III	129	38·2‡	395	30·5
Unknown	1	0·3		
TOTAL	338	100·0	1293	100·0

†Figures for the general population of Finland reported by Rauhala (1966).
*Almost significant difference ($\chi^2 = 4\cdot0$, p $<0\cdot05$).
‡Significant difference ($\chi^2 = 7\cdot1$, p $<0\cdot01$).

Maternal Marital Status

Thirty-eight (11.2 per cent) of the patients in this series were born to unmarried mothers, whereas according to the Statistical Yearbook of Finland for 1952 (Finland, Central Statistical Office 1954) the figure for the general population is only 4.7 per cent. This difference is highly significant ($\chi^2 = 35.2$; p <0.001).

Family History of Mental Retardation

Twenty-five patients (7 per cent) had one or more mentally retarded siblings, and forty-seven (14 per cent) had one or more mentally retarded persons among their close relatives (*i.e.* amongst their grandparents, their grandparents' children, and their grandparents' children's children). These percentages agree well with those reported by Penrose in 1938 (6 to 9 per cent for parents and siblings of mentally retarded patients), and are higher (approximately 1 per cent) than those quoted for the general population.

Previous Abortions and Stillbirths

Sixty-two (18 per cent) of the mothers of the patients in this series had had previous abortions or stillbirths. In a Finnish control series reported by Klemetti and Saxén (1970), the frequency of previous abortions was 14 per cent, and that of previous stillbirths was 2 per cent. However, comparison between these two sets of data is not really valid, because the figures for this series were obtained predominantly from the subjective evidence given in spoken and/or written form by the mothers, often several years later. Thus, the frequency of 18 per cent is a minimal figure, and is unreliable. Nevertheless, it seems likely that the frequency of abortions and stillbirths in this series is higher than that in the general population.

Maternal Age

The mean maternal age at the time of the birth of the patients in this series was 28.5 years, which is similar to the figure reported in the Statistical Yearbook of Finland for the general population for 1952 (Finland, Central Statistical Office 1954) Also, when the mothers were divided into five-year age groups, the distribution in this series did not differ significantly from the distribution within the general population (Table VII). It is worth noting in connection with these figures that there were only four cases of Down's syndrome in this series.

TABLE VII

Maternal age distribution

Age in Years	Present series		General population†	
	No. of cases	Per cent	No. of cases	Per cent
19 or under	18	5·3	4086	4·3
20-24	86	25·5	25839	26·8
25-29	94	27·8	27037	28·1
30-34	72	21·3	19812	20·6
35-39	44	13·0	12644	13·1
40-44	15	4·4	5915	6·1
45 or over	3	0·9	793	0·8
Unknown	6	1·8	3	0·0
TOTAL	338	100·0	96129	100·0

†Statistical Yearbook of Finland, 1952 (Finland, Central Statistical Office 1954).

Abnormalities During Pregnancy

The retrospective recording of abnormalities of pregnancy is unreliable (Klemetti 1966, Klemetti and Saxén 1967). In the present study, therefore, evidence of abnormalities during pregnancy was only sought when these abnormalities seemed likely to be of causal significance for mental retardation.

The most common abnormality during pregnancy was toxaemia, which had occurred in fifty-five cases (16 per cent). If this figure is compared with that presented in a report from the Helsinki Institute of Midwifery (1952), it appears that the incidence of toxaemia was significantly higher ($p < 0.001$) in this series than in the general population of mothers in Finland.

27

Other important complications during the first trimester of pregnancy were infection in seventeen cases (5 per cent), trauma in seventeen cases (5 per cent), ionizing radiation in ten cases (3 per cent), and the continuous use of drugs in seven cases (2 per cent). The actual names of the drugs used in the last seven cases were impossible to clarify retrospectively, but were known to include thalidomide, chloramphenicol, meclozine, phenacetine, penicillin, sedatives and several other medicines.

Only in a few of the cases listed above were the complications during pregnancy considered to be of aetiological significance as far as the mental retardation of the offspring was concerned: toxaemia of pregnancy in fifteen cases (eclampsia in one, pre-eclampsia gravis in twelve, and pre-eclampsia levis in two—classified according to Nelson 1955), infection in nine cases (rubella in three, severe maternal tonsillitis in two, syphilis in two, and toxoplasmosis in two), trauma in one case, and ionizing radiation in one case. In the case of trauma, the mother had had a haemorrhage *ex utero* immediately after the abdominal bruising. In the case complicated by high doses of ionizing radiation, the mother's abdominal region had been radiated in connection with colography, urography, biligraphy and ventricular examination. The apparatus used had been old-fashioned, without any image intensifier, and with a fluoroscope. A few days after the examination, the mother had had bleeding *ex utero*.

Primiparous Mothers

The number of infants of primiparae in this series was 113 (33.4 per cent), a figure which did not differ significantly from the corresponding figure for the general population in 1952—29.1 per cent according to the Statistical Yearbook of Finland (Finland, Central Statistical Office 1954). This finding does not confirm the results of some earlier studies (Gupta and Virmani 1968, Roboz and Pitt 1968b), which found a rather higher incidence of primiparae amongst the mothers of mentally retarded patients, suggesting that birth injuries associated with primiparity are a risk factor for mental retardation. This difference is unlikely to be due to the criteria by which the patients were selected, because there are no obvious reasons why the indications for neuroradiological examinations should lead to exclusion of a high proportion of cases of birth injury. It seems possible that if the infant of a primiparous mother is treated in hospital, the primiparous pregnancy *per se* should not put him at any more risk.

Delivery Without Skilled Assistance

Two hundred and fifty-seven (76 per cent) of the patients in this series were born in maternity hospitals. Of the rest, 36 (11 per cent) were born at home attended by midwives, and 45 (13 per cent) at home, or on a journey or somewhere else without trained help. The corresponding figures for the general population in 1952 (the mean year of birth in this series) were 67, 31 and 2 per cent (Finland Central Statistical Office 1954, Finland, Central Medical Board 1955). The difference between the numbers of births without trained help in this series and in the general population was statistically significant when tested by the χ^2 test (p $<$ 0.01).

TABLE VIII
Mode of delivery

Mode of delivery	Present series		Control group†	
	No. of cases	Per cent	No. of cases	Per cent
Breech	20	5·9	116	3·9
Forceps	17	5·0*	80	2·7
Caesarean section	6	1·8‡	164	5·5
TOTAL SERIES	338		2997	

†Helsinki, Institute of Midwifery (1952).
*Almost significant difference ($\chi^2 = 6·0$, p $< 0·05$).
‡Significant difference ($\chi^2 = 8·8$, p $< 0·01$).

Obstetrical Procedures

Some kind of obstetrical operation was used in 26 deliveries, *i.e.* suction cup in three, caesarean section in six, and low forceps delivery in seventeen. The number of breech presentations in this series was twenty, which represented a slightly, but not significantly, greater prevalence than in the general population. Forceps deliveries were found to have been significantly more common and caesarian sections significantly less common in this series than in the general population (Table VIII) (Helsinki Institute of Midwifery 1952).

Because of the great differences between different countries with regard to the number of obstetrical operations carried out, it is not reasonable to compare these figures with the corresponding figures in foreign countries.

Birthweight

The birthweight was 2500g or less in fifty-one cases (15 per cent), more than 4500g in six cases (2 per cent) and unknown in twenty-three cases (7 per cent). There was a significantly higher proportion of patients with low birthweight in this series than in the general population (Table IX) (Helsinki Institute of Midwifery 1952).

TABLE IX
Birthweight distribution

Birthweight	Present series		Healthy infants†		General population‡	
	No. of cases	Per cent	No. of cases	Per cent	No. of cases	Per cent
2500g or less	51	16·7*	110	3·2	105	3·5
2501-3000g	56	18·4*	341	9·9		
3001-4000g	175	57·4*	2438	70·3		
4001-4500g	17	5·6*	473	13·7	2892	96·5
More than 4500g	6	2·0	101	2·9		
TOTAL	305	100·0	3463	100·0	2997	100·0

†Klemetti (1966).
‡Helsinki, Institute of Midwifery (1952).
*Highly significant difference ($\chi^2 <_{2500} = 128·1$, $\chi^2_{2501-3000} = 21·6$, $\chi^2_{3001-4000} = 22.4$, $\chi^2_{4001-4500} = 16·2$; p $< 0·001$).

29

The finding that mental retardation is particularly associated with low birthweight agrees well with earlier reports on patients with cerebral palsy and/or mental retardation and/or congenital malformations (Malamud et al. 1964, Drillien 1968b, Saxén and Klemetti 1970).

Maturity

The maturity of the child at birth, which was ascertained from the case records, was abnormal in fifty-seven cases (17 per cent). Fourteen (4 per cent) were small-for-dates, thirty-seven (11 per cent) were born more than two weeks pre-term, and six (2 per cent) were born more than two weeks post-term.

Short gestation, which is not now considered to be a primary cause of serious conditions (McDonald 1967, Drillien 1968a), was thought to be of aetiological importance in only three cases in this series.

Multiple Pregnancy

Fifteen (4.4 per cent) of the patients in this series were twins, nine of them A twins, and six of them B twins.* Two of the mentally retarded patients in this series resulted from the same twin pregnancy. Twin births were found to have occurred significantly ($p < 0.01$) more frequently in this series than in the general population in 1952—1.6 per hundred births according to the Statistical Yearbook of Finland (Finland Central Statistical Office 1954).

Condition of Child Immediately After Birth

The condition of the child immediately after birth was reported to have been in some way abnormal in 141 cases (42 per cent). Seventy-four cases (22 per cent) had been reported to have suffered slight neonatal asphyxia (cyanosis and/or delayed cry), and in a further 31 (9 per cent) marked asphyxia had been observed. Where possible, the later records of these patients were checked for findings consistent with the occurrence of asphyxia. Although the figure for mild cases may be unreliable, this is unlikely to be so for the more marked cases. Marked asphyxia occurred significantly more frequently in this series than it did amongst the 7024 live-born infants born in the Obstetric Departments of the University of Helsinki during 1952, of whom 322 (4.6 per cent) were markedly asphyxiated at birth ($\chi^2 = 15.3$, $p < 0.001$) (University of Helsinki 1952).

Abnormalities During the Later Neonatal Period

Abnormalities in the child's condition during the later neonatal period had been recorded in 139 cases (41 per cent), whereas Kantero (1973) describes such abnormalities as occurring in only 7 out of 156 non-retarded healthy children (4.5 per cent). This difference is statistically significant ($\chi^2 = 68.9$, $p < 0.001$).

---

* A twin = Born as the first of the twins.
  B twin = Born as the second of the twins.

30

Early Manifestations of Mental Retardation

The mental retardation had been diagnosed during the first year of life in 245 cases (73 per cent), and during the second year of life in 37 cases (11 per cent). The oldest age at which the mental retardation had been detected was seven years (in 4 cases or 1 per cent). The retardation was probably apparent from the beginning in 271 cases (80 per cent), had an acute onset in 33 cases (10 per cent), and was progressive in 13 cases (4 per cent). In the remaining six per cent of the patients, the picture was less clear, and the form of onset varied.

Epileptic Seizures

Epileptic seizures had been observed in 210 cases (62 per cent). The type of epilepsy was diagnosed from the historical data and the EEGs, and was classified as focal in 47 cases (14 per cent), generalised in 61 cases (18 per cent), and miscellaneous in 102 cases (30 per cent).

Physical Examination

Height, Weight and Head Circumference

The mean *height* of the male patients, grouped according to age, was below the 2.5 percentile for healthy Finnish males (Bäckström-Järvinen 1964) in groups aged 6, 16, 19 and over 20 years of age. In all other groups, the means were between the 2.5 and 50th percentiles (Fig. 2). The mean heights of the female patients were relatively smaller compared with the means for the normal Finnish population than those of the males. The mean heights in the age groups of 3, 4, 8, 12 and 13 years were between the 2.5 and 50th percentiles, while the means in all other groups were below the 2.5 percentile (Fig. 3).

The mean *weights* of the male patients were between the 2.5 and 50th percentiles in all age groups except for those of 16, 17, 18 and 19 years, in which the values were below the 2.5 percentile (Fig. 4). The mean weights of the female patients were below the 2.5 percentile in the 2- and 5-year-old age groups. In all the other age groups, the mean was between the 2.5 and 50th percentiles, except in the group aged 13 years, in which it was between the 50th and 97.5 percentiles (Fig. 5).

The mean *head circumference* of the male patients was between the 2nd and 50th percentiles in all except the 5-year-old group, in which it was between the 50th and 98th percentiles (Fig. 6). The mean head circumferences of the female patients in each age group were as follows: between the 2nd and 50th percentiles in the groups aged 2, 3, 4, 12, 17 and over 20 years, over the 98th percentile in the 5-year-old group, and below the 2nd percentile in all the other groups (Fig. 7).

Grouping all the cases into three categories, according to whether they were more than 2 s.d. (standard deviations) below, between 2 s.d. below and 2 s.d. above, or more than 2 s.d. above the norm, showed that more than half the cases were abnormally small in height, whereas less cases showed deviation from normal with regard to weight and head circumference.

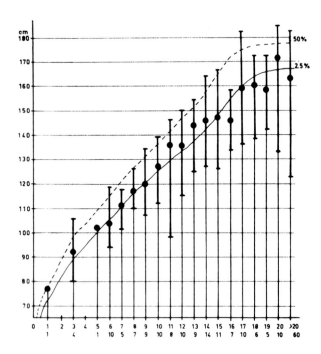

Fig. 2. Mean heights (with extreme values) of males, according to age (in years). The great majority of means lie between the 50th and 2.5 percentiles of males of the corresponding age in the general population. On the horizontal axis, the upper row of figures indicates the age in years, while the lower row indicates the number of patients.

Fig. 3. Mean heights (with extreme values) of females, according to age (in years). The majority of means lie below the 2.5 percentile of females of the corresponding age in the general population. On the horizontal axis, the upper row of figures indicates the age in years, while the lower row indicates the number of patients.

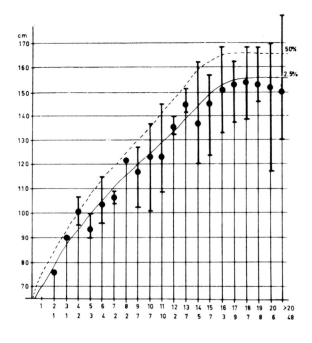

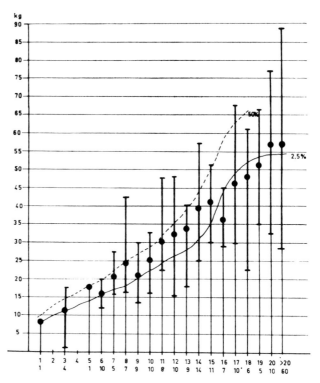

Fig. 4. Mean weights (with extreme values) of males, according to age (in years). The great majority of means lie between the 50th and 2.5 percentiles of males of the corresponding age in the general population. On the horizontal axis, the upper row of figures indicates the age in years, while the lower row indicates the number of patients.

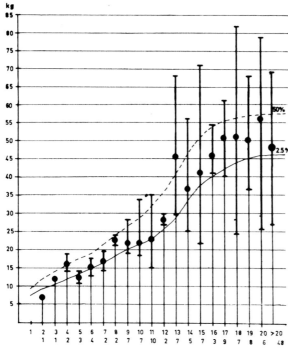

Fig. 5. Mean weights (with extreme values) of females, according to age (in years). The great majority of means are between the 50th and 2.5 percentiles of males of the corresponding age in the general population. On the horizontal axis, the upper row of figures indicates the age in years, while the lower row indicates the number of patients.

33

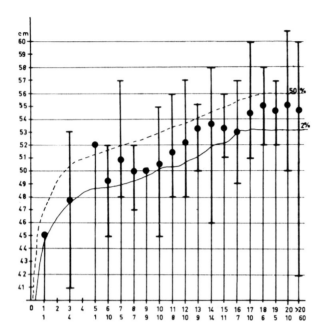

Fig. 6. Mean head circumferences (with extreme values) of males, according to age (in years). The great majority of means are between the 50th and 2nd percentiles of males of the corresponding age in the general population. On the horizontal axis, the upper row of figures indicates the age in years, while the lower row indicates the number of patients.

Fig. 7. Mean head circumferences (with extreme values) of females, according to age (in years). The majority of means lie below the 2nd percentile of females of the corresponding age in the general population. On the horizontal axis, the upper row of figures indicates the age in years, while the lower row indicates the number of patients.

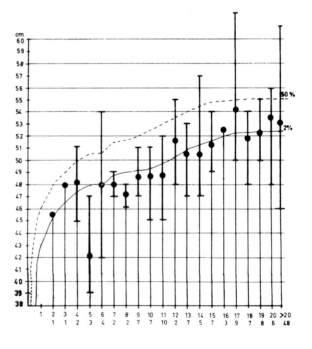

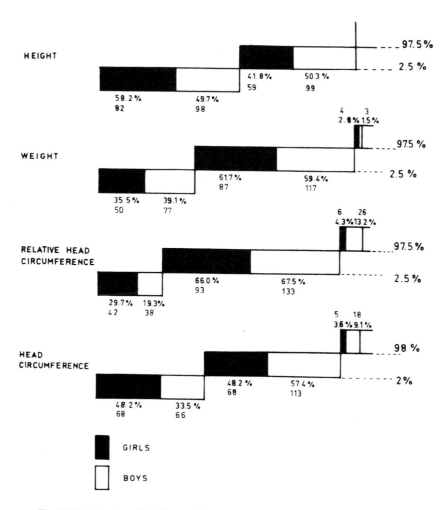

Fig. 8. Distribution of heights, weights, relative head circumferences and absolute head circumferences into three categories, according to whether they were below the 2.5 (2.0 for head circumferences), between the 2.5 and 97.5 (2 and 98 for head circumferences) or over the 97.5 (98 for head circumferences) percentiles of the normal population. The proportion of patients who were abnormally small is strikingly high. Note the difference between relative and absolute head circumferences.

When assessed in relation to height, the head circumference measurements for each age group were closer to normal than when they were taken in isolation and simply compared with the normal for the patients' ages (Fig. 8). It would therefore seem more natural when assessing the head circumferences of mentally retarded patients to use a 'relative' method, whereby the head circumference is related both to the age and stature of the patient, than an 'absolute' method, which does not take account of stature, and tends to indicate a higher incidence of abnormally small head circumference.

TABLE X

TABLE X

Cephalic index distribution

Cephalic index	Present series		General population[†]	
	No. of cases	Per cent	No. of cases	Per cent
74·9 or less (dolichocephaly)	65	19·2*	164	10·5
75·0-80·9 (mesocephaly)	106	31·4*	768	49·0
81·0-85·4 (brachycephaly)	92	27·2‡	525	33·5
85·5 or more (hyperbrachycephaly)	75	22·2*	111	7·1
TOTAL	338	100·0	1568	100·0

[†]The figures for the general population are arithmetical means from the results of studies in Häme and Uusimaa counties in Finland (Löfgren 1937, Telkkä 1952).

‡Almost significant difference ($\chi^2 = 5\cdot2$, p $<0\cdot05$).

*Highly significant difference ($\chi^2_{<75\cdot0} = 22\cdot0$, $\chi^2_{75\cdot0-80\cdot9} = 35\cdot5$, $\chi^2_{>85\cdot4} = 78.8$; p <0.001).

Cephalic Index

When the patients' skulls were classified according to cephalic index, the most common abnormal finding was flat skull (cephalic index more than 81.0), which was found in 167 cases (49 per cent). The extreme forms of abnormality, dolichocephaly and hyperbrachycephaly, were significantly more common in this series than in the general population (Table X). The mean cephalic index in this series was a little, but not significantly, greater (82.7 for the males; 81.5 for the females; and 82.2 for the whole series) than in the general population (81.0 for males; 81.1 for females; and 81.0 for both sexes together—according to Takkunen and Telkkä 1964).

Handedness

Handedness was assessed by observing the patients during their daily activities. Forty-three (12.5 per cent) of the patients in this series were left-handed, and 231 (68.5 per cent) were right-handed, whereas, according to a survey of 65,600 Finnish school children reported by Kallio and Mäki (1934), only 4.8 per cent of the general population is left-handed. This difference is highly significant ($\chi^2 = 46.5$; p <0.001).

Handedness could not be determined in 64 (19 per cent) of the patients in this series, in most cases because of a severe degree of extremital paresis.

Dyscrania

Dyscrania, or some kind of maldevelopment of the skull, was found at physical examination in 232 cases (69 per cent).

Major Malformations

Of the 54 patients (16 per cent) who were found to have major congenital malformations, 20 (37 per cent) had a congenital cataract defect (Table XI). Congenital

TABLE XI

Major congenital malformations at physical examination

Malformation	Present series		Control
	No. of cases	Per cent	Per cent
Congenital cataract	20	5·9	0·26†
Syndactyly of fingers and/or toes	9	2·7	
Congenital heart anomaly	8	2·4	0·11‡
Harelip and/or cleft palate	8	2·4	0·13‡
Eye anomaly	8	2·4	0·01‡
microphthalmia	(5)	(1·5)	
keratoconus and/or coloboma	(2)	(0·6)	
anophthalmia	(1)	(0·3)	
Supernumerary fingers and/or toes	1	0·3	
TOTAL	54	16·0	1·17*

†Prevalence at the Department of Ophthalmology, University of Helsinki (Liesmaa 1972).
‡Prevalence among newborns in Finland (Saxén and Härö 1964).
*See Klemetti and Saxén (1970): The Finnish Register of Congenital Malformations.

cataract defect was significantly more common (6 per cent) in this series than in either the patient population of the Department of Ophthalmology, University of Helsinki (Liesmaa 1972) or other series of mentally retarded patients reported in the literature (*e.g.* Warburg 1963), although the prevalence depends, of course, on the criteria by which the patients are selected for study.

Cutaneous Findings

The most striking cutaneous findings were as follows: abnormalities of skin pigmentation in 36 cases (16 per cent), cutis verticis gyrata in 16 cases (5 per cent), cutis marmoratus in 15 cases (4 per cent), striae albicantes in 10 cases (3 per cent), adenoma sebaceum in 3 cases (1 per cent), and anhydrotic cutaneous dysplasia, congenital ichthyosis, naevus flammeus, pseudoxanthoma elasticum and xeroderma pigmentosum each in one case.

Abnormal Neurological Findings at Physical Examination

The classification of different neurological syndromes followed classical lines. Thus, a child with increased reflexes, fickle distribution of loss of power, and up-going plantar responses was regarded as having an upper motor neurone lesion. A child with involuntary movements, unsteadiness, variable tone or rigidity was regarded as having an extra-pyramidal syndrome. Signs of a cerebellar syndrome included truncal and/or limb ataxia, intention tremor, and, sometimes, a positive Romberg sign. In a group of patients such as the present one, however, one inevitably finds these classical lines hard to follow. Thus, for example, a child with rigidity but increased reflexes, that is to say, with evidence of both upper motor neurone and extra-pyramidal signs, was placed in a miscellaneous group.

Neurological signs indicative of an upper motor neurone lesion were present in nearly half the patients in this series (151 or 45 per cent) (Table XII). Extra-pyramidal

TABLE XII

TABLE XII

Distribution of the different neurological syndromes

Neurological findings indicative of	No. of cases	Percentage of 338
Upper motor neurone lesion	151	45
Cranial nerve lesion	54	16
Cerebellar lesion	37	11
Extrapyramidal lesion	28	8
Miscellaneous abnormal findings	49	15
TOTAL	319	95

syndromes were seen in 28 (8 per cent). A cerebellar syndrome was diagnosed in 37 patients (11 per cent), but it could not be excluded in a further 50 with severe paresis of the extremities.

Atrophy of one or both optic discs was found in 39 cases (12 per cent), and papilloedema in four (1 per cent). The papilloedema in two cases was fluctuating. Sixteen patients (5 per cent) were blind, and three (1 per cent) were deaf. Decreased muscular strength was found in 140 cases (41 per cent), of which 137 showed signs of an upper motor neurone lesion, and 3 (1 per cent) signs of muscular disease. Muscular hypotonia was found in 22 cases (7 per cent), dystonia in 4 (1 per cent), and rigidity in 3 (1 per cent). Decreased sensitivity to pain stimulus was difficult to record, but 12 patients (4 per cent) certainly did not react.

Cerebral Palsy

Cerebral palsy was diagnosed in 183 patients (54 per cent), of whom 101 (55 per cent) had spasticity, 41 (22 per cent) had dyskinesia, 4 (2 per cent) had ataxia, and 37 (20 per cent) had a combination of these different forms.

Diplegia was the most common of the spastic pareses, being present in 46 (34 per cent) of the 137 patients with spasticity, either alone or in combination with other forms of cerebral palsy. Tetraplegia and paraplegia were also common (see Table XIII). Altogether, 70 patients (38 per cent of those with cerebral palsy) exhibited some

TABLE XIII

Distribution of spastic extremital pareses

Form of paresis	No. of cases	Per cent
Diplegia	46	34
Tetraplegia	27	20
Paraplegia	26	19
Triplegia	13	9
Right hemiplegia	13	9
Left hemiplegia	7	5
Monoplegia	5	4
TOTAL	137	100

form of dyskinesia. Of these, 15 (21 per cent) had athetosis, 7 (10 per cent) tremor, 4 (6 per cent) dystonia, and 44 (63 per cent) miscellaneous and/or unspecified forms.

Disturbances of Functional Skills

Three hundred and three cases (90 per cent) had speech disturbances, 230 (68 per cent) could not dress themselves properly, 220 (65 per cent) had inadequate bowel and bladder control, 208 (62 per cent) had difficulty undressing, 172 (51 per cent) could not walk normally, of whom 50 (15 per cent) could not walk at all, 111 (33 per cent) were unable to feed themselves, and 62 (18 per cent) could not sit without support.

Psychiatric Evaluation

Formal psychiatric evaluation was not really possible, because of the severity of the mental retardation in many of the patients in this series. Thus, estimation of behavioural problems was based largely on observations made during the course of the doctor's examination, and by independent observers when the patients were on the wards and involved in normal activities. These observations were discussed with the psychologist and child psychiatrist before a final diagnosis was made.

Signs of psychosis, *i.e.* restlessness in 11 cases, autism in 10 cases, and hallucinations in 6 cases, were found in 27 cases (8 per cent).

Laboratory Investigations

Almost without exception, the laboratory tests carried out on cerebrospinal fluid and blood serum samples taken from the patients in this series (see Methods, page 22) showed non-specific changes, which have been reported elsewhere (Iivanainen and Collan 1968, Iivanainen and Kostiainen 1971, Palo *et al.* 1973), and were obviously without significance as far as the aetiology of mental retardation was concerned.

The largely negative results obtained from the extensive CSF investigations indicate that, although such investigations may obviously be very important and revealing during the period of the acute insult, during the chronic stage of mental retardation they are of very limited value.

A diagnosis of infection had been made in 38 of the patients before this study was begun (see Table XLIII), by means of the conventional isolation of micro-organisms and/or follow-up of antibody titres. Wassermann's complement fixation test, and Kahn's flocculation test were positive in the CSF of three additional cases, but in all three, all the other blood serum and CSF investigations carried out, including *Treponema pallidum* immobilisation test (TPI), and Reiter's test, gave negative findings.

The results of some of the biochemical studies (*i.e.* analysis of amino acid and carbohydrate concentrations in urine and/or blood) performed on a number of patients have been presented elsewhere (Palo 1966, 1967). These studies revealed two cases of cystinuria, one case of peptiduria, and one case of probable renal glucosuria. Later, the case of peptiduria was identified as having aspartylglucosaminuria (Palo and Mattson 1970). In all the other cases studied, amino acid chromatography revealed normal findings. The glucose loading tests performed in five cases with convulsions revealed a pathologically high blood glucose content in two cases.

However, it was difficult to establish the aetiological significance of this finding, since both patients also had brain injuries. In one case of muscular atrophy, previously undiagnosed, the low concentration of serum phosphorus was normalised, and the osteoporosis improved, after treatment with high doses of vitamin D.

Electroencephalography

All the EEGs were examined by Dr. Seppäläinen. The EEG recordings were normal or on the borderline of normal in 20 of the 320 cases examined (6 per cent). Mild disturbances were found in 80 cases (25 per cent), and marked disturbances in 220

TABLE XIV

Prevalence of specific abnormalities in the 320 patients submitted to EEG

EEG abnormality	No. of cases	Percentage of 320
Diffuse slow wave abnormalities		
slight	92	29
moderately severe	165	52
severe	26	8
Abnormal β-activity	41	13
Extreme spindles	1	0
Asymmetry or depression of background activity	33	10
Focal slow wave abnormalities		
slight	24	8
moderate	22	7
severe	3	1
Intermittent delta rhythms	3	1
Paroxysmal slow activity	56	18
Focal spikes and sharp waves		
a few	29	9
abundant	32	10
Generalised irregular spikes and waves	53	17
Generalised regular 3 Hz spikes and waves	5	2
Rhythmical 2-2·5 Hz spikes and waves	13	4
Hypsarrhythmia	1	0
14 and 6 positive spikes	1	0
Other generalised bilateral changes	2	1

TABLE XV

Localisation of focal EEG abnormalities

Localisation	No. of cases	Per cent
Temporal	36	35
Occipital	17	15
Frontal	14	12
Parietal	7	6
Miscellaneous	40	35
TOTAL	114	100

cases (69 per cent). Table XIV shows the prevalence of specific EEG findings, as classified according to Dumermuth (1965). Diffuse slow wave abnormalities were recorded in the great majority of cases (89 per cent). Focal slow wave abnormalities were found in 49 cases (15 per cent), and focal spikes and sharp waves in 61 cases (19 per cent). The focal EEG changes were most frequently localised in the temporal region (36 cases or 11 per cent) (see Table XV); they were also recorded slightly, thought not significantly, more often on the right than on the left side (Table XVI). It is hoped that a fuller report on these findings will be published at a later date.

TABLE XVI
Lateralisation of focal EEG abnormalities

Lateralisation	No. of cases	Per cent
Right	52	46
Left	47	41
Bilateral	8	7
Fluctuating asymmetry	7	6
TOTAL	114	100

Auditory Evoked Potentials

The elicitation of auditory evoked potentials, recorded by means of an electro-encephalograph and a computer, indicated hearing loss in 54 of the 94 cases studied. The loss of hearing was severe in three cases, moderate in twelve, and slight in 39. The hearing ability of the 40 remaining cases was regarded as normal in 38 cases, and uncertain in two. A clear evoked response to a 60dB tone of 250 to 4000 Hz was set as the upper limit of normal hearing ability.

The recording of auditory evoked potentials is not a very reliable way of determining hearing ability in the mentally retarded, for two main reasons: (1) even though an auditory evoked response is elicited, it is still possible that the patient does not understand what he hears (*i.e.* the association functions may not be intact); (2) it may not be possible to elicit a response even though the auditory system is in order, because the secondary intracerebral system giving rise to the non-specific evoked response is faulty.

Electromyography

Myotonic paroxysms after mechanical stimulation and a typical myotonic pattern were found in two of the three cases studied with electromyography. In the third case, electromyography revealed nothing definitely abnormal.

The motor nerve conduction velocities of these three cases were within normal limits.

Chromosome Karyotyping and the Determination of the Presence of Sex Chromatin

Chromosome analysis revealed an abnormal karyotype in 13 of the 124 cases investigated. Four had Down's syndrome, six had an autosomal aberration involving

41

TABLE XVII

Karyotypes of chromosome aberrations

Karyotype	No. of cases
46,XY,Bp −	1
46,XY,Bq +	1
46,XX,Cq fragility	1
46,XY,t(Cq − ;Dp +)	1
47,XX, ?E +	1
46,XX,Er	1
47,XY,G +	3
46,XY,G −,t(GqGq) +	1
45,X	1
45,X/46,XXq −	1
45,X/46,XXqi/47,XXqiXqi	1
TOTAL	13

other than the G chromosome, and three had a sex chromosome aberration (Table XVII). The two cases of Turner's syndrome with mosaicism had been diagnosed previously (de la Chapelle 1962, 1963; de la Chapelle *et al.* 1966).

The presence of sex chromatin was determined from buccal smears in 10 cases. The findings were pathological in the three cases with sex chromosome aberrations, *viz* no sex chromatin in the case of 45,X; no and one sex chromatin in the case of 45,X/46,XXq−; no, one and two sex chromatins in the case of 45,X/46,XXqi/47, XXqiXqi.

Neuroradiological Investigations

Skull X-ray

The findings in the 331 cases given skull x-rays were classified, with some modifications, according to the system of classification suggested by Epstein and Epstein (1967). In half the cases (166), the findings had no clinical significance, *i.e.* they were asymptomatic or normal (Table XVIII). Asymptomatic anomalies were found in 96 cases (29 per cent). These included asymmetry of the frontal sinuses in 82 cases (22 per cent), slight digital markings in 53 cases (16 per cent), persistent metopic fontanelle or cranium bifidum occultum frontalis in 19 cases (6 per cent), and hypertrophy of the sutures in one case.

Congenital cranial deformities were found in 33 cases (10 per cent). Most of these patients had some form of craniosynostosis, such as hyperbrachycephaly (20 cases), scaphocephaly (9 cases), and oxycephaly (3 cases). In addition there was one case of meningoencephalocele.

Neoplasms or haematomas were revealed by the skull x-ray in five cases, *i.e.* through the signs of high intracranial pressure in two cases of cerebral neoplasm (astrocytoma, Figs. 28 and 29) and in one case of acute subdural haematoma, and through typical intracranial calcifications in one case of tuberose sclerosis and in one

42

TABLE XVIII
Skull X-ray findings

Finding	No. of cases	Per cent
Asymptomatic anomaly	96	29
Congenital cranial deformity	33	10
Neoplasm or haematoma	5	2
Skull defect due to trauma	3	1
Asymmetry (small right-sided lesion)	19	6
Asymmetry (small left-sided lesion)	35	11
Infective changes (calcifications)	3	1
Miscellaneous pathological	67	20
Normal	70	21
TOTAL	331	100

case of chronic subdural haematoma (Fig. 23). The signs of high intracranial pressure consisted of clear digital markings in three cases, diastasis of the sutures in two cases, and atrophy of the dorsum of the sella turcica in one case.

The three cases of skull defect due to trauma comprised one case of skull fracture, and two of post-operative skull defect.

In 54 cases (16 per cent) skull x-ray examination showed certain other unilateral or asymmetrical changes, which assisted in the determination of the lateralisation of the intracranial lesion. These asymmetrical changes, which were located on the right side in 19 cases, and on the left side in 35, included asymmetry of the vault (unilateral bulging included) and/or of the base of the skull, sometimes combined with lateral dislocation of the crista galli. Lateral displacement of the calcified pineal gland was observed in four cases.

Infective changes shown by the skull x-rays included calcifications in two cases of toxoplasmosis and in one case with an undefined infection.

Miscellaneous pathological findings (*i.e.* mixed forms of the other findings described above) were found in about one fifth of the skull x-rays.

The volume of the sella turcica was abnormally large (*i.e.* over 1092 mm³; see DiChiro and Nelson 1962) in eight cases. A bone bridge over the sella turcica was found in seven cases (2 per cent).

When the patients in this series were grouped according to their ages in years, the mean cranial volume of each age group was compared with the normal value for British children of the same age, as reported by Gordon (1966). The mean was below the limit of the 5th percentile in all age groups except those of four years or less (Figs. 9 and 10). However, the number of very young patients in this series was small.

Classification of the cranial volumes into three categories (below the 5th percentile, between the 5th and 95th percentiles, and over the 95th percentile) showed that there were few cases of macrocephaly (10 cases or 4 per cent), while there was a preponderance of microcephalics (207 cases or 74 per cent) (Table XIX).

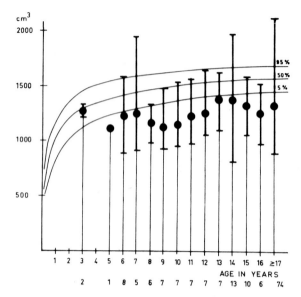

Fig. 9. Mean cranial volumes (with extreme values) of males, according to age (in years). All the means are similar, almost all of them being below the 5th percentile of normal males of the corresponding age in the general population. The lower row of figures on the horizontal axis indicates the number of patients in each age group.

Fig. 10. Mean cranial volumes (with extreme values) of females, according to age (in years). All the means are similar, almost all of them being below the 5th percentile of normal females of the corresponding age in the general population. The lower row of figures on the horizontal axis indicates the number of patients in each age group.

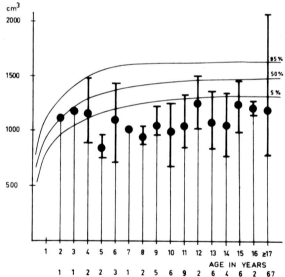

TABLE XIX

Distribution of the cranial volumes measured on the skull X-rays

Cranial volume*	No. of cases	Per cent
Below 5th percentile (microcephaly)	207	74
Between 5th and 95th percentiles (normocephaly)	61	22
Above 95th percentile (macrocephaly)	10	4
TOTAL	278	100

*Assessed according to the method described by Gordon (1966).

44

Echoencephalography

The echoencephalographic findings were pathological in 67 per cent of the 70 patients examined. Displacement or suspected displacement of the cerebral mid-line was found in 16 cases, microventriculy without dislocation of the mid-line in 11 cases, and an additional echo spike alone in 10 (Table XX).

TABLE XX

Distribution of the findings at echoencephalography

Finding	No. of cases
Macroventriculy without displacement of the cerebral mid-line	11
Additional echo spike alone	10
Displacement of cerebral mid-line	8
Suspected displacement of cerebral mid-line	8
Hemimacroventriculy or local ventricular dilatation	2
Miscellaneous abnormal findings	8
Nothing definitely pathological	23
TOTAL	70

Cerebral Angiography

The main findings from the 105 angiograms performed on 90 patients are listed in Table XXI.

The most common finding was displacement of cerebral vessels. Lateral displacement of the pericallosal artery and/or the internal cerebral vein indicated a lateral shift of the cerebral mid-line structures in 23 cases, and displacement of the striothalamic vein revealed a large lateral ventricle in 44 cases. The latter group of cases also had a tightened and large pericallosal arch. Displacement of the anterior cerebral artery

TABLE XXI

Distribution of the main findings at cerebral angiography

Finding	No. of cases	Per cent
Displacement of cerebral vessels due to a non-expansive process	42	47
Dysplasia of cerebral vessels	8	9
Subdural haematoma	4	4
Arterial aneurysm	2	2
Cerebral angiopathy	2	2
Cerebral neoplasm	2	2
Occlusion of cerebral vessels	2	2
Miscellaneous pathological findings	2	2
Nothing definitely pathological	26	29
TOTAL	90	100

was observed in 14 cases, of the middle cerebral artery in 22 cases, and of the posterior cerebral artery in 5 cases.

From the evidence provided by the angiograms and the other neuroradiological studies performed on these 90 patients, the cause of the shift of the cerebral vessels appeared to be a non-expanding process in 42 cases (Table XXI). Three of the four subdural haematomas were acute, and one was chronic (Fig. 23). A cerebral neoplasm was the cause of the displacement of the cerebral vessels in two cases. One was a right-sided thalamic expansion without pathological vascularization (Fig. 28), and the other was a right-sided temporal expansion, also without pathological vascularization (Fig. 30). Neither had been identified clinically at the time of the investigation. Later, both were verified as astrocytomas (the former at autopsy, the latter at operation).

Cerebrovascular disorders other than subdural haematomas were detected in a further fourteen cases (see Table XXI). In one of the two cases of vascular occlusion, the occlusion was in the arterial system (occlusion of the internal carotid artery in a girl with moyamoya disease) (Fig. 24), and in the other it was in the venous system (the deep veins, *i.e.* the great cerebral vein of Galen, sinus rectus, and transverse sinus, were not visualized) (Fig. 25). One of the two cases with a single arterial aneurysm had a small saccular aneurysm in the posterior cerebral artery. The cerebral angiopathy was visualized in both cases as an unevenness of the walls of the cerebral arteries and changes of the calibre of the arterial lumen. In addition, the cerebral circulation time was markedly slowed in one of these two cases. The hypoplasia of the cerebral vessels was moderate or severe in all eight cases. It involved the branches of the middle cerebral artery and the corresponding veins in six cases, and the branches of the pericallosal and/or posterior cerebral arteries and the corresponding veins in the other two cases.

One of the two cases of miscellaneous pathological findings at cerebral angiography had hypoplasia of the middle cerebral artery and a persisting trigeminal artery, in association with a slowed cerebral circulation rate. The other had a very narrow anterior cerebral artery on the left side, and an enlarged anterior cerebral artery on the right side. These findings were interpreted as constituting a variation of the circle of Willis, and were considered to have no clinical significance. This patient gave the appearance of having the Rubinstein-Taybi syndrome (Fig. 38).

In less than one third of the cases (26 out of the 90 cases, or 29 per cent) did cerebral angiography reveal no definite pathological findings.

Pneumoencephalography

Main Findings. In about 90 per cent of the 334 cases studied with pneumoencephalography, the findings were pathological (Table XXII). Macroventriculy appeared to be the most important finding, being observed in 204 (*i.e.* over 60 per cent). In 84 (41 per cent) of the patients with macroventriculy, the supratentorial ventricles were symmetrically large, while 38 (19 per cent) had asymmetrical macroventriculy and 45 (22 per cent) hemimacroventriculy; localised enlargement of the ventricles was the main finding in 37 cases (18 per cent of all the cases found to have

TABLE XXII

Distribution of the main findings at pneumoencephalography

Finding	No. of cases	Per cent
Symmetrical macroventriculy	84	25
Asymmetrical macroventriculy	38	11
Hemimacroventriculy	45	13
Temporal horn dilatation	31	9
Other localised ventricular dilatation	6	2
Cortical atrophy or dysplasia	13	4
Cerebral malformation	52	16
Intracranial expansion (neoplasm)	3	1
Cerebellar atrophy or dysplasia	20	6
Miscellaneous pathological findings	5	1
Insufficient gas filling	4	1
Nothing definitely pathological	33	10
TOTAL	334	100

macroventriculy), of whom 31 had unilateral or bilateral enlargement of the temporal horns.

Although it is traditional to talk about enlargement of the ventricles, it is clear that, in fact, in many instances these ventricles have not enlarged, but have always been large. It is perhaps wiser, therefore, to use the term macroventriculy to distinguish this phenomenon of a big ventricle from enlargement of the ventricles such as one sees, for example, in hydrocephalus.

Cerebral malformation was diagnosed in 52 cases (16 per cent of all the cases submitted to pneumoencephalography), and cerebellar atrophy or dysplasia in 20 cases (6 per cent).

Supratentorial Ventricular Size. In Table XXIII, the 107 older patients (over 20 years) submitted to pneumoencephalography are classified according to the size of the supratentorial ventricles, using the criteria suggested by Nielsen *et al.* (1966a). The

TABLE XXIII

Size of supratentorial ventricular space in patients aged over twenty years

Category	No. of cases	Per cent
Microventriculy	5	5
Normoventriculy	15	14
Ventricular asymmetry	7	7
Symmetrical macroventriculy	28	26
Asymmetrical macroventriculy	15	14
Hemimacroventriculy	19	18
Temporal horn deformity	10	9
Other ventricular deformity	3	3
Not measurable	5	5
TOTAL	107	100

TABLE XXIV

Cases aged over twenty years with macroventriculy classified according to the degree of ventricular enlargement (Nielsen et al. 1966a)

Type of macroventriculy	Degree of macroventriculy			Total
	Slight	Moderate	Severe	
Symmetrical macroventriculy	15	10	3	28
Asymmetrical macroventriculy	0	5	10	15
Hemimacroventriculy	8	9	2	19
TOTAL	23	24	15	62

lateral ventricles and the third ventricle were found to be normal-sized in nearly one fifth of the cases. Various types of macroventriculy were the most common abnormal finding. In Table XXIV, the cases of symmetrical and asymmetrical macroventriculy and hemimacroventriculy are divided into the sub-groups of slight, moderate and severe (Nielsen *et al.* 1966a).

In the majority of cases of ventricular asymmetry, the left side of the ventricular system was larger than the right side. This was true of all types of asymmetry (including asymmetry of the ventricular horns). Thus, the left lateral ventricle was larger than the right one in six of the cases with normal-sized ventricles, in eleven of the cases of asymmetrical macroventriculy, in fifteen of the cases of hemimacroventriculy, and in four of the cases with 'other ventricular asymmetries', whereas the figures for right-sided dominance in each group were one, four, four and three, respectively. In other words, altogether, the left lateral ventricle was larger than the right one in 36 out of 48 cases of ventricular asymmetry who were aged over 20 years.

Bilateral macroventriculy without ratio difference and without displacement was the most common finding (about two thirds) among the patients aged 20 years or less, when the ventricular sizes were classified according to Evans' (1942) ratio (Table XXV). The second largest group comprised cases of bilateral macroventriculy with ratio difference and without displacement (about 16 per cent). Evans' ratio was not measurable in 11 of the 227 cases. The remainder were subdivided into smaller groups of microventriculy, bilateral macroventriculy with ratio difference and with displacement, unilateral macroventriculy, normoventriculy, and bilateral macroventriculy without ratio difference and with displacement.

Tables XXVI to XXX show the widths of the cellae mediae, of the nucleus caudatus septum lines, of the frontal horns, of the temporal horns, and of the occipital horns, as measured from the pneumoencephalograms (see page 24). From these data it can be seen that the left lateral ventricle was enlarged more often than the right one in this series. The greatest difference was found in respect of the widths of the temporal horns.

The third ventricle showed no enlargement (*i.e.* width below 6 mm) in about one quarter of the cases submitted to pneumoencephalography (Table XXXI). In fifteen cases (4 per cent), the third ventricle was very small (width 3 mm or less). The third ventricle was severely enlarged (width 12 mm or more) in 34 cases (10 per cent), and was not visualized in another 34.

TABLE XXV

Classification of cerebral ventricular size by means of Evans' ratio in patients aged twenty years or less

Category	Evans' ratio	No. of cases	Per cent
Symmetrical microventriculy	less than 0·20	2	1
Symmetrical normoventriculy	0·20 to 0·24	5	2
Asymmetrical normoventriculy	0·20 to 0·24	1	0
Bilateral macroventriculy with a	0·25 to 0·29	45	20
ratio difference of 0·05 or	0·30 to 0·34	59	26
less and with ventricular displacement	0·35 to 0·39	22	10
of less than 5 mm (*i.e.* with no ratio	0·40 to 0·49	18	8
difference and no displacement)	0·50 or more	9	4
Bilateral macroventriculy with no ratio	0·25 to 0·29	1	0
difference (*i.e.* 0·05 or less), and with	0·30 to 0·34	1	0
ventricular displacement of 5 mm or more	0·35 to 0·39	1	0
	0·40 to 0·49	3	1
Bilateral macroventriculy with a ratio difference	0·25 to 0·29	5	2
of more than 0·05, but without ventricular	0·30 to 0·34	13	6
displacement of 5 mm or more	0·35 to 0·39	8	4
	0·40 to 0·49	9	4
	0·50 or more	3	1
Bilateral macroventriculy with a ratio	0·30 to 0·34	1	0
difference of more than 0·05 and	0·40 to 0·49	3	1
with ventricular displacement of 5 mm or more			
Unilateral macroventriculy without	only one ratio	5	2
ventricular displacement of 5 mm or more	more than 0·25		
Unilateral macroventriculy with	only one ratio	2	1
ventricular displacement of 5 mm or more	more than 0·25		
Unclassified	not measurable	11	5
TOTAL		**227**	**100**

TABLE XXVI

Widths of the cellae mediae

Width in mm	Right		Left	
	No. of cases	Per cent	No. of cases	Per cent
15 or less	29	9	21	6
16-18	84	25	79	24
19-20	68	20	55	16
21-22	40	12	39	12
23-25	37	11	49	15
26-28	18	5	32	10
29-30	13	4	14	4
More than 30	21	6	22	7
Not measurable	24	7	23	7
TOTAL	**334**	**100**	**334**	**100**

The width of both cellae mediae was graded as follows (Nielsen *et al.* 1966a).

    Less than 40 mm = no enlargement   45 to 49 mm = moderate enlargement
    40 to 44 mm = slight enlargement   50 mm or more = severe enlargement

TABLE XXVII

Septum caudate lines

| Length in mm | Right | | Left | |
	No. of cases	Per cent	No. of cases	Per cent
6 or less	4	1	6	2
7- 8	25	7	27	8
9-10	52	16	40	12
11-12	61	18	46	14
13-14	54	16	49	15
15-16	40	12	41	12
17-18	20	6	35	10
19-20	12	4	15	4
21-22	4	1	6	2
More than 22	25	7	30	9
Not measurable	37	11	39	12
TOTAL	334	100	334	100

The lengths of the septum caudate lines (*i.e.* the heights of the lateral ventricles) were graded as follows (Nielsen *et al.* 1966*a*).

    Less than 15 mm = no enlargement
    15 to 16 mm = slight enlargement
    17 to 18 mm = moderate enlargement
    19 mm or more = severe enlargement

TABLE XXVIII

Widths of the frontal horns

| Width in mm | Right | | Left | |
	No. of cases	Per cent	No. of cases	Per cent
15 or less	4	1	7	2
16-18	31	9	17	5
19-21	74	22	64	19
22-24	91	27	85	25
25-27	49	15	69	21
28-30	30	9	33	10
31-33	9	3	14	4
More than 33	21	6	20	6
Not measurable	25	7	25	7
TOTAL	334	100	334	100

The widths of the frontal horns were graded as follows (Engeset and Skraastad 1964).

    Less than 25 mm = no enlargement
    25 mm or more = enlargement

TABLE XXIX

Widths of the temporal horns

Width in mm	Right		Left	
	No. of cases	Per cent	No. of cases	Per cent
Less than 5	202	60	154	46
5-6	57	17	64	19
7-8	12	4	35	10
9-10	9	3	17	5
11-12	9	3	12	4
13-14	3	1	7	2
15-16	2	1	5	1
17-18	1	0	2	1
19-20	1	0	2	1
More than 20	7	2	7	2
Not measurable	31	9	29	9
TOTAL	334	100	334	100

The widths of the temporal horns were graded as follows (Engeset and Skraastad 1964).

Less than 5 mm = no enlargement

5 mm or more = enlargement

TABLE XXX

Widths of the occipital horns

Width in mm	Right		Left	
	No. of cases	Per cent	No. of cases	Per cent
10 or less	31	9	26	8
11-15	106	32	97	29
16-20	90	27	82	25
21-25	34	10	46	14
26-30	22	7	22	7
31-35	8	2	16	5
36-40	2	1	7	2
41-45	4	1	1	0
46-50	1	0	3	1
More than 50	3	1	3	1
Not measurable	33	10	31	9
TOTAL	334	100	334	100

TABLE XXXI

Width of the third ventricle

Width in mm	No. of cases	Per cent
Less than 4	15	4
4-5	65	19
6-8	128	38
9-11	58	17
12-14	27	8
More than 14	7	2
Not measurable	34	10
TOTAL	334	100

The width of the third ventricle was graded as follows (Nielsen *et al.* 1966*a*).

  Less than 6 mm = no enlargement
  6 to 8 mm = slight enlargement
  9 to 11 mm = moderate enlargement
  12 mm or more = severe enlargement

TABLE XXXII

Findings in the cerebral mid-line region at pneumoencephalography

Finding	No. of cases	Per cent
Agenesis of the septum pellucidum	7	2
Communicating cavity in the septum pellucidum	7	2
Broad septum pellucidum (non-communicating cavity)	8	2
Agenesis of the corpus callosum	3	1
Cup-shaped corpus callosum	14	4
Insufficient visualisation	28	8
Nothing definitely pathological	267	80
TOTAL	334	100

Mid-line Structures. Anomalous findings in the region of the cerebral mid-line structures were found in 39 cases (12 per cent) (Table XXXII). The most common of these anomalies were those involving the septum pellucidum (*i.e.* agenesis, and communicating and non-communicating cavities), which were identified in 22 cases. Pathological deformities of the corpus callosum (cupular configuration and agenesis) were observed in the remainder of these 39 patients. One of the three cases of agenesis of the corpus callosum exhibited partial agenesis. All the cases of agenesis of the septum pellucidum and corpus callosum had additional supratentorial pathology (*e.g.* hemidysplasia) at pneumoencephalography. Lateral displacement of the cerebral

TABLE XXXIII

TABLE XXXIII

Displacement of mid-line structures shown at pneumoencephalography

Degree of displacement of mid-line structures	No. of cases	Per cent
No displacement (*i.e.* less than 2 mm displacement to either side)	297	89
Displaced to right by 3 to 4 mm	6	2
Displaced to right by 5 to 10 mm	10	3
Displaced to left by 3 to 4 mm	8	2
Displaced to left by 5 to 10 mm	6	2
Displaced to left by more than 10 mm	1	0
Insufficient visualisation	6	2
TOTAL	334	100

TABLE XXXIV

Cortical atrophy or dysplasia at pneumoencephalography

	Slight No.	Moderate No.	Pro-nounced No.	Severe No.	Un-classified No.	Total	Per cent
Bilateral diffuse cortical atrophy or dysplasia	19	32	2	4	2	59	18
Unilateral diffuse cortical atrophy or dysplasia	3	3	1	1	1	9	3
Localised cortical atrophy or dysplasia	2	6	3	4	1	16	5
Nothing abnormal	–	–	–	–	–	90	27
Insufficient visualisation	–	–	–	–	–	160	48
TOTAL	24	41	6	9	4	334	100

Cortical atrophy or dysplasia was graded as slight, moderate, pronounced, and severe according to the criteria suggested by Nielsen *et al.* (1966*b*).

mid-line structures was observed in nearly 10 per cent of the 334 cases. There was little difference between the numbers of left-sided and right-sided displacements (Table XXXIII).

Cortical Subarachnoid Space. In nearly half the 334 patients, the cortical sub-arachnoid space was poorly visualised due to insufficient filling (Table XXXIV). Pathologically large sulci (> 4 mm, according to Nielsen *et al.* 1966*b*) were found in about half the remainder. Localised cortical atrophy or dysplasia was found most frequently in the frontal and temporal lobes, and on the left more frequently than the right side (Table XXXV).

TABLE XXXV
Main areas affected by localised and unilateral cortical atrophy or dysplasia

Area of cortex mainly affected	No. of cases	Per cent
Left frontal	6	24
Right frontal	4	16
Left temporal	4	16
Right temporal	4	16
Left parietal	3	12
Right parietal	1	4
Other	3	12
TOTAL	25	100

TABLE XXXVI
Findings in the infratentorial space at pneumoencephalography

Finding	No. of cases	Per cent
Cerebellar atrophy or dysplasia	79	24
Narrow posterior fossa	22	7
Small cerebellum	15	4
Atrophy or dysplasia of brain stem alone	12	4
Occlusion of the sylvian aqueduct (including a case of agenesis of the cerebellar vermis)	4	1
Megalocisterna magna	3	1
Insufficient visualisation	17	5
Nothing abnormal	182	54
TOTAL	334	100

TABLE XXXVII
Height of the fourth ventricle

Height in mm	No. of cases	Per cent
Less than 10	24	7
10-11	47	14
12-13	90	27
14-15	78	23
16-17	20	6
18-19	33	10
20-21	8	2
More than 21	4	1
Not measurable	30	9
TOTAL	334	100

The height of the fourth ventricle was graded as follows (Salomonsen *et al.* 1957).

Less than 18 mm = no enlargement

18 mm or more = enlargement

Infratentorial Space. Pathological findings in the infratentorial space were recorded in nearly half the cases submitted to pneumoencephalography (Table XXXVI). Half of these were identified as atrophy-like changes of the cerebellum. The rest of the pathological findings were malformations (*i.e.* abnormally large cisterna magna, narrow posterior fossa, agenesis of the cerebellar vermis), apart from twelve cases of brain stem atrophy and four cases of occlusion of the sylvian aqueduct.

The height of the fourth ventricle appeared to be small (9 mm or less) in 24 cases, and large (18 mm or over) in 45 (13 per cent) (Table XXXVII).

The spaces between the cerebellar folia in the superior cerebellar cistern were regarded as pathologically large (*i.e.* 3 mm or more) in 49 cases (15 per cent).

Brain Scanning with a Radioisotope

Brain scanning with a radioisotope (Technetium 99^m) was performed in five cases. Pathological or suspected pathological findings were revealed in two; of these, one had a focal finding in the right temporo-posterior basal area. Pneumoencephalography confirmed the former as a case of tumour, and the latter as one of internal hydrocephalus with enormous enlargement of the left temporal horn.

Neuropathological Studies

Autopsy examinations were performed on ten of the fourteen patients who died. The ages of these patients ranged from 12 to 30 years. Their brain weights ranged from 780g to 1750g, with a mean of 1140g. The cerebral ventricles were abnormally small in one case, of normal size in one, and abnormally large in eight, of which two had asymmetrical macroventriculy.

Macroscopic examination at autopsy revealed the following cortical findings: microgyria in three cases, cortical atrophy in three cases, cortical dysplasia in two cases, and nothing definitely pathological in two cases. Additional findings were cerebellar atrophy and a ruptured aneurysm of the left middle cerebral artery, each in one case.

Microscopic examination of the brain was performed in two cases during life (brain biopsy at operation), and in five cases *post mortem*. The brain biopsy in both the former cases showed a histological picture of astrocytoma (Figs. 29 and 30). The pathological-anatomical diagnoses for the other five cases were as follows: astrocytoma (Fig. 28), micrencephaly, slight diffuse fibrous gliosis of the cerebral white matter, numerous ectopic nerve cells in the cerebral white matter, and cortical dysplasia.

Microscopic examination of skin biopsies taken from five cases of skin disorder confirmed the following diagnoses: pseudoxanthoma elasticum, congenital ichthyosis, xeroderma pigmentosum, tuberose sclerosis, and anhidrotic cutaneous dysplasia.

Muscle biopsy tissue was studied in three patients with muscular diseases. Microscopic examination showed slight dystrophic changes in the first case, a rare form of atrophy of muscle fibres in the second, and no detectable changes in the third. In the first and third cases the diagnosis was myotonic dystrophy, and in the second muscular atrophy of Dent and Harris.

CHAPTER 4

The Aetiological Classification of the 338 Patients, with Selected Examples of Characteristic Neuroradiological Findings

When all the historical data were collated with the results of the psychological, physical, biochemical, microbiological, serological, neurophysiological, neuroradiological, and neuropathological examinations, the cause of the mental retardation was evaluated in each case separately. This aetiological diagnosis was made 'blind', without knowledge of any previously recorded diagnosis. Individual cases were discussed with paediatric and neurological colleagues when the diagnosis presented difficulties. The patients were classified in two ways: (1) according to the timing of the insult or the onset of the process, using the criteria laid down by Yannet (see page 2); and (2) using the aetiological categories of the WHO (see page 4).

Yannet's Classification

The distribution of the cases amongst the categories of Yannet is shown in Table XXXVIII. The aetiological timepoint was considered to have been prenatal in about half the 338 cases. In about one fifth it was postnatal, and in another fifth it could not be determined. In the remainder (less than one fifth), the aetiological timepoint was perinatal.

TABLE XXXVIII

Aetiological classification of 338 mentally retarded patients according to Yannet (1945)

Category	No. of cases	Per cent
Prenatal	151	45
Perinatal	42	12
Postnatal	61	18
More than one category	17	5
Undeterminable	67	20
TOTAL	338	100

The WHO's Classification

The distribution of the 338 cases amongst the aetiological categories of the WHO (1968) is shown in Table XXXIX.

Selected cases from each of the main categories are illustrated with neuroradiological pictures (Figs. 11 to 51).

It should be noted that some of the pneumoencephalographic pictures described in the figure legends as antero-posterior and postero-anterior views are angled obliquely. This is because, in addition to 'direct' or 'true' antero-posterior and postero-

56

TABLE XXXIX

Aetiological classification of the 338 mentally retarded patients according to the WHO (1968)

Aetiological categories	No. of cases	Per cent
Infections and intoxications	58	17
prenatal infections ⎫ see Table XL	(9)	
postnatal infections ⎬	(34)	
toxaemia of pregnancy ⎭	(12)	
other infections and intoxications	(3)	
Trauma or physical agents	46	14
prenatal trauma	(2)	
mechanical trauma at birth	(18)	
hypoxia at birth	(18)	
postnatal trauma (see Table XLI)	(8)	
Disorders of metabolism	11	3
Spielmeyer-Vogt's disease	(3)	
Prader-Willi syndrome	(3)	
myotonic dystrophy	(2)	
myopathy of Dent and Harris	(1)	
aspartylglucosaminuria	(1)	
syndrome of infantile hypercalcaemia, with		
typical facies and aortic stenosis	(1)	
Gross brain diseases	9	3
tuberose sclerosis	(3)	
Von Recklinghausen's disease with astrocytoma	(1)	
astrocytoma	(2)	
spinocerebellar degeneration with		
encephalopathy	(1)	
telangiectatic ataxia of Louis-Bar	(1)	
xeroderma pigmentosum	(1)	
Unknown prenatal influence	106	31
cerebral defect (see Appendix Table I)	(70)	
primary skull anomaly	(6)	
cutis verticis gyrata syndrome	(10)	
other prenatal disorder (see Appendix Table II)	(20)	
Chromosome aberrations	12	4
Down's syndrome	(4)	
other autosomal aberration	(5)	
sex chromosome aberration	(3)	
Prematurity	3	1
Major psychiatric disorder	1	0
More than one probable cause (see Table XLII)	25	7
Other and unspecified causes (see Appendix		
Table III)	67	20
TOTAL	338	100

57

TABLE XL

Infections as aetiology of mental retardation

Diagnosis	No. of cases
Prenatal	
Rubella	3
Influenza	2
Syphilis	2
Toxoplasmosis	2
Postnatal	
Non-defined encephalitis	16
Measles encephalitis	3
Pertussis encephalitis	2
Influenzal encephalitis	2
Varicella encephalitis	1
Non-defined meningitis	3
Pneumococcal meningitis	3
Tuberculous meningitis	1
Non-defined meningo-encephalitis	3
TOTAL	43

anterior views, pneumoencephalograms were always taken with the central ray parallel with the skull base (or clivus), to give the best view of the ventricles.

When studying the angiograms, the reader may wish to refer to the diagrams of the cerebral arterial system on page 160 (Appendix V).

The captions also give details of the most important clinical findings in each case. The ages given are the patients' ages at the time of the present investigation. Although not mentioned in the captions, mental retardation was, of course, present in all cases. The phrase 'minor malformations' is used to describe findings which are of no functional significance, such as abnormalities of the skin, webbing of the toes and clinodactyly.

Infections and Intoxications

The diagnoses in the 43 cases in which pre- and postnatal infections were considered to be the primary cause of the mental retardation (see Table XXXIX) are listed in Table XL.

The diagnoses in the two patients whose mothers had had a serious illness of a viral type (*e.g.* influenza) during the first trimester of pregnancy were only speculative, because although the illness in both mothers was severe there was a shortage of viral and other supportive evidence.

In 15 of the 34 cases of postnatal infection, the organism was identified, but in 19, although there were well-defined signs of encephalitis or meningoencephalitis with characteristic changes in the cerebrospinal fluid, no specific diagnosis could be made. Many of these children had had an illness many years before this investigation was initiated, at a time when fewer routine viral studies were carried out than would be the case today. It is likely that, had these patients been infected more recently, the number of cases in which the organism responsible for the encephalitis remained unidentified would have been much smaller.

The main sequelae of postnatal encephalitis shown at the neuroradiological examinations included various types of supratentorial macroventriculy, and lesions of the cerebral cortex, cerebellum and brain stem (Figs. 11 to 16). Calcifications are common in post-encephalitic disease, and may serve to confirm the diagnosis.

The twelve cases in this category in which the mother had had toxaemia of pregnancy are discussed on pages 28 and 128. In all but two the toxaemia had been severe. Typical pneumoencephalographic findings in these cases were symmetrical or asymmetrical supratentorial macroventriculy and, not infrequently, cerebellar atrophy or dysplasia.

The suspected primary causes of the mental retardation in the three cases of 'other infections and intoxications' were as follows: variola vaccination in one case; Rh hyperbilirubinaemia in the second; and diarrhoea intoxication in the third. The second of these cases was one of kernicterus. The third was a patient who had had very severe gastroenteritis at an early age, with clouding of consciousness during the course of the illness; since her previous development had been normal, it was considered reasonable to include her in this category.

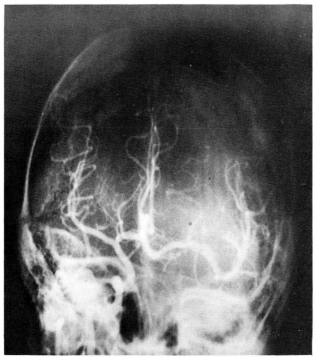

Fig. 11. Carotid angiogram (compression picture) showing elevation of the right middle cerebral artery, which was due to dilatation of the right temporal horn (shown by pneumoencephalography) and pyramidal asymmetry (shown by plain skull X-ray).
Clinical details. Male aged 21 years with left hemiplegia. This boy had had pertussis encephalitis at the age of one year.

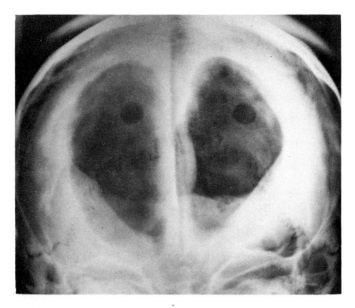

Figs. 12 a and b. (*a*) *Upper picture*. Antero-posterior ventriculogram showing macroventriculy.

(*b*) *Lower picture*. Lateral ventriculogram showing macroventriculy and marked digital impression suggesting raised intracranial pressure (the latter finding was confirmed on plain skull X-ray, which also showed some separation of the sutures and atrophy of the sella turcica). The patient was tilted, and gas failed to enter the aqueduct of Sylvius, the upper part of which is arrowed.

Clinical details. Female aged 10 years with triplegia, ataxia and optic atrophy. This girl had had measles encephalitis at six years, and her previous development had been normal.

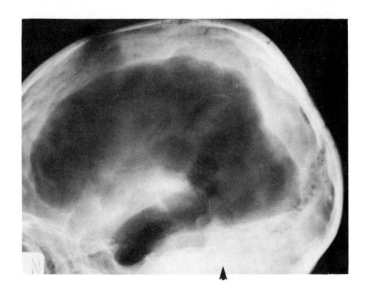

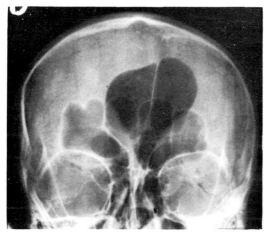
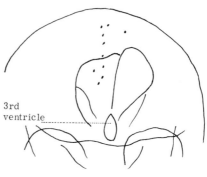

3rd
ventricle

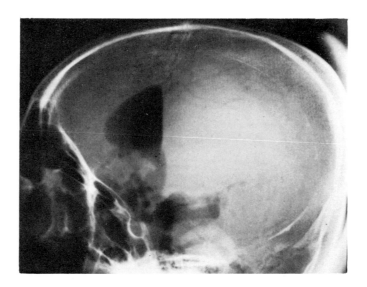

Figs. 13 a and b. (*a*) *Upper pictures.* Antero-posterior lumbar pneumo-encephalogram showing severe macroventriculy. Slight intracranial calcification can be seen as indicated in the sketch.

(*b*) *Lower picture.* Lateral lumbar pneumoencephalogram showing severe macroventriculy and a clear circular calcification in the falx.

Clinical details. Male aged 15 years with right hemiplegia. This boy had had a severe illness in the first year of life, which the calcifications and deformed, enlarged ventricles found at pneumoencephalography suggest may have been encephalitis—a likely cause of his present marked mental retardation.

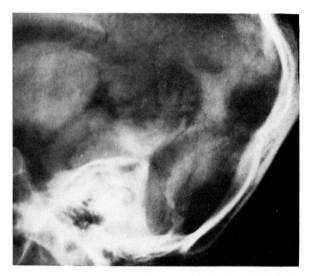

Fig. 14. Lateral lumber pneumoencephalogram, with patient in sitting position, showing widened cerebellar sulci in the culmen of the vermis, suggesting atrophy or dysplasia.

Clinical details. Female aged 19 years with epilepsy, poor vision and marked optic atrophy. At the age of two weeks this girl had suffered an attack of encephalitis (of unknown type).

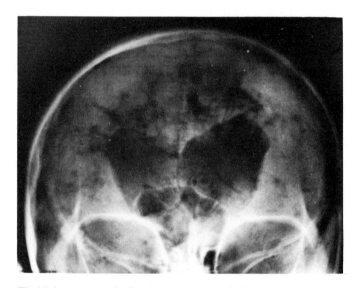

Fig. 15. Antero-posterior lumbar pneumoencephalogram showing severe asymmetrical macroventriculy. Excessive gas in sulci suggests moderate cortical atrophy. (Enlarged ambient cisterns were seen on postero-anterior pneumoencephalogram, suggesting atrophy of the brain stem.)

Clinical details. Female aged 22 years with epilepsy, diplegia and some atypical dyskinesia. She had had encephalitis of unknown type at two months.

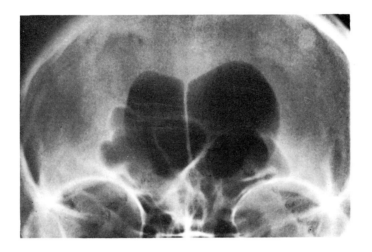

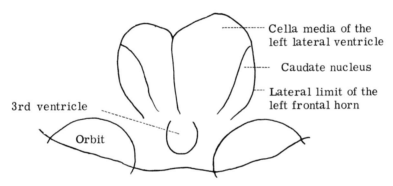

Cella media of the
left lateral ventricle

Caudate nucleus

Lateral limit of the
left frontal horn

3rd ventricle

Orbit

Fig. 16. Antero-posterior lumbar pneumoencephalogram showing severe asymmetrical (left larger than right) macroventriculy and severe enlargement of the third ventricle (see sketch).

Clinical details. Male aged 23 years with epilepsy. He had had encephalitis of unknown type at two years of age.

Trauma and Physical Agents

In the two cases of prenatal trauma, the mothers had had bleeding *ex utero* following a traumatic injury. Both these injuries had been sustained in domestic accidents, one involving a horse.

Eighteen cases who had been in a poor condition immediately after delivery were considered to have sustained mechanical trauma at birth. In the majority of these cases, blood had been found in the cerebrospinal fluid. In all eighteen there was obstetric evidence to support the belief that birth trauma had been of primary aetiological significance for the mental retardation. The most frequent encephalographic findings in cases of mechanical trauma at birth were unilateral or asymmetrical bilateral cerebral lesions, associated in some cases with an extra cavity due to intracerebral haemorrhage, and in others with a cerebellar lesion (Figs. 17 to 20).

A further eighteen cases had had marked hypoxia in the immediate postnatal period, being what would formerly have been described as 'pseudo deaths'. Today such babies would be described as having low Apgar scores at between five and ten minutes, but at the time at which most of them were born such standardised methods of measuring the degree of anoxia in the period immediately after delivery were not in use. Unilateral or asymmetrical bilateral cerebral atrophy plus, in some cases, a cerebellar lesion was a common finding in cases thought to have sustained hypoxic brain damage at birth (Figs. 21 and 22).

Some of the eight cases of postnatal trauma (Table XLI) had had traffic accidents, and others, it was suspected, had been battered. However, the exact causes of the injuries in these latter infants, all of whom showed visible evidence of physical damage to the skull, were difficult to ascertain, and they were mostly described as having had domestic accidents. One case of chronic subdural haematoma was diagnosed nineteen years after the injury (Fig. 23). The other patients who had suffered postnatal trauma had had neurological and neuroradiological examinations at the time of the injury.

Cases of cerebrovascular occlusive disease have been put in the category of postnatal trauma, although some of them may more correctly belong in the category of prenatal trauma. It seems that 'moyamoya' disease may be commoner in Europe than previously thought and not almost specific to Japanese patients (Suzuki and Takaku 1969, Taveras 1969), for a number of cases have been found in Finland in a relatively short time (Halonen *et al.* 1973). Figure 24 shows occlusions of main intracranial arteries with collateral networks and intracranial calcifications in a case of cerebrovascular 'moyamoya' disease. In another case a phlebogram and an encephalogram revealed what appeared to be a sinus occlusion (Fig. 25).

TABLE XLI

Postnatal trauma or physical agents as aetiology of mental retardation

Diagnosis	*No. of cases*
Subdural haematoma	4
Traumatic brain contusion	2
Occlusion of cerebral vessels ('moyamoya' disease, sinus thrombosis)	2
TOTAL	8

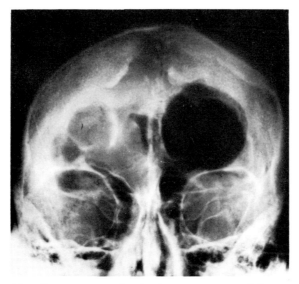

Fig. 17. Antero-posterior lumbar pneumo-encephalogram showing severe left hemimacroventriculy, with displacement of the septum pellucidum to the left side. There is asymmetrical thickening of the cranial vault corresponding to the hemiatrophy. Lateral pictures suggested cerebellar atrophy.

Clinical details. Female aged 18 years with right hemiplegia and epilepsy. Maternal disproportion had been found during the course of labour, and the infant had eventually been delivered by Caesarian section.

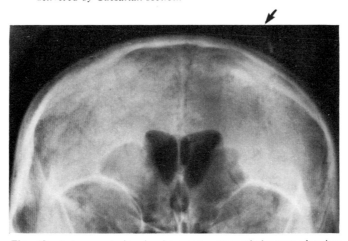

Fig. 18. Antero-posterior lumbar pneumoencephalogram showing mild left hemimacroventriculy, with moderate enlargement (width 9mm) of the third ventricle. A parietal calcification is arrowed in the left dura mater.

Clinical details. Female aged 20 years with epilepsy and squint. A prolonged labour had been followed by mild asphyxia and positive neurological findings in the neonatal period, which suggested a diagnosis of birth injury. This diagnosis has been confirmed by the findings of the present neuroradiological investigations.

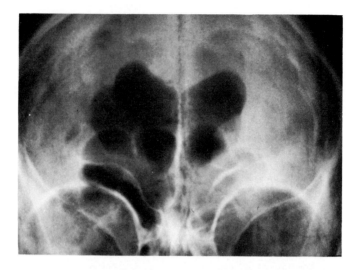

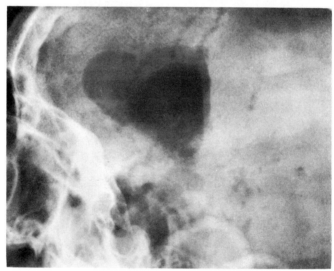

Figs. 19 a and b. (*a*) *Upper picture*. Antero-posterior lumbar pneumo-encephalogram showing an extra cavity in the right frontal lobe which communicates with the severely dilated right lateral ventricle.

(*b*) *Lower picture*. Lateral lumbar pneumoencephalogram, with the patient in the brow-up position, which demonstrates that the cavity is anteriorly situated in the frontal lobe.

Clinical details. Male aged 20 years with diplegia and epilepsy. An intracranial haemorrhage had been diagnosed immediately after birth in the Children's Hospital.

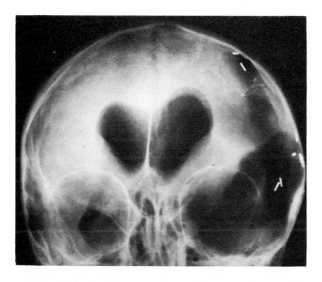

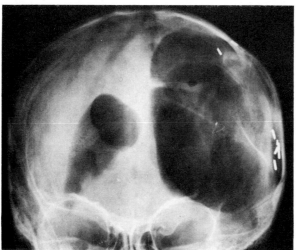

Figs. 20 a and b. (*a*) *Upper picture*. Antero-posterior lumbar pneumoencephalogram showing severe asymmetrical (left larger than right) macroventriculy, with slight displacement of the anterior ventricular system to the right side. The left temporal lobe shows large defects.

(*b*) *Lower picture*. Postero-anterior lumbar pneumo-encephalogram. This view shows that there is also a large defect of the occipital lobe on the left side.

Clinical details. Female aged 18 years with left hemiplegia and epilepsy. Four days after birth an intracranial haemorrhage had been diagnosed, and at one month a subdural haematoma had been evacuated.

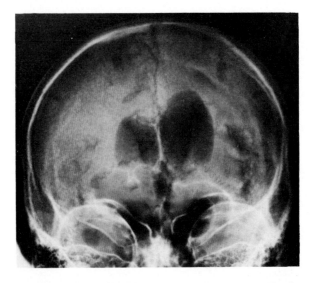

Fig. 21. Antero-posterior lumbar pneumoencephalogram showing moderate left hemimacroventriculy, with some gas in the sulci, particularly in the left Sylvian fissure, suggesting cortical atrophy.

Clinical details. Female aged 18 years with tetraplegia and epilepsy. Asphyxia and respiratory difficulties had been reported in the neonatal period. Six months after the present neuroradiological investigations the patient died, and at autopsy anoxic brain lesions were seen.

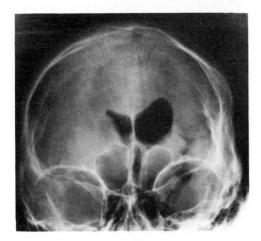

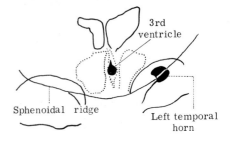

Fig. 22a

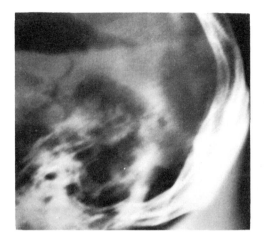

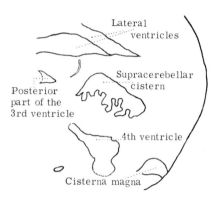

Lateral
ventricles

Posterior
part of the
3rd ventricle

Supracerebellar
cistern

4th ventricle

Cisterna magna

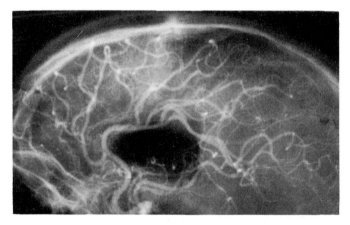

Figs. 22 a, b and c. (*a*) *Facing page, lower pictures.* Antero-posterior lumbar pneumoencephalogram showing marked hemimacroventriculy with a thickened cranial vault. The left sphenoidal plate (see sketch) and the left pyramis are both raised. Some gas can be seen in the left temporal horn of the ventricle, which is increased in size. The right temporal horn, which is normal, contains no gas in this view.

(*b*) *This page, upper pictures.* Lateral 'auto'-tomogram showing gas in the supracerebellar cistern and an enlarged fourth ventricle. (The cisterna magna has gas in it but is not enlarged.)

(*c*) *This page, lower picture.* Left lateral carotid angiogram in the arterial phase. The middle cerebral artery and its main branches are thinned. (In the antero-posterior views, the pericallosal artery was shown to be 2 to 3 cm to the left of the mid-line, and the striothalamic vein was displaced laterally.)

Clinical details. Male aged 18 years with triplegia and epilepsy. At birth the onset of respiration had been delayed, and it was suspected in the neonatal period that hypoxic brain damage had occurred.

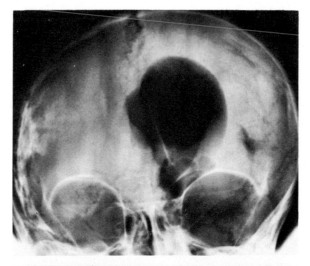

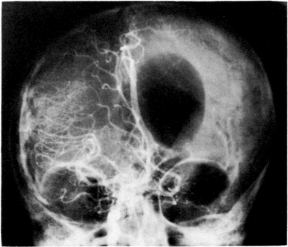

Figs. 23 a and b. (a) *Upper picture*. Postero-anterior lumbar pneumoencephalogram showing severe left macroventriculy, with a flattened right lateral ventricle and an oblique septum pellucidum. The third ventricle is severely enlarged (13 mm). There is a large intracranial calcification over the right cerebral hemisphere. The whole skull is asymmetrical.

(b) *Lower picture*. Antero-posterior right carotid angiogram, which confirms the presence of an avascular area of calcification 2 cm thick between the tabula interna and the peripheral edges of the cerebral arteries.

Clinical details. Female aged 19 years with epilepsy. A probable case of battering in infancy, this child had attended hospital at the age of five months with raised intracranial pressure and focal convulsions. The left sided findings described above suggest a cerebral contusion at that time due to a contre-coup mechanism. Prior to the present investigations, this girl's mental retardation had been regarded as being due to psychosis, because of her profound restlessness.

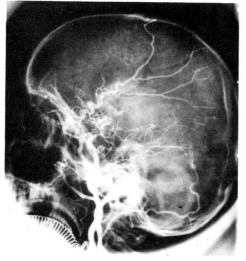

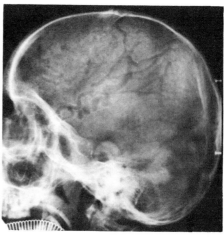

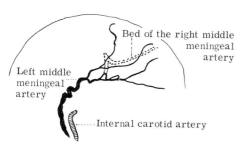

Bed of the right middle meningeal artery

Left middle meningeal artery

Internal carotid artery

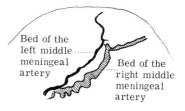

Bed of the left middle meningeal artery

Bed of the right middle meningeal artery

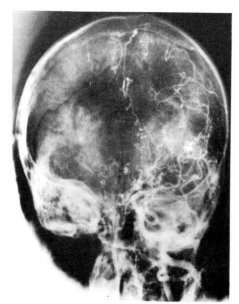

Figs. 24 a, b and c. (a) *Upper left.* Carotid angiogram showing occlusion of the left internal carotid artery and a collateral circulation via an enlarged and meandering middle meningeal artery. The corresponding bed of the contralateral middle meningeal artery in the cranial vault can be clearly seen, suggesting that there is a carotid occlusion on the right side also.

(b) *Upper right.* Lateral plain skull X-ray showing the enlarged beds of the middle meningeal arteries (see a).

(c) *Left.* Antero-posterior carotid angiogram (half-axial view) showing left carotid occlusion and well-developed collateral circuit.

Clinical details. Female aged 11 years with diplegia and epilepsy. Occlusive cerebro-vascular disease of unknown origin, with onset in infancy. (The angiographic picture is similar to that seen in other cases of 'moyamoya' disease (Halonen *et al.* 1973).)

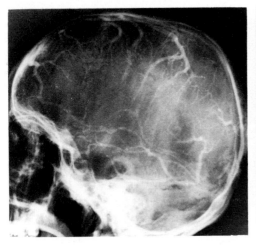
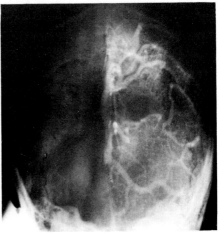
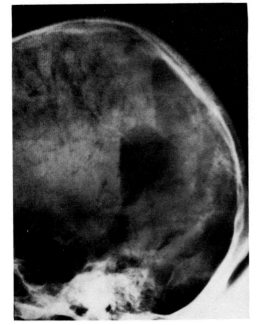

Figs. 25 a, b and c. (a) *Above left*. Venous phase of carotid angiogram, showing sinus occlusion. The deep venous system (for example the internal cerebral vein and the great vein of Galen) is not seen.

(b) *Above right*. Antero-posterior half-axial view of the venous phase of the carotid angiogram.

(c) *Left*. Lateral lumbar pneumoencephalogram with patient in brow-down position showing an enlarged occipital horn and a parieto-occipital cavity, which a postero-anterior picture showed to be inter-hemispheric.

Clinical details. Female aged 19 years with no specific clinical findings apart from the mental retardation. The newborn period had been unremarkable, but mental retardation was noted during the first year.

Disorders of Metabolism

Most of the metabolic disorders listed in Table XXXIX have been well described in the literature, and were diagnosed along classical lines. However, cases of aspartyl-glucosaminuria have rarely been described, although the disorder has been the subject of a special study in Finland (Autio 1972). Patients in the category of metabolic disorders generally exhibited symmetrical cerebral defects (Figs. 26 and 27).

Gross Brain Diseases

The one example of Von Recklinghausen's disease in this series died during the course of investigations. In this case, both carotid angiography and pneumoen-cephalography, which had been performed before the patient's death, had revealed the presence of a tumour (Fig. 28), which was discovered at autopsy to be an astro-cytoma.

The neuroradiological examinations in patients with other gross brain diseases, such as tuberous sclerosis associated with the cutis verticis gyrata and mental retarda-tion syndrome, astrocytoma alone (Figs. 29 and 30), and xeroderma pigmentosum, revealed mostly heterogeneous findings, ranging from a cerebral mass shift due to intracranial expansion in cases of neoplasm, to varying degrees of supratentorial and infratentorial central and cortical atrophy in other conditions.

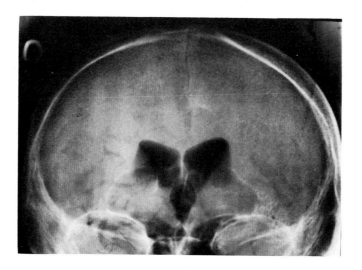

Fig. 26. Antero-posterior lumbar pneumoencephalogram showing moderate symmetrical macroventriculy. The third ventricle is greatly enlarged.
Clinical details. Female aged 24 years with epilepsy and optic atrophy. The retardation had first been noted when the girl was six years old. A diagnosis of Spielmeyer-Vogt's disease was confirmed during the present investigations.

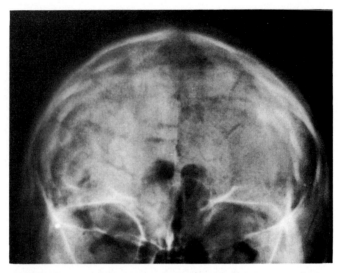

Fig. 27. Antero-posterior lumbar pneumoencephalogram showing microventriculy and an enlarged septum pellucidum. There is increased gas in the sulci of the right cerebrum, whereas filling on the left is poor. A lateral view demonstrated a small cerebellum. Other projections confirmed the presence of marked cortical dysplasia or atrophy in the right fronto-parietal region.

Clinical details. Female aged 24 years. A striking feature is her deep voice. A case of infantile hypercalcaemia with typical facies and supra-valvular aortic stenosis.

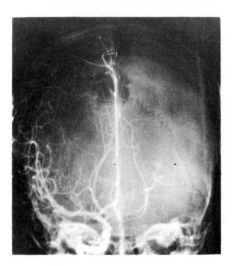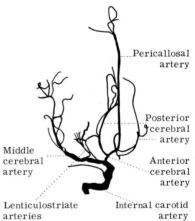

Middle
cerebral
artery

Lenticulostriate
arteries

Pericallosal
artery

Posterior
cerebral
artery

Anterior
cerebral
artery

Internal carotid
artery

Figs. 28 a, b and c. (*a*) *This page, lower pictures*, and (*b*) *Facing page, upper pictures*. Right carotid angiograms (a = antero-posterior half-axial view, and b = lateral view). There is an avascularised expansion in the region of the thalamus, and either an enlarged ventricular system or internal hydrocephalus. The branches of the middle cerebral artery in the Sylvian fissure are slightly elevated. The middle cerebral artery and the lenticulostriate arteries are displaced laterally, and the posterior cerebral artery is depressed. The pericallosal artery shows a prominent curve and the syphon is straightened.

74

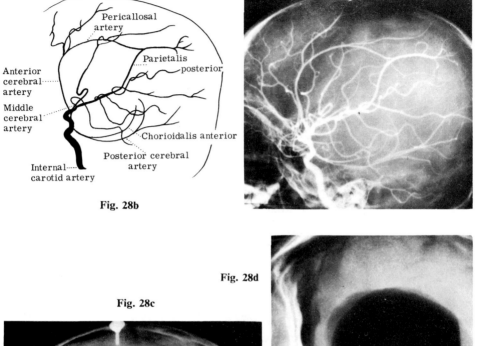

Fig. 28b

Fig. 28d

Fig. 28c

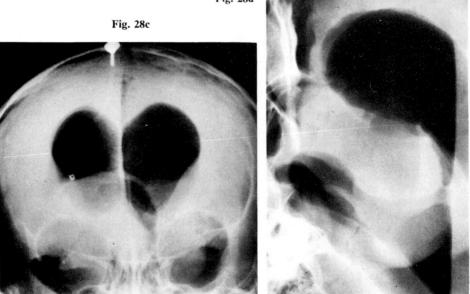

(c) *This page*, *lower left*. Antero-posterior ventriculogram (with patient in brow-up position) showing macroventriculy, which partially accounts for the angiographic findings. The third ventricle is pushed over to the left.

(d) *This page*, *lower right*. Lateral ventriculogram with patient in brow-up position. Below the enlarged ventricle there is a shadowing (which can also be seen in (c)), suggesting a tumour.

Clinical details. Male aged five years with tetraplegia, bilateral optic atrophy, nystagmus and expressive dysphasia. Von Recklinghausen's neurofibromatosis had been diagnosed one year previously. The patient died some time after the present neuroradiological investigations had been completed, and the inoperable tumour was diagnosed at autopsy as an astrocytoma.

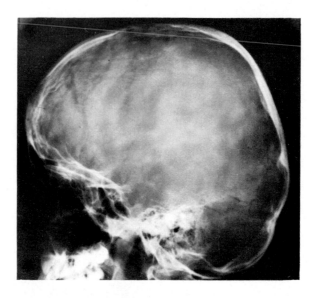

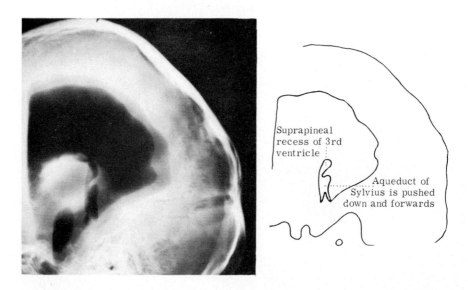

Figs. 29 a and b. (*a*) *Upper picture*. Lateral plain skull X-ray showing signs of high intra-cranial pressure with prominent digital markings and atrophy of the dorsum.

(*b*) *Lower picture*. Lateral ventriculogram with patient in brow-down position showing macroventriculy and occlusion of the kinked and deformed aqueduct of Sylvius, findings which strongly suggest the presence of a posterior fossa tumour.

Clinical details. Male aged 20 years with epilepsy, ataxia and optic atrophy. Pictures (a) and (b) were not taken at the time of the present investigations, but had been taken by the neurosurgical department when the patient was 10 years old. At that time a posterior fossa astrocytoma grade I had been removed.

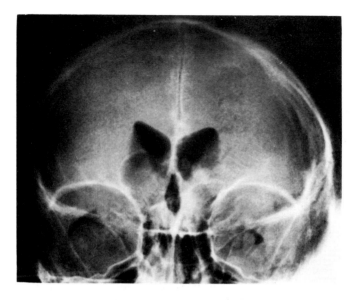

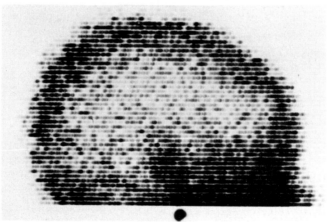

Figs. 30 a and b. (*a*) *Upper picture.* Antero-posterior lumbar pneumo-encephalogram with patient in brow-up position. The right temporal horn (seen behind the right orbit) is displaced upwards and laterally in contrast to the left temporal horn (seen behind the centre of the left orbit).

(*b*) *Lower picture.* Isotope scan showing a localisation in the posterior temporal region.

Clinical details. Male aged 14 years. In this boy the mental retardation has been present from infancy. At the time of the present investigation he was having ten to twenty fits per month, and had transient ataxia (due to phenytoin intoxication) and dysphasia. Subsequent to the present investigations a grade II astrocytoma has been removed, and the boy's condition has improved markedly.

Unknown Prenatal Influence

Seventy of the cases placed in this category had major cerebral defects (see Appendix Table I). In all of them, the cerebral pathology revealed by pneumoencephalography and/or other techniques was such that it was considered to be a likely cause of the severe mental retardation.

Signs of cerebral damage were also found in a further twenty cases (see Appendix Table II), but in none of these was the defect considered serious enough to necessarily account for the mental retardation. Many of these patients had congenital malformations (Appendix Table II), and in all 20 there were findings which suggested that the mental retardation was caused by some disorder of prenatal development. It seems likely that, as investigative techniques become more sophisticated, a number of as yet unrecognised syndromes will be identified amongst such patients.

Cutis verticis gyrata (ten cases) is a syndrome in which the staff of the Rinnekoti Institution have taken a particular interest. Although the number of such cases in this series would seem to be large, it is possible that this is merely because a higher proportion of cases of cutis verticis gyrata in other populations remain unidentified. Many cases are only identified in adult life by shaving the heads of patients with long hair in whom the syndrome is suspected. The fact that so many cases have been identified in this relatively small series of mentally retarded patients suggests that shaving the heads of suspected cases might lead to the identification of larger numbers of cases in other institutions. At the moment, it is not known whether there are differences in the prevalence of the syndrome in different parts of the world.

Only two of the cases previously described in the literature were in children (Truffi 1929, Palo and Iivanainen 1971). This syndrome had traditionally been classified as a metabolic disorder, but the pneumoencephalographic findings and the maldevelopment of the skull strongly suggest that it is a generalised disorder of prenatal development rather than a specific metabolic disease.

Typical findings in patients classified in the category of unknown prenatal influence were various types of supratentorial ventricular and cortical dysplasia, often combined with brain stem and/or cerebellar maldevelopment (Figs. 31 to 40).

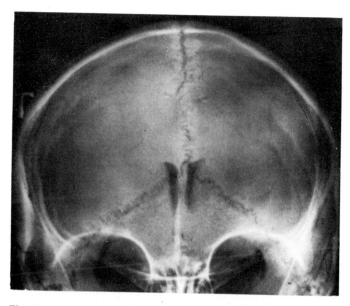

Fig. 31. Antero-posterior pneumoencephalogram showing micro-ventriculy and broad septum pellucidum. The frontal sinuses are absent.

Clinical details. Male aged 11 years with hypacusis and psychotic symptoms. Physical examination showed some minor malformations but no gross signs. The mental retardation was first noted when the patient was two years old.

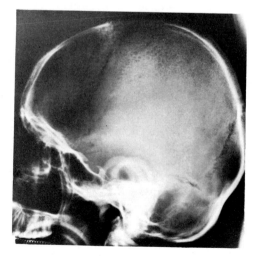

Fig. 32. Lateral plain skull X-ray showing marked platybasia and basilar impression.

Clinical details. Male aged 15 years with paraplegia, harelip and cleft palate (repaired) and other minor malformations. The mental retardation had been first recognised shortly after birth.

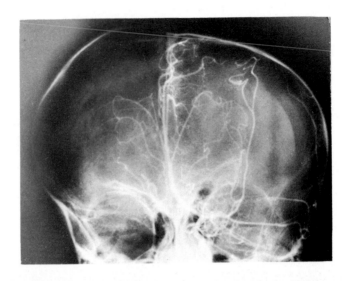

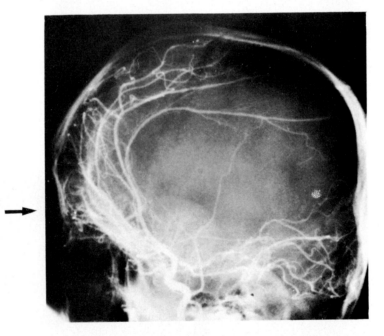

Figs. 33 a, b, c *and* **d.** (*a*) and (*b*) *This page, upper and lower pictures.* Left carotid angiograms (a = antero-posterior view and b = lateral view) showing a large avascular area mainly in the parietal region. In (b) the lenticulo-striate branches can be seen supplying the basal ganglia, and there is a clear boundary (arrowed) between this area and the avascular area. From (a) it was suspected that there might be large defects in the right cerebral cortex, and this suspicion was confirmed by a right carotid angiogram.

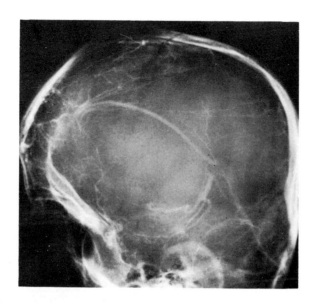

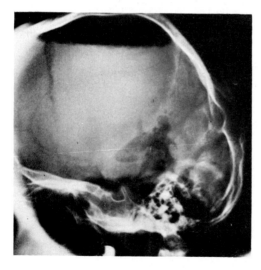

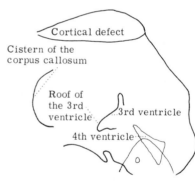

Cortical defect

Cistern of the
corpus callosum

Roof of
the 3rd
ventricle

3rd ventricle

4th ventricle

Fig. 33 (cont.)

(c) *This page, upper picture*. Venous phase of cerebral angiogram (lateral view) showing downward displacement of the internal cerebral vein corresponding exactly to the appearance of the roof of the third ventricle in the lateral encephalogram (see figure (d)). This finding suggests that it is impossible for gas to enter the lateral ventricles through the foramen of Monro.

(d) *This page, lower pictures*. Lateral lumbar pneumoencephalogram (with patient in upright position) showing a clear large cortical defect. A deformed third ventricle can be faintly seen, but gas has not yet entered the lateral ventricles because of the avascular expanded area of which the outline can be defined (see sketch).

Clinical details. Male aged 9 years with tetraplegia, epilepsy, optic atrophy and minor malformations. His development had been abnormal since birth.

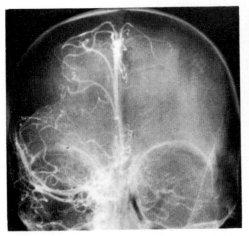 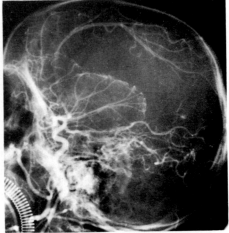

Figs. 34 a, b and c. (*a*) *Above left and* (*b*) *Above right*. Right carotid angiograms (a = antero-posterior view and b = lateral view) showing the distal branches of the middle cerebral artery ending in the bottom of the Sylvian fissures. The whole operculum appears avascularised. The pericallosal arch is prominent and raised.

(*c*) *Below*. Lumbar pneumoencephalogram showing a large cortical defect in the corresponding area (see *a* and *b*). On the opposite side the lateral ventricle continues as a hole through the brain substance, and no normal ventricular configuration is visible. In other views a megalocisterna magna and a hypoplastic brain stem were seen.

Clinical details. Male aged five years with epilepsy, tetraplegia and minor malformations. This boy had been mentally retarded since infancy.

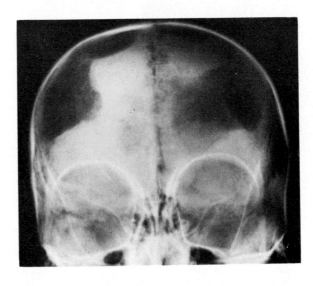

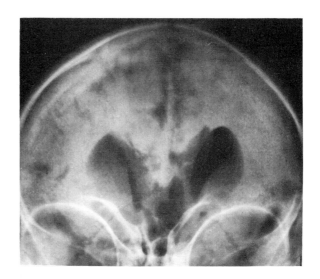

Figs. 35 a and b. (*a*) *Right*. Antero-posterior lumbar pneumoencephalogram. An elevated third ventricle can be seen between the enlarged lateral ventricles which are unusually far apart. There is enlargement of the cisterns of the corpus callosum. These findings suggest partial agenesis of the corpus callosum.

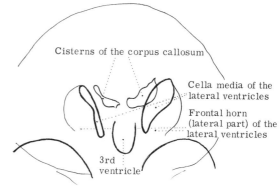

Cisterns of the corpus callosum

Cella media of the lateral ventricles

Frontal horn (lateral part) of the lateral ventricles

3rd ventricle

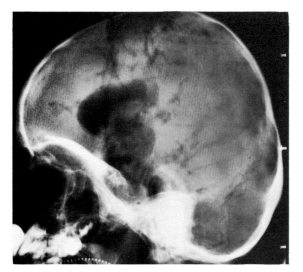

(*b*) *Left*. Lateral lumbar pneumoencephalogram. The elevation of the third ventricle can again be clearly seen. As in (a), gas in cortical sulci suggests atrophy or dysplasia.

Clinical details. Female aged five years with microcephaly (head circumference 40.5 cm), diplegia, epilepsy, optic atrophy and squint. Birth weight: 1700 g. This girl's development had been abnormal from birth.

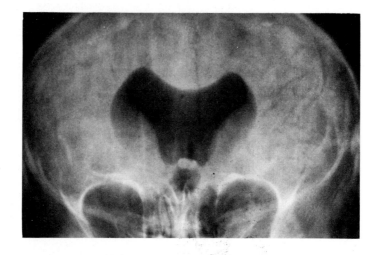

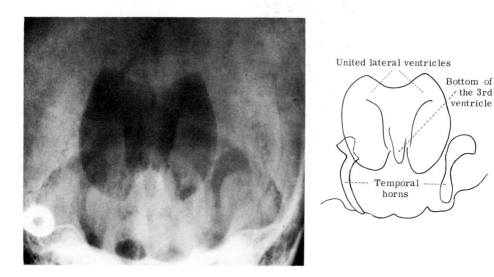

United lateral ventricles

Bottom of
the 3rd
ventricle

Temporal
horns

Figs. 36 a and b. (*a*) *Upper picture*. Antero-posterior lumbar pneumoencephalogram, with patient in brow-up position, showing moderately large united lateral ventricles (so-called cyclops ventricle). Note small orbits and absent frontal sinuses.

(*b*) *Lower pictures*. Half-axial antero-posterior lumbar pneumoencephalogram showing the mis-shaped temporal horns, which are abnormally medially situated.

Clinical details. Female aged 9 years with bilateral anophthalmia and minor malformations. Her development had been abnormal since birth.

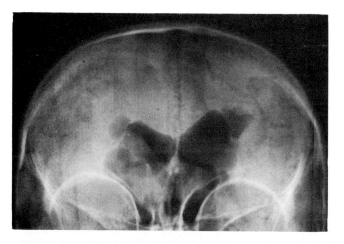

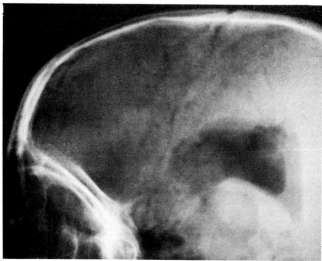

Figs. 37 a and b. (*a*) *Upper picture*. Antero-posterior lumbar pneumo-encephalogram showing mild asymmetrical (left larger than right) macroventriculy. On both sides there is an additional communicating cavity on the upper border of the lateral ventricle.

(*b*) *Lower picture*. Lateral lumbar pneumoencephalogram (taken with patient in brow-up position) showing shortness of the frontal horns of the lateral ventricles. These findings suggest the presence of a malformation of the frontal lobes.

Clinical details. female aged 16 years, with diplegia and minor malformations. Her development had been abnormal since birth.

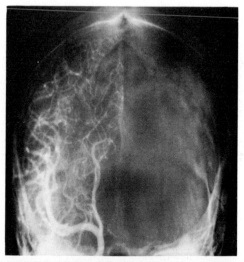

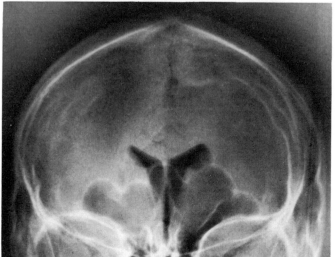

Figs. 38 a and b. (*a*) *Upper picture*. Antero-posterior right carotid angiogram (half-axial view). The pericallosal arteries (which should be seen alongside the mid-line) did not fill. (Subsequently, however, with left carotid angiography they were both shown to fill from the left side.) The right anterior cerebral artery, which is very thin and thread-like, can be seen rising medially from the internal carotid artery.

(*b*) *Lower picture*. Antero-posterior lumbar pneumoencephalogram showing small lateral ventricles and a thick corpus callosum (the latter is demonstrated by the distance between the upper border of the lateral ventricle and the cistern of the corpus callosum—seen here most clearly on the right side about 5 mm above the ventricle. An autotomogram displayed an anomalous cerebellum.

Clinical details. Male aged 15 years with left optic atrophy, right cataract, paraplegia and left cryptorchidism. As a result of the present investigations, this patient was diagnosed as having Rubinstein-Taybi's syndrome (classical beaked nose and broad toes and thumbs). His development had been abnormal since birth.

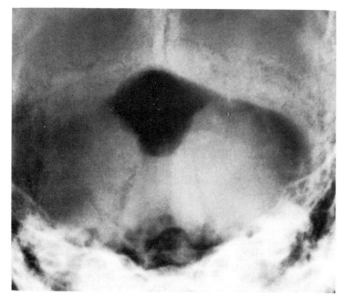

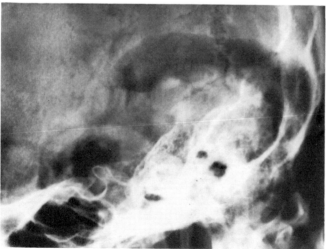

Figs. 39 a and b. (*a*) *Upper picture*. Half-axial postero-anterior lumbar pneumoencephalogram (taken with patient in sitting position). No gas has entered the supratentorial space and the ventricles have failed to fill. The gas shadow in this picture is infratentorial and supracerebellar, and is grossly enlarged.

(*b*) *Lower picture*. Lateral lumbar pneumoencephalogram. The gas shadow shown in (a) is seen extending above the entire cerebellum, indicating marked cerebellar hypoplasia.

Clinical details. Male aged 21 years with epilepsy, truncal ataxia and minor malformations. His development had been abnormal since birth.

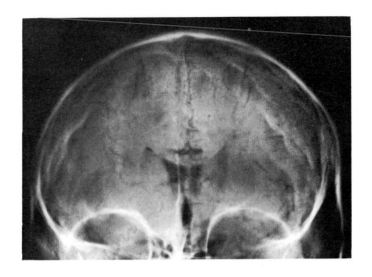

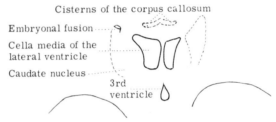

Cisterns of the corpus callosum

Embryonal fusion

Cella media of the
lateral ventricle

Caudate nucleus

3rd
ventricle

Figs. 40 a and b. (*a*) *Above*. Antero-posterior lumbar pneumoencephalo-gram showing small asymmetrical ventricles. On the right a small communicating cavity can be seen. There is embryonal fusion between the caudate nucleus and the corpus callosum. The corpus callosum is hyperplastic.

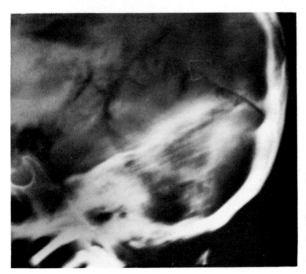

(*b*) *Left*. Lumbar pneumoencep-halogram (autotomogram) showing no gross abnormalities. The cere-bellum appears normal.
Clinical details. Male aged 8 years with autism and epilepsy, but no significant physical findings. This boy had been considered normal up to the age of two years, but at that age he had presented with behaviour and communication difficulties.

Chromosome Aberrations

The category of chromosome aberrations is somewhat smaller than might be expected, mainly because in many patients with such anomalies at the Rinnekoti there were no indications for pneumoencephalography and/or other neuroradiological investigations, so they were not selected for this study. There were in the institution many other children with Down's syndrome who are not reported on here.

Both infratentorial and supratentorial maldevelopment of the brain were encountered in cases of chromosome aberration (Figs. 41 to 44).

More Than One Probable Cause (Table XLII)

In twenty-five cases in this series, classification was difficult, because it was felt that more than one of the aetiological factors described above could have been responsible for the mental retardation. For example, one patient had a proven chromosomal abnormality (in the C chromosome), but also had been diagnosed as having encephalitis in the neonatal period. Others, in whom pneumoencephalographic evidence of cerebral defect suggested a prenatal origin, had also suffered a severe anoxic episode at birth. Although in most of the latter cases pneumoencephalography alone had revealed enought pathological findings for them to be placed in the 'unknown prenatal influence' category, both factors had probably contributed to the mental retardation. Nevertheless, it may be that the congenital cerebral defect was the primary cause, and that the subsequent condition merely aggravated the already severe damage.

The cases in this category exhibited symmetrical and asymmetrical cerebral lesions in both the supratentorial and infratentorial spaces (Figs. 45 to 47).

TABLE XLII

Aetiological diagnoses in cases of mental retardation due to more than one probable cause

First Condition	Second Condition	Third condition	No. of cases
Unknown prenatal influence	Hypoxia at birth	Neonatal hypoglycaemia	1
Unknown prenatal influence	Hypoxia at birth		5
Unknown prenatal influence	Mechanical injury at birth		2
Unknown prenatal influence	Hypothyreosis		1
Unknown prenatal influence	Postnatal infection		3
Chromosome aberration	Postnatal infection		1
Toxaemia of pregnancy	Hypoxia at birth		3
Toxaemia of pregnancy	Mechanical injury at birth		2
Toxaemia of pregnancy	Postnatal infection		1
Prematurity	Postnatal brain injury		1
Cultural-familial mental retardation	Hypoxia at birth		1
Hypoxia at birth	Postnatal infection		3
Hypoxia at birth	Hyperbilirubinaemia		1
TOTAL			25

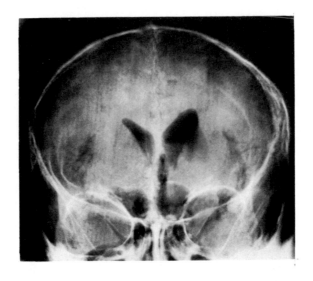

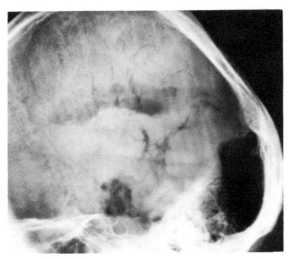

Figs. 41 a and b. (*a*) *Upper picture*. Antero-posterior lumbar pneumoencephalogram showing moderate left macroventriculy with a broad septum pellucidum.

(*b*) *Lower picture*. Lateral lumbar pneumoencephalogram showing a grossly enlarged cisterna magna, a small fourth ventricle and a small cerebellum.

Clinical details. Male aged 14 years with congenital ichthyosis, a crooked thumb and several minor malformations. This child's development had been abnormal since birth. Shortly before the present investigations he had been shown to have a chromosome abnormality (46,XY, Bq+).

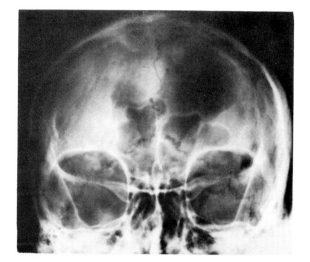

Fig. 42a.

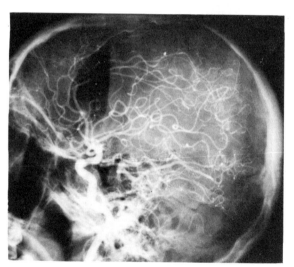

Fig. 42b.

Figs. 42 a and b. (*a*) *Upper picture*. Antero-posterior lumbar pneumoencephalogram showing a large defect in the left frontal lobe. The definition is not sharp because there was too little gas to display its full extent. The right lateral ventricle is also enlarged. There are unusually, though not necessarily abnormally, large frontal sinuses.

(*b*) *Lower picture*. Left carotid angiogram. The gas remaining in the lateral ventricle shows an enlarged frontal horn. The displaced vascularisation confirms the enlargement of the ventricles.

Clinical details. Female aged 34 years. Looks older than her age. Reddish cheeks. Head circumference: 51.5 cm (below 2nd percentile). Height: 150 cm (below 2.5 percentile). Weight: 40 kg (below 2.5 percentile). Brachycephalic (cephalic index 82.3). Monoplegia. Pseudoxanthoma elasticum diagnosed by skin biopsy. Chromosome analysis showed the karyotype of 46, XX, Cq fragility.

This patient's mother had had 15 pregnancies, 5 of which had ended in stillbirths. One brother was profoundly mentally retarded. The patient's development had been abnormal from birth, but in addition she had had encephalitis at one year.

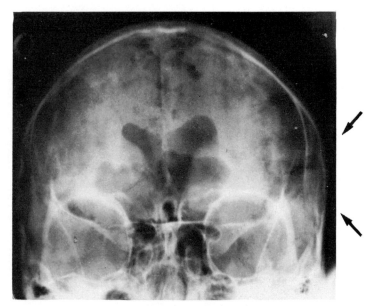

Fig. 43a

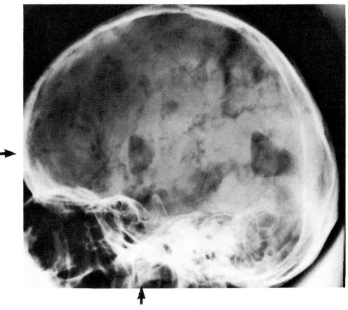

Fig. 43b

92

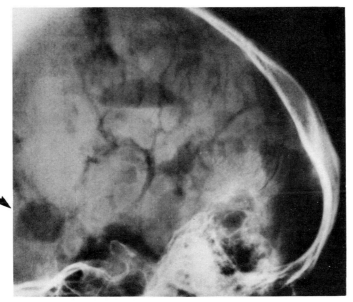

Fig. 43c

Figs. **43 a, b and c.** (*a*) *Facing page, upper picture.* Antero-posterior
lumbar encephalogram showing moderate left macroventriculy. There
is a cavity in the left temporal lobe (arrowed), which can be seen clearly
in the lateral views.

(*b*) *Facing page, lower picture.* Lateral lumbar pneumoencephalogram
(taken with patient in prone position) again showing the temporal
cavity (arrowed). The occipital horn of the lateral ventricle is enlarged,
and there is increased gas all over the cortex.

(*c*) *Above.* Lateral lumbar pneumoencephalogram (taken with
patient in sitting position). Again, the temporal cavity can be seen
(arrowed left). There is a small cerebellum.

Clinical details. Female aged 41 years with scanning speech
(cerebellar dysarthria) and minor malformations. No gross neurological
signs. Chromosomal findings (made in the course of the present
investigations): 47,XX, ?E+. This patient's development had been
abnormal from birth.

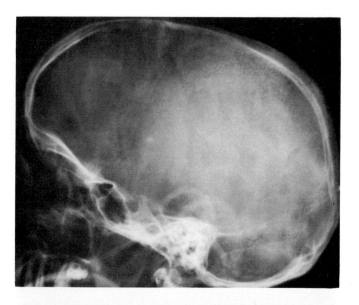

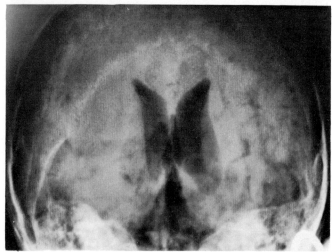

Figs. 44 a, b and c. (*a*) *This page, upper picture.* Plain skull X-ray showing platybasia, dolichocephaly and increased digital markings.

(*b*) *This page, lower picture.* Antero-posterior half-axial lumbar pneumoencephalogram showing normal ventricular system. There is an increase of gas in the cortex, which can be seen more clearly in (c).

(*c*) *Facing page, upper picture.* Lateral lumbar pneumoencephalogram showing large cortical gas shadow.

Clinical details. Female aged 15 years with clinical findings typical of Turner's syndrome, which was diagnosed during the course of the present study.

Fig. 44c

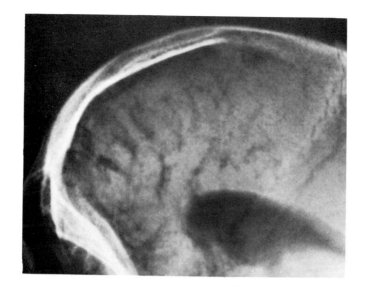

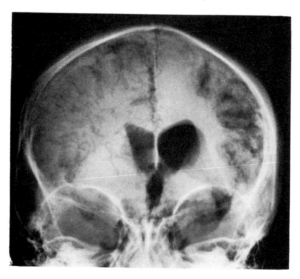

Fig. 45. Antero-posterior pneumoencephalogram showing moderate left macroventriculy and some enlargement of the third ventricle. There is an increase of gas in the cortex on the left side (the right side is normal).

Clinical details. Female aged 11 years at the time of the present study. This girl had been regarded as dysmature at birth and had had toxaemia. She had developed epilepsy at 10 months. At the age of six years, following a fit, she had presented with right hemiplegia, expressive dysphasia and paresis in the area of the facial nerve. The epilepsy remained intractible, and after the present investigations had been completed a left hemispherectomy was performed. This has improved the epilepsy, and the patient now has only a mild right hemiplegia, but she is still retarded.

95

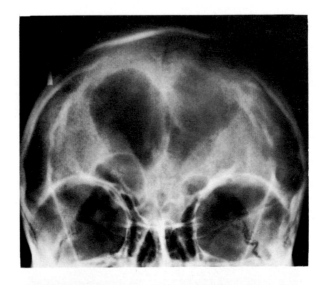

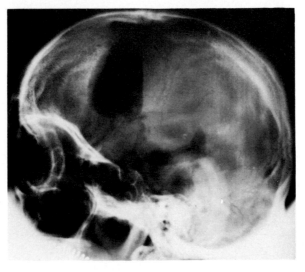

Figs. 46 a, b and c. (a) *This page, upper picture.* Antero-posterior lumbar pneumoencephalogram showing severe asymmetrical macroventriculy (the left side is larger than the right, although the right is more clearly shown as there is more gas in it). The temporal horns are slightly enlarged.

(b) *This page, lower picture.* Lateral lumbar pneumo-encephalogram (with patient in brow-up position) showing enlarged frontal horns.

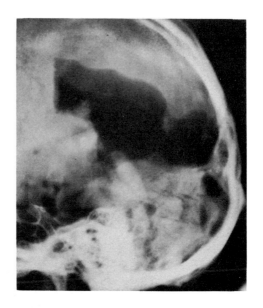

Fig. 46c. Right. Lateral lumbar pneumoencephalogram (with patient in prone position) showing enlargement of occipital horns. As in (a) and (b) calcifications can be seen in the right choroid plexus.

Clinical details. Male aged 23 years with diplegia, epilepsy, optic atrophy, right congenital cataract, nystagmus, cutis verticis gyrata and minor malformations. The patient had been born by a difficult forceps delivery, and his development had been abnormal since birth.

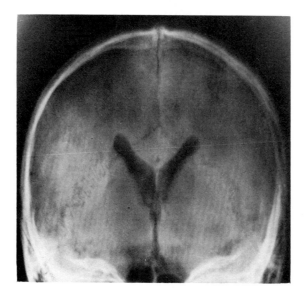

Fig. 47. Antero-posterior half-axial pneumoencephalogram showing mild macroventriculy, with a cup-shaped hypoplastic corpus callosum. (Other views showed enlargement of the temporal horns.) These findings suggest a prenatal cause.

Clinical details. Male aged 9 years with diplegia and epilepsy. Birth had been by a breech delivery and the patient's birthweight had been 2200 g (short gestation). He had had severe asphyxia at birth, and had suffered severe anoxic episodes and shown abnormal neurological findings in the neonatal period.

Other and Unspecified Causes

The main findings in these 67 cases are listed in Appendix Table III. In many of them, pneumoencephalography had revealed some abnormalities (*e.g.* enlargement of the cerebral ventricles), but no evidence of gross cerebral malformations which would have justified classifying them in the 'Unknown Prenatal Influence' category (*c.f.* the cases listed in Appendix Table II). However, quite a number of them had epilepsy, and several had cerebral palsy. It is possible that in the majority of these cases the mental retardation was of prenatal origin, but there was not enough evidence to place them in that group.

Various non-specific atrophy-like changes were the most frequent neuroradiological findings in patients in this category (Figs. 48-51).

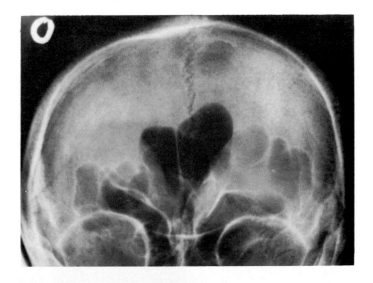

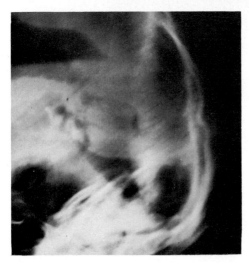

Figs. 48 a and b. (*a*) *Above.* Antero-posterior lumbar pneumoencephalogram showing severe left hemimacroventriculy with displacement of the septum pellucidum.

(*b*) *Left.* Lateral lumbar pneumoencephalogram. The tent-shaped fourth ventricle can be clearly seen and is not enlarged, but the cerebellum is small.

Clinical details. Male aged 17 years with epilepsy, mild ataxia and minor malformations, but no other clinical signs. The patient's development has been abnormal from birth.

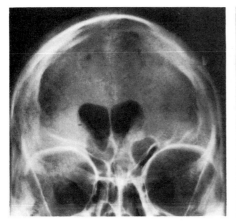
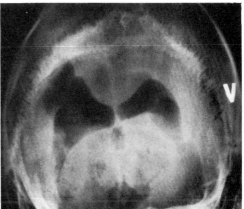
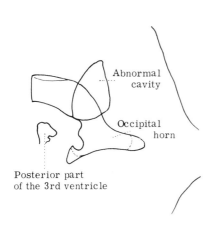
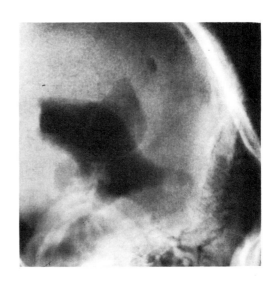

Abnormal
cavity

Occipital
horn

Posterior part
of the 3rd ventricle

Figs. 49 a, b and c. (*a*) *Upper left*. Antero-posterior lumbar pneumoencephalogram (taken with patient in brow-up position) showing mild macroventriculy, but no marked abnormal findings.

(*b*) *Upper right*. Postero-anterior lumbar pneumoencephalogram (taken with patient in brow-up position) demonstrating a cavity in the right parietal occipital region communicating with the right lateral ventricle.

(*c*) *Lower picture*. Lateral (occipital) lumbar pneumoencephalogram (taken with patient in brow-down position) showing the posterior part of the abnormal cavity.

Clinical details. Male aged 27 years with epilepsy and minor malformations. No information is available as to when the retardation was first noted.

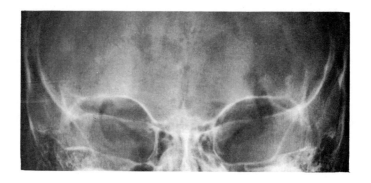

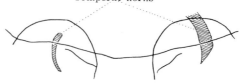

Temporal horns

Fig. 50. Antero-posterior lumbar pneumoencephalogram taken with patient in brow-up position. There is enlargement of the left temporal horn suggesting a lesion of the left temporal lobe. Other views suggested atrophy or dysplasia of the cerebellum.

Clinical details. Female aged 10 years with expressive dysphasia. Regarded as typical autistic retarded child, with no abnormal findings apart from some hyperpigmentation of the skin. Her development had been abnormal from birth.

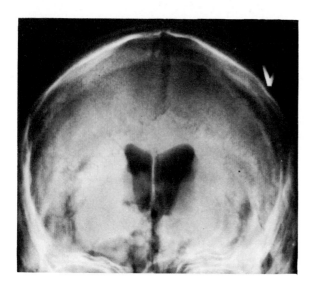

Figs. 51 a, b and c. (*a*) *Left.* Antero-posterior lumbar pneumoencephalogram showing moderate left hemi-macroventriculy. There is some suggestion of temporal cortical atrophy.

100

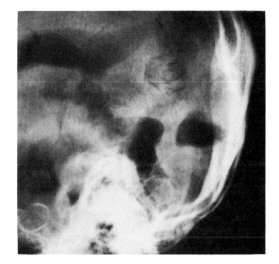

Fig. 51b

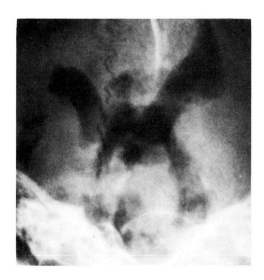

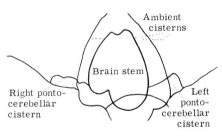

(b) *Upper picture.* Lateral lumbar pneumoencephalogram showing very enlarged fourth ventricle and cisterna magna. There is little supra-cerebellar gas. Severe cerebellar atrophy.

(c) *Lower pictures.* Posterio-anterior half-axial lumbar pneumoencephalogram taken with patient in sitting position. Enlarged ambient cisterns indicate atrophy of the brain stem. The ponto-cerebellar cisterns, which are poorly seen, are also enlarged.

Clinical details. Female aged 27 years with diplegia, epilepsy (with chronic phenytoin intoxication) and some minor malformations. Her development had been abnormal from birth.

Comparison of Present Diagnosis with Previous Diagnosis

At the time when the patients in this series were first admitted to the Rinnekoti, the aetiological diagnoses were classified according to Heber (1961) (see page 3). Thus, in order that the diagnoses made in connection with the present study might be compared with those made previously, the former were re-classified according to Heber's system.

In as many as 146 cases (43 per cent), the aetiological diagnosis had to be changed as a result of this investigation. As can be seen from Table XLIII, these changes did not greatly affect the number of cases within each diagnostic category, because some changes compensated for each other. The statistically significant changes ($p < 0.001$) in the proportional distribution of cases amongst the various categories were as follows: there was a decrease in the proportion of cases placed in the categories of 'trauma and physical agents' (from 28 to 15 per cent), and 'uncertain (or presumed psychological) cause with the functional reaction alone manifest' (from 12 to 1 per cent); on the other hand there was an increase in the category of '(unknown) prenatal influence' (from 21 to 37 per cent).

TABLE XLIII

Aetiological classification of the 338 mentally retarded patients according to Heber (1961), before and after the present study

Aetiological category	Before		After	
	No. of cases	Per cent	No. of cases	Per cent
Infection	38	11	48	14
Intoxication	16	5	19	6
Trauma or physical agents	95	28*1	52	15
Metabolic disorder	9	3	12	4
New growths	6	2	7	2
Unknown prenatal influence	72	21*2	125	37
Uncertain cause with the structural reactions manifest	61	18	73	22
Uncertain cause with the functional reaction alone manifest	41	12*3	2	1
TOTAL	338	100	338	100

*Highly significant difference between numbers before and after present study ($\chi^2_1 = 16\cdot1$; $\chi^2_2 = 20\cdot1$; $\chi^2_3 = 38\cdot1$); $p < 0\cdot001$.

Conclusions

Perhaps the most important result of this diagnostic study was the demonstration of some pathology in every case investigated, and the consequent reduction in the number of cases in which, before the study began, the aetiology had been completely unknown. Although the categories of unknown prenatal influence and other and unspecified causes did comprise cases in which a definite aetiological diagnosis still could not be made, the finding that the majority of these patients had suffered a cerebral insult before birth was in itself an important step forward. It is to be hoped that, with more careful studies of babies in the perinatal period and more detailed collection of historical data, we shall, in future, be able to make more definite diagnoses of the causes of some of these pathological conditions.

The Aetiology of the Mental Retardation in Those Patients Who Were not Selected for Further Neuroradiological Studies

In Tables XLIV, XLV and XLVI, the aetiological diagnoses made in the 662 patients out of the original 1000 who were not selected for cerebral angiography and/ or pneumoencephalography are classified according to Yannet, the WHO and Heber. A comparison of Table XLIV with Table XXXVIII, of Table XLV with Table XXXIX and of Table XLVI with Table XLIII reveals a number of significant differences. Amongst the patients not selected for further neuroradiological investigation, cases in Yannet's prenatal category were more prevalent (361/662 vs. 151/338; $p < 0.001$). Cases in the WHO's category of unknown prenatal influence were less common (111/ 662 vs. 106/338; $p < 0.001$), and those in the WHO's category of chromosome aberrations were more common (156/662 vs. 12/338; $p < 0.001$). Finally, cases in Heber's category of 'unknown or uncertain cause with the structural reactions manifest' were less prevalent (83/662 vs. 73/338; $p < 0.001$), and those in Heber's category of 'uncertain or presumed psychological cause with the functional reaction alone manifest' were more prevalent (81/662 vs. 2/338; $p < 0.001$).

TABLE XLIV

Aetiological classification of the 662 mentally retarded patients not included in the present series, according to Yannet (1945)

Category	No. of cases	Per cent
Prenatal	361	55
Perinatal	75	11
Postnatal	95	14
More than one category	17	3
Undeterminable	114	17
TOTAL	662	100

TABLE XLV

Aetiological classification of the 662 mentally retarded patients not included in the present study, according to the WHO (1968)

Category	No. of cases	Per cent
Infections and intoxications	90	14
Trauma or physical agents	73	11
Disorders of metabolism	34	5
Gross brain diseases	20	3
Unknown prenatal influence	111	17
Chromosomal aberrations	156	24
Prematurity	5	1
Major psychiatric disorders	16	2
Psycho-social deprivation	1	0
More than one probable cause	25	4
Other and unspecified causes	130	20
Not classifiable	1	0
TOTAL	662	100

103

TABLE XLVI

Aetiological classification of the 662 mentally retarded patients not included in the present study, according to Heber (1961)

Category	No. of cases	Per cent
Infection	71	11
Intoxication	28	4
Trauma or physical agent	81	12
Disorder of metabolism	34	5
New growths	10	2
Unknown prenatal influence	273	41
Uncertain cause with the structural reactions manifest	83	13
Uncertain cause with the functional reaction alone manifest	81	12
Not classifiable	1	0
TOTAL	662	100

Statistical Correlations Between the Various Sets of Data and the Aetiological Categories of Mental Retardation

In this chapter, the diagnoses described in the previous chapter are correlated with items of information which had been collected about the patients (see Appendix Table IV). Obvious correlations, such as those between a history of infection and the aetiological category of infections, in which the data collected were directly linked with the diagnosis made, are not listed here. This chapter is mainly concerned with statistically significant correlations which would not necessarily have been expected from the diagnosis. These statistical findings are discussed in Chapter 6.

Throughout this chapter, the items selected for analysis have been correlated both with Yannet's (1945) categories, based on the timing of the insult (see Table XXXVIII), and with the WHO's (1968) aetiological categories (see Table XXXIX).

Correlations with categories in which there were few cases (*e.g.* the WHO's categories of 'metabolic disorders', 'gross brain diseases', 'chromosome aberrations', 'prematurity' and 'major psychiatric disorder') were not tested by the χ^2 test. The reliability of the results presented is considered in the final discussion (see page 127).

Sex, Age and Degree of Retardation

Sex

One hundred and ninety-seven (58 per cent) of the patients in this series were males and 141 (42 per cent) were females. The male/female ratio varied considerably amongst the aetiological categories of Yannet. The smallest percentage of males was in the category of unknown aetiological timepoint (51 per cent). In the perinatal category 52 per cent, in the prenatal category 62 per cent, and in the category of more than one aetiological timepoint 65 per cent were males. These figures suggest that males sustain better than females disorders with an unknown or perinatal aetiology, while females sustain better than males disorders of prenatal origin. However, all these differences were without statistical significance when tested by the χ^2 test.

Using the WHO's system of classification, the following categories contained a higher proportion of males than did the series as a whole: metabolic disorders (82 per cent males), gross brain diseases (67 per cent), infections and intoxications (62 per cent), unknown prenatal influence (61 per cent), and more than one probable cause (60 per cent). A particularly high predominance of males was found in certain sub-groups, *i.e.* in the sub-group of 'other' unknown prenatal influences (82 per cent), and in that of toxaemia of pregnancy (75 per cent). Females predominated in the sub-groups of congenital brain defects (80 per cent) and hypoxic birth injuries (61 per cent). The predominance of males in the category of unknown prenatal influence is largely due to the high male:female ratio amongst mentally retarded patients with the cutis verticis gyrata syndrome (see Palo *et al.* 1970).

In view of these findings, it seems logical to suggest that females may be more vulnerable to developmental diseases of the brain. However, the differences were without statistical significance, using the χ^2 test.

Age at Time of Investigation

Not surprisingly, among Yannet's categories the mean age of the patients was highest in the category of unknown causative timepoint (mean = 18.5 years). This was significantly higher than the mean age of the patients in the perinatal category (mean = 15.5; $p < 0.05$).

There were no statistically significant differences between the various categories of the WHO in respect of the mean age of the patients, and those differences which did exist were not large enough to be of clinical significance. It should be remembered that a number of diseases, *e.g.* Spielmeyer-Vogt's disease, occur particularly commonly in patients in specific age groups. This is not evident from the statistical results because of the rarity of these conditions in the present study.

Degree of Mental Retardation

There were no statistically significant differences between the various aetiological categories of Yannet in respect to the mean degree of mental retardation as assessed by intelligence tests. However, there were fewer cases with IQs of 36 or less than with IQs of more than 36 in the categories of postnatal and unknown aetiological timepoints, and more cases with IQs of 36 or less than with IQs of more than 36 in the perinatal and prenatal categories (Table XLVII).

When the degree of mental retardation was classified according to the WHO (1968), and scored 0 (borderline), 1 (mild), 2 (moderate), 3 (severe) or 4 (profound), the Student's 't' test revealed some significant differences between the various aetiological categories of the WHO. The patients in the category of metabolic disorders had a significantly higher mean IQ (mean score = 2.4) than those in the categories of unknown prenatal influence (mean score = 3.4; $p < 0.01$), trauma and physical agents

TABLE XLVII

Correlations between the degree of mental retardation and the aetiological
categories of Yannet (1945)

| Aetiological category | I.Q. more than 36 | | I.Q. 36 or less | |
	No.	*Per cent*	*No.*	*Per cent*
Prenatal	26	37	124	47
Perinatal	5	7	37	14
Postnatal	17	24	44	17
Several aetiological timepoints	6	9	11	4
Unknown aetiological timepoint	17	24	50	19
TOTAL	71	100	266	100

TABLE XLVIII

Correlations between the degree of mental retardation and the aetiological
categories of the WHO (1968)

Aetiological category	I.Q. more than 36		I.Q. 36 or less	
	No.	Per cent	No.	Per cent
Infections and intoxications	9	13	49	18
Trauma or physical agents	8	11	38	14
Disorders of metabolism	7	10†	4	2†
Gross brain diseases	1	1	8	3
Unknown prenatal influence	18	25	87	33
Chromosomal aberrations	1	1	11	4
Prematurity	1	1	2	1
Major psychiatric disorders	0	0	1	0
More than one probable cause	6	8	19	7
Other and unspecified causes	20	28*	47	18*
TOTAL	71	100	266	100

*Almost significant difference ($\chi^2 = 3 \cdot 9$; p $< 0 \cdot 05$).
†Highly significant difference ($\chi^2 = 12 \cdot 6$; p $< 0 \cdot 001$).

(mean score = 3.4; p < 0.01), infections and intoxications (mean score = 3.4; p < 0.01),
chromosome aberrations (mean score = 3.5; p < 0.05), and other and unspecified causes
(mean score = 3.2; p < 0.05).

Patients with IQs of 36 or less were more common than those with IQs of more
than 36 in the WHO's categories of infections and intoxications and unknown prenatal
influence, and less common in the categories of metabolic disorders and other and
unspecified causes (Table XLVIII).

When tested by the χ^2 test, the distribution of cases with an IQ of 36 or less throughout the main aetiological categories of the WHO (*infections and intoxications: disorders
of metabolism: unknown prenatal influence: other and unspecified causes: other
categories*) was significantly different from the distribution of cases with an IQ score
of more than 36 (49: 4: 87: 47: 79 vs 9: 7: 18: 20: 17; p < 0.001).

One factor which should be considered in connection with these results is that
many metabolic disorders are progressive, and the degree of mental retardation found
will depend on the stage the disease has reached when the IQ is determined. For this
reason, the statistically significant findings in this category are not necessarily of
clinical significance.

Statistical Correlations Between Information Taken From Case Histories and the Aetiology of Mental Retardation.

Social Class

When the patients in this series were classified according to the system of the
WHO, the highest mean social class was in the category of prematurity (mean = 4.7;
using Rauhala's 1966 classification into nine social classes, see page 26) and the lowest
in that of metabolic disorders (mean = 6.7). Although this difference between the
two categories was significant (p < 0.05) when tested by the Student's 't' test, this

finding is of doubtful significance, because there were only three cases in the category of prematurity. No other statistically significant correlations were found between social class and the various aetiologies of mental retardation as classified by Yannet and the WHO.

Unmarried Mothers

Although the number of patients in this series whose mothers were unmarried at the time of their birth was high, none of these were in the WHO's category of infections and intoxications. There was a statistically significant difference between the number of children with unmarried mothers in this category and the number in all the other categories of the WHO (nobody out of 58 cases as against 38 out of 280 cases, or 0/58 vs 38/280; p <0.01). The statistical significance of this finding is obscure. It may be a chance finding, or it could be that unmarried mothers are more immune than married mothers to infections and intoxications.

Mentally Retarded Siblings and Close Relatives

A study of the distribution of patients with mentally retarded siblings and close relatives revealed no significant differences between the various aetiological categories of Yannet or the WHO.

Previous Abortions and Stillbirths

Patients whose mothers had had previous abortions or stillbirths were found significantly more frequently in Yannet's category of more than one causative time-point than in all his other categories (7/17 vs 50/321; p <0.01). When the patients were classified according to the WHO, previous abortions and stillbirths were found to be significantly less frequent in the category of trauma and physical agents (3/46 vs 54/292; p <0.05), and significantly more frequent ($\chi^2 = 4.4$; p <0.05) in the category of more than one probable cause (8/25 vs 49/313; p <0.05), than in all the other categories.

Maternal Age

Using the WHO's classification, the mean maternal age was highest in the category of chromosome aberrations (31.3 years). The maternal age of patients in this category differed significantly from that of patients in the categories of metabolic disorders (mean = 26.0 years; p <0.05) and more than one probable cause (mean = 27.1 years; p <0.05).

Births Without Trained Help

The proportion of patients born without trained help was significantly higher in Yannet's category of unknown aetiological timepoint than in the rest of the series (15/67 vs 30/271; p <0.05).

Obstetrical Operations

Fifteen of the 42 patients in Yannet's perinatal category, but only 28 out of the 296 in other categories, had required obstetrical operations (*i.e.* forceps delivery, caesarian section, and breech delivery). This significant difference is hardly surprising in view of the definition of the category. Sixteen of the 43 patients who had required obstetrical operations were among the 46 patients in the WHO's category of trauma and physical agents (16/46 vs 27/292; p <0.001).

Birthweights

The mean birthweight of patients in Yannet's postnatal category (3500 g) was significantly higher than that of patients in the prenatal (p <0.001), perinatal (p <0.05), and more than one aetiological timepoint (p <0.001) categories. In addition, the mean birthweight of the patients in the category of unknown aetiological timepoint was significantly higher than that of patients in the category of more than one aetiological timepoint (p <0.05) (Table XLIX).

TABLE XLIX

Statistically significant correlations between birthweights and Yannet's (1945) aetiological categories of mental retardation

	Aetiological categories				
	Prenatal	*Perinatal*	*Postnatal*	*Several*	*Unknown*
Mean birth-weight (grams)	3110	3200	3500	2820	3260
Deviation	690	650	510	920	740
No. of cases	138	41	54	17	55
Student t values for pairs of means					
Postnatal	3·8†	2·6*			
Several			3·9†		
Unknown				2·0*	

*Almost significant difference (p <0.05).
†Highly significance difference (p <0.001).

Of all the WHO's categories, that of gross brain diseases contained patients with the highest mean birthweight (4020 grams; see Table L). The mean birthweight of the patients in this category was significantly greater when tested by the Student's 't' test than that of patients in any other categories. (The category of psychiatric disorder included one case only and was not tested statistically. The mean birthweight of patients in the category of prematurity without other cause (1300 g) was significantly lower than the corresponding means in all the other categories (see Table L). However, it is not possible to attach much clinical significance to this finding as there were only three patients in the category. The mean birthweight in the category of birth trauma and physical agents (3310 g) was significantly higher than that in the categories of metabolic disorders (p <0.05), prematurity (p <0.001) and more than one probable cause (p <0.001), and lower than that in the category of gross brain diseases (p <0.01).

TABLE L

Statistically significant correlations between birthweights and the aetiological categories of mental retardation according to the classification of the WHO (1968)

	Infections and intoxications	Trauma and physical agents	Disorders of metabolism	Gross brain disease	Unknown prena-tal influence	Chromosome aberrations	Prematurity	Major psychiat-ric disorder**	More than one probable cause	Other and un-specified causes
Mean birthweight (g)	3230	3310	2810	4020	3210	3080	1300	3800	2840	3320
Deviation	670	550	600	510	660	470	200	0	840	650
No. of cases	55	44	7	6	98	10	3	1	25	56

Student t values for pairs of means

	Infections and intoxications	Trauma and physical agents	Disorders of metabolism	Gross brain disease	Unknown prena-tal influence	Chromosome aberrations	Prematurity	Major psychiat-ric disorder**	More than one probable cause	Other and un-specified causes
Disorders of metabolism		2·2*								
Gross brain disease	2·8‡	3·0‡	3·9‡							
Unknown pre-natal influence				2·9‡						
Chromosome aberrations				3·7‡						
Prematurity	4·9†	6·2†	4·2‡	8·6†	5·0†	6·3†				
Major psychi-atric disorder**										
More than one probable cause	2·3*	2·8‡		3·3‡	2·4*		3·1‡			
Other and un-specified causes				2·5*			5·3†		2·8‡	

*Almost significant difference (p < 0·05).
‡Significant difference (p < 0·01).
†Highly significant difference (p < 0·001).
**Category not tested statistically because it contained only one case.

Abnormal Maturity of the Fetus

A significantly low proportion of the cases in which the fetus was of abnormal maturity (*i.e.* pre-term, small-for-dates, and post-term) was in Yannet's postnatal category (4/61 vs 52/277; p <0.05), and a significantly high proportion was in the category of several causative timepoints (7/17 vs 49/321; p <0.01).

Cases in which the fetus was of abnormal maturity were less frequent in the WHO's category of trauma and physical agents (2/46 vs 54/292; p <0.05), and more frequent in that of more than one probable cause (10/25 vs 46/313; p <0.01) than in the rest of the series.

Slight Asphyxia Immediately After Birth

Cases in which slight asphyxia or cyanosis had been found immediately after birth were significantly more common in Yannet's categories of perinatal aetiology (23/42 vs 51/296; p <0.001) and more than one causative timepoint (12/17 vs 62/321; p <0.001), and significantly less common in Yannet's categories of postnatal aetiology (2/61 vs 72/277; p <0.001) and unknown aetiological timepoint (6/67 vs 68/271; p <0.01) than in the rest of the series. When the WHO's classification was used, cases of slight asphyxia after birth were found to be significantly more common in the categories of trauma and physical agents (22/46 vs 52/292; p <0.001) and more than one probable cause (16/25 vs 58/313; p <0.001) and significantly less common in the category of infections and intoxications (3/58 vs 71/280; p <0.001) than in the other categories.

Marked Asphyxia Immediately After Birth

Cases in which marked asphyxia had occurred immediately after birth were significantly more common in Yannet's categories of perinatal aetiology (11/42 vs 20/296; p <0.001) and more than one aetiological timepoint (6/17 vs 25/321; p <0.001), and significantly less common in the categories of postnatal aetiology (1/61 vs 30/277; p <0.05) and unknown aetiological timepoints (2/67 vs 29/271; p <0.05) than in the other categories.

Cases of marked asphyxia immediately after birth were more frequently found in the WHO's categories of mechanical trauma at birth and physical agents (11/46 vs 20/292; p <0.001) and more than one probable cause (9/25 vs 22/313; p <0.001) than in the other categories.

Abnormalities During the Later Neonatal Period

These had been found significantly more frequently in the patients in Yannet's categories of prenatal aetiology (79/151 vs 60/187; p <0.001), perinatal aetiology (34/42 vs 105/296; p <0.001) and more than one aetiological timepoint (11/25 vs 128/321; p <0.05) than in the rest of the series. On the other hand, they had been found significantly less frequently in the patients in Yannet's categories of postnatal aetiology (1/61 vs 138/277; p <0.001) and unknown aetiological timepoint (14/67 vs 125/271; p <0.001).

Using the WHO's classification, abnormalities during the later neonatal period were found to have occurred significantly more frequently in patients in the categories of mechanical trauma at birth and physical agents (29/46 vs 110/292; p <0.01) and more than one probable cause (18/25 vs 121/313; p <0.01) and significantly less frequently in patients in the category of infections and intoxications (13/58 vs 126/ 280; p <0.01) than in the rest of the series.

Types of Development of Mental Retardation

The mental retardation had been apparent from birth in 148 out of 151 cases in Yannet's category of prenatal aetiology. In this respect, the findings in this category differed significantly from those in the rest of the series (p <0.001). The distribution of the various types of development of mental retardation (*apparent from birth: of acute onset: other*) was significantly different from the distribution throughout the rest of the series in the following categories: Yannet's categories of postnatal aetiology (16: 29: 16 vs 258: 4: 15; p <0.001) and unknown aetiological timepoint (58: 1: 8: vs 216: 32: 23; p <0.05), and the WHO's categories of infections and intoxications (29: 24: 5 vs 245: 9: 26; p <0.001), unknown prenatal influence (105: 1: 0 vs 169: 32: 31; p <0.001) and other and unspecified causes (54: 1: 12: vs 220: 32: 19; p <0.01). In the WHO's category of unknown prenatal influence, the development of the mental retardation was apparent from birth in 105 out of the 106 cases. In this respect, the difference between this category and the rest of the series was significant (p <0.001).

Epilepsy

The patients were divided into four groups according to whether they had *no epilepsy*, *focal epilepsy*, *centrencephalic epilepsy*, or *other miscellaneous forms of epilepsy*. The distribution of patients amongst these groups in the following categories differed from the corresponding distribution in the remainder of the series: Yannet's prenatal (75: 13: 21: 42 vs 53: 34: 40: 60; p <0.001) and perinatal categories (6: 11: 10: 15 vs 122: 36: 51: 87; p <0.01), and the WHO's category of mechanical trauma at birth and physical agents (8: 15: 10: 13 vs 120: 32: 51: 89; p <0.001).

Statistical Correlations Between Physical and Other Non-neuroradiological Findings and the Aetiology of Mental Retardation

The statistically significant differences between the various aetiological categories with respect to height, weight, and head circumference are set out in Table LI.

Height

Dwarfing (below the 2.5 percentile in height) occurred significantly more frequently, and normal height (between the 2.5 and 97.5 percentiles) less frequently (p <0.05), in Yannet's category of prenatal aetiology than in the other categories. In the postnatal category, dwarfing was significantly less frequent, and normal height more frequent (p <0.05), than in the rest of the series.

Weight

Low weight occurred more frequently (p <0.05) and normal weight less frequently (p <0.05) in Yannet's prenatal category than in the rest of the series. In

TABLE LI

Statistically significant correlations between heights, weights, and head circumferences and the aetiological categories of mental retardation (Yannet and the WHO)

Aetiological category	Height† Small (No. of cases)	Height† Normal (No.)	Weight† Small (No.)	Weight† Normal (No.)	Head circumference (relat.)‡ Small (No.)	Head circumference (relat.)‡ Normal (No.)	Head circumference (relat.)‡ Large (No.)	Head circumference (absolute)† Small (No.)	Head circumference (absolute)† Normal (No.)	Head circumference (absolute)† Large (No.)
Prenatal (Yannet)	90*↑	61*↓	68*↑	80*↓	45*↑			71*↑	70*↓	
Postnatal (Yannet)	25*↓	36*↑					12‡↑	17*↓		8*↑
Unknown (Yannet)			16‡↓	50‡↑		54‡↑				
Unknown pre-natal influence (WHO)			49*↑		34*↑	63*↓				
Other and un-specified causes (WHO)			17*↓	49*↑		54‡↑		19*↓	45*↑	

*Almost significant difference (p <0·05).

‡Significant difference (p <0·01).

†Small = below 2·5 percentile (except in head circumference = below 2·0 percentile).

Normal = between 2·5 and 97·5 percentiles (except in head circumference = between 2·0 and 98·0 percentiles).

Large = over 97·5 percentile (except in head circumference = over 98·0 percentile).

↑ = high frequency.

↓ = low frequency.

Yannet's category of unknown aetiological timepoint and in the WHO's category of other and unspecified causes, low weight was found significantly less frequently (Yannet p <0.001; WHO p <0.05) and normal weight more frequently (Yannet p <0.01; WHO p <0.05) than in the rest of the series. Low weight was also found significantly more frequently in the WHO's category of unknown prenatal influence than in the other categories.

Head Circumference

Small relative head circumferences (determined in relation to height and age) were found more frequently in Yannet's prenatal category than in the rest of the series (p <0.05), and large relative head circumferences (over the 98th percentile) were found more frequently in his postnatal category (p <0.01). Normal head circumferences (between the 2nd and 98th percentiles) were found significantly more often in Yannet's category of unknown aetiological timepoint and in the WHO's category of other and unspecified causes, than in the rest of the series (p <0.01). Small head circumferences were significantly more frequent (p <0.05), and normal head circumferences significantly less frequent (p <0.05) in the WHO's category of unknown prenatal influence than in the rest of the series.

The correlations between small, normal and large *absolute head circumferences* (determined only in relation to age) and the aetiological categories were mostly similar to the correlations between small, normal and large *relative head circumferences* and the various aetiological categories listed above (see Table LI). However, unlike normal relative head circumferences, normal absolute head circumferences were significantly less common in Yannet's prenatal category than in the rest of the series (p <0.05). Unlike small relative head circumferences, small absolute head circumferences were found significantly less frequently in Yannet's postnatal category (p <0.05) and in the WHO's category of other and unspecified causes (p <0.05), but were no more prevalent in the WHO's category of unknown prenatal influence, than in the rest of the series.

Cephalic Index

The finding that the three cases in the WHO's category of prematurity had a mean cephalic index of only 74.3 suggests a possible association between dolichocephaly and mental retardation due to short gestation alone. The mean cephalic index in this small category differed significantly from the means in the categories of chromosome aberrations (mean = 84.3; p <0.05) and other and unspecified causes (mean = 82.0; p <0.05). On average the skulls of patients in the category of chromosome aberrations were significantly more brachycephalic than those of patients in the category of more than one probable cause (mean cephalic index = 79.8; p <0.05).

Dyscrania

This was found significantly more frequently in cases in Yannet's prenatal category than in the rest of the series (114/151 vs 118/187; p <0.05).

114

Handedness and Psychotic Signs

As far as handedness and psychotic signs were concerned, no significant differences were found between the various aetiological categories.

Other Neurological Findings

Cranial nerve syndromes were found significantly more frequently in patients in Yannet's category of more than one causative timepoint than in the rest of the series (6/17 vs 48/321; $p < 0.05$). Signs indicative of an upper motor neurone lesion were more common in cases in the WHO's category of more than one probable cause than in the rest of the series (16/25 vs 135/313; $p < 0.05$). Upper motor neurone syndromes were significantly less common in Yannet's category of unknown aetiological timepoint (17/67 vs 134/271; $p < 0.001$) and in the WHO's category of other and unspecified causes (20/67 vs 131/271; $p < 0.01$) than in the rest of the series.

A study of the prevalence of atrophy of the optic discs in this series showed that no one aetiological category contained a significantly high proportion of cases of blindness.

Muscular hypotonia was found in patients in Yannet's prenatal category more frequently than in the rest of the series (16/151 vs 6/187; $p < 0.01$).

Extrapyramidal syndromes were found in Yannet's perinatal category significantly more frequently than in the rest of the series (7/42 vs 21/296; $p < 0.05$).

Cerebral palsy was found less often in patients in Yannet's category of unknown aetiological timepoint (27/67 vs 156/271; $p < 0.05$) and in the WHO's category of other and unspecified causes (29/67 vs 154/271; $p < 0.05$). Of the different forms of cerebral palsy, spastic right hemiplegia was more common in Yannet's postnatal category (7/61 vs 6/277; $p < 0.001$) and in the WHO's category of infections and intoxications (7/58 vs 6/280; $p < 0.001$) than in the rest of the series. Spastic diplegia was evenly spread throughout the categories. Triplegia occurred more frequently in Yannet's category of more than one aetiological timepoint (3/25 vs 10/313; $p < 0.05$) and tetraplegia more frequently in the WHO's category of unknown prenatal influence (13/106 vs 14/232; $p < 0.05$) than in the rest of the series. Ataxia was found significantly more frequently in Yannet's postnatal category than elsewhere (8/61 vs 14/277; $p < 0.05$).

Motor and Social Skills

At the time of examination, more children could walk, feed themselves and sit without support in Yannet's category of unknown aetiological timepoint than in the rest of the series. (Unable to walk normally: 21/67 vs 152/271; $p < 0.001$. Unable to feed themselves: 14/67 vs 97/271; $p < 0.05$. Unable to sit-up unsupported: 6/67 vs 56/271; $p < 0.05$). Similar differences were found in the WHO's category of other and unspecified causes. (Unable to walk normally: 24/67 vs 149/271; $p < 0.01$. Unable to feed themselves: 14/67 vs 97/271; $p < 0.05$. Unable to sit up unsupported: 6/67 vs 56/271; $p < 0.05$).

Malformations

The distribution of major malformations and of cutaneous abnormalities was not studied statistically because of the significance of these findings in deciding the causes of particular forms of mental retardation. For instance, major malformations were considered as one of the indications of a prenatal aetiology, and some cutaneous findings (*e.g.* xeroderma pigmentosum, adenoma sebaceum, and cutis verticis gyrata) were known to be closely associated with certain disorders or syndromes (see page 133).

Other correlations between the findings on physical examination and the various aetiological categories of mental retardation were without statistical significance.

Statistical Correlations Between EEG Findings and the Aetiology of Mental Retardation

Using a crude form of classification (*normal or borderline: slightly disturbed: markedly disturbed*), the distribution of the different types of EEG recording in the following categories differed significantly from that in the rest of the series: Yannet's postnatal category (5: 7: 47: vs 15: 73: 173; p <0.05), the WHO's category of trauma and physical agents (3: 5: 48 vs 17: 75: 172; p <0.01) and the WHO's category of other and unspecified causes (6: 22: 34 vs 14: 58: 186; p < 0.05).

Diffuse slow wave abnormalities were found significantly more frequently in Yannet's prenatal category than in the rest of the series (133/143 vs 151/177; p <0.05).

Cases in which abnormal β-activity and extreme spindles were recorded were significantly more common in Yannet's prenatal category (28/143 vs 14/177; p <0.01), and significantly less common in the WHO's category of other and unspecified causes (3/63 vs 39/257; p <0.05) than in the rest of the series. On the other hand, asymmetry or depression of background activity and focal slow wave abnormalities were found significantly less frequently in Yannet's prenatal category than elsewhere in the series (29/143 vs 53/177; p <0.05).

Paroxysmal slow activity in the EEG was found more frequently in the cases in the WHO's category of unknown prenatal influence than in the rest of the series (24/100 vs 32/220; p <0.05).

Focal spikes and waves were recorded significantly more frequently in patients in the WHO's category of infections and intoxications than in all the other patients (17/56 vs 44/264; p <0.05).

Generalised irregular spikes and waves, generalised regular 3 Hz spikes and waves, hypsarrhythmia, 14 and 6 positive spikes, and other bilateral generalised changes, were all seen more frequently on the EEGs of patients in the WHO's category of trauma and physical agents than on those of other patients (16/44 vs 59/276; p <0.05).

Occipital localisation of focal EEG changes occurred less frequently in Yannet's category of unknown aetiological timepoint than elsewhere in the series (0/23 vs 17/91; p <0.05).

There was a significant difference between Yannet's postnatal category and the rest of the series (16/25 vs 31/89; p <0.01) and between the WHO's category of infections and intoxications and the rest of the series (18/29 vs 29/85; p <0.01), in that focal EEG changes in patients in these categories were more frequently recorded on the left than the right side. Of all the cases with focal EEG findings, those in the WHO's category of more than one probable cause showed right-sided lateralisation of EEG abnormalities more frequently (7/7 vs 45/107; p <0.01), and left-sided lateralisation less frequently (0/7 vs 47/107; p <0.05), than the others.

All the other correlations between the EEG findings and the various aetiological categories of mental retardation, as defined by Yannet and the WHO, were without statistical significance.

Statistical Correlations Between the Neuroradiological Findings and the Aetiology of Mental Retardation.

Skull X-Rays

The relative distribution of the main skull x-ray findings (*normal: asymptomatic anomaly: congenital cranial deformity: unilateral intracranial lesion: other findings*) differed from that in the rest of the series in Yannet's prenatal (27: 46: 29: 15: 29 vs 43: 50: 4: 39: 49; p <0.001) and perinatal (6: 13: 1: 6: 6 vs 64: 83: 32: 38: 72; p <0.001) categories.

The distribution of the various skull radiological findings was also significantly different in the WHO's categories of trauma and physical agents (9: 10: 2: 15: 10 vs 61: 86: 31: 39: 68; p <0.05), unknown prenatal influence (12: 29: 24: 11: 26 vs 58: 67: 9: 43: 52; p <0.001), and other and unspecified causes (21: 17: 1: 7: 20 vs 49: 79: 32: 47: 58; p <0.01), compared with the rest of the series.

The prevalence of each of the major skull x-ray findings in the various aetiological categories of Yannet and the WHO is shown graphically in Figures 52 and 53.

Normal x-ray views of the skull were obtained significantly more often in patients in Yannet's category of unknown aetiological timepoint (20/66 vs 50/265; p <0.05) and in the WHO's category of other and unspecified causes (21/66 vs 49/265; p <0.05),

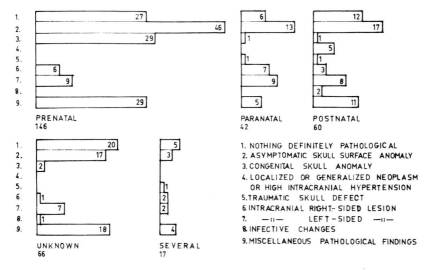

Fig. 52. Distribution of the main findings at skull X-ray examination throughout the aetiological categories of Yannet. The proportion of congenital skull anomalies in the prenatal category is particularly high.

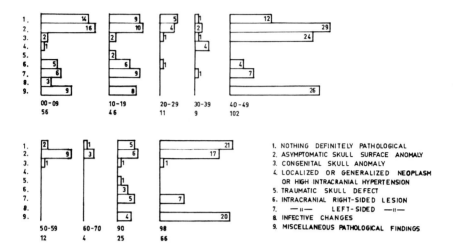

Fig. 53. Distribution of the main findings at skull X-ray examination throughout the aetiological categories of the WHO. 00-09 = infections and intoxications (56 patients); 10-19 = trauma and physical agents; 20-29 = metabolic disorders; 30-39 = gross brain diseases; 40-49 = unknown prenatal influence; 50-59 = chromosome aberrations; 60-70 = prematurity and major psychiatric disorder; 90 = more than one probable cause; 98 = other and unspecified causes.

Unilateral intracranial lesions were found most frequently in the category of trauma and physical agents, and congenital skull anomalies most frequently in the category of unknown prenatal influence; normal findings were found most frequently in the category of other and unspecified causes. Note the similarity between the distribution of findings in these three categories and the distribution in Yannet's categories of perinatal, prenatal and unknown aetiological timepoint (*c.f.* Fig. 52).

and significantly less often in patients in the WHO's category of prenatal influence (12/102 vs 171/229; p <0.01), than in the other patients.

Small or slightly large skulls were regarded as normal for the purposes of this statistical analysis.

With regard to the distribution of asymptomatic skull anomalies, no significant differences were found between the various aetiological categories.

Congenital cranial deformities were found significantly more frequently in Yannet's prenatal category (29/146 vs 4/185; p <0.001) and in the WHO's category of unknown prenatal influence (24/102 vs 9/229; p <0.001), than in the rest of the series. They were found significantly less frequently in Yannet's categories of postnatal aetiology (1/60 vs 32/271; p <0.05) and unknown aetiological timepoint (2/66 vs 31/265; p <0.05), and in the WHO's categories of infections and intoxications (1/56 vs 32/275; p <0.05) and other and unspecified causes (1/66 vs 32/265; p <0.05).

Other asymmetrical skull findings, indicative of a unilateral intracranial lesion, were found more frequently in the x-rays of patients in Yannet's perinatal category (16/42 vs 38/289; p <0.001) and in the WHO's categories of trauma and physical agents (15/46 vs 39/285; p <0.01) and more than one probable cause (8/25 vs 46/306; p <0.05), and less frequently in the x-rays of patients in Yannet's prenatal category (15/146 vs 39/185; p <0.01) than in those of the other patients in the series.

118

Asymmetry of the frontal sinuses was found to be more common in Yannet's prenatal (26/145 vs 56/186; p <0.05) and postnatal categories (21/60 vs 61/271; p <0.05) and in the WHO's category of unknown prenatal influence (18/102 vs 64/229; p <0.05) than in the rest of the series.

Persistent metopic fontanelle or cranium bifidum occultum frontalis occurred more frequently in Yannet's prenatal category (14/146 vs 15/185; p <0.01) and in the WHO's category of unknown prenatal influence (10/102 vs 9/229; p <0.05) than in the other categories.

The smallest mean volume of the sella turcica was found in Yannet's prenatal category (551 ml). In this respect the patients in this category differed significantly from those in the categories of postnatal aetiology (mean volume = 633 ml; p < 0.05) and unknown causative timepoint (mean = 621 ml; p <0.05). Of all the WHO's categories, that of gross brain diseases contained patients with the largest mean volume of the sella turcica (mean = 823 ml). The mean volume in this category differed significantly from that in the categories of unknown prenatal influence (mean = 553 ml; p <0.01), trauma and physical agents (mean = 594 ml; p <0.01), more than one probable cause (mean = 553 ml; p <0.01) and other and unspecified causes (mean = 625 ml; p <0.05).

There were no significant differences between the various aetiological categories as far as the mean cranial volume was concerned.

Cerebral Angiography

The distribution of the main angiographic findings (*normal: dislocation of cerebral vessels due to non-expanding process: other findings*) in Yannet's categories of postnatal aetiology (2: 12: 8 vs 24: 30: 14; p <0.05) and unknown aetiological timepoint (8: 4: 1: vs 18: 38: 21; p <0.05) and in the WHO's category of other and unspecified causes (8: 4: 0: vs 18: 38: 22; p <0.01), was significantly different from the corresponding distribution amongst the rest of the series.

Pathological angiographic findings were found significantly more frequently in Yannet's postnatal category (20/22 vs 44/68; p <0.05), and significantly less frequently in Yannet's category of unknown aetiological timepoint (5/13 vs 59/77; p <0.01) and in the WHO's category of other and unspecified causes (4/12 vs 60/78; p <0.01), than in the rest of the series.

No statistically significant correlations were found between the finding of displacement of cerebral vessels due to a non-expansive process and any of the aetiological categories of Yannet or the WHO.

Some rare and unusual angiographic findings such as occlusion and dysplasia of the cerebral vessels were pathognomic in the aetiological diagnosis of mental retardation. They were not tested statistically (see Fig. 54).

Pneumoencephalography

In respect of the distribution of the main pneumoencephalographic findings (*normal findings: symmetrical macroventriculy: asymmetrical macroventriculy: hemimacroventriculy: temporal horn dilatation: cerebral malformation: cerebellar atrophy or dysplasia: other findings*), there were significant differences between the

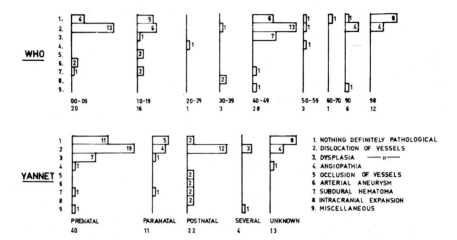

Fig. 54. Distribution of the main findings at cerebral angiography throughout the aetiological categories of the WHO (*above*) and Yannet (*below*). Normal findings were relatively uncommon in Yannet's postnatal category, but there were no marked differences between the various aetiological categories in either classification.

The WHO's categories: 00-09 = infections and intoxications (total 20 patients); 10-19 = trauma and physical agents; 20-29 = metabolic disorders; 30-39 = gross brain diseases; 40-49 = unknown prenatal influence; 50-59 = chromosome aberrations; 60-70 = prematurity and major psychiatric disorder; 90 = more than one probable cause; 98 = other and unspecified causes.

following categories and the rest of the series: Yannet's categories of prenatal aetiology (11: 35: 15: 10: 8: 48: 11: 8 vs 22: 49: 23: 35: 23: 4: 9: 19; p <0.001), perinatal aetiology (4: 8: 7: 9: 9: 0: 1: 3 vs 29: 76: 31: 36: 22: 52: 19: 24; p <0.01), postnatal aetiology (4: 16: 11: 13: 5: 1: 2: 7 vs 29: 68: 27: 32: 26: 51: 18: 20; p <0.01), and unknown aetiological timepoint (13: 19: 5: 9: 7: 1: 6: 7 vs 20: 65: 33: 36: 24: 51: 14: 20; p <0.01), and the WHO's categories of infections and intoxications (4: 14: 11: 12: 5: 2: 5: 3 vs 29: 70: 27: 33: 26: 50: 15: 24; p <0.05), unknown prenatal influence (6: 23: 10: 8: 4: 40: 7: 5 vs 27: 61: 28: 37: 27: 12: 13: 22; p <0.001), and other and unspecified causes (14: 19: 6: 9: 7: 1: 5: 6 vs 19: 65: 32: 36: 24: 51: 15: 21; p <0.01).

The proportion of patients in each of the WHO's and Yannet's aetiological categories with each of the above eight main pneumoencephalographic findings is shown graphically in Figures 55 and 56.

Pathological findings on pneumoencephalography were less common in Yannet's category of unknown aetiological timepoint (54/67 vs 243/263; p <0.01) and in the WHO's category of mental retardation due to other and unspecified causes (53/67 vs 244/263; p <0.001) than amongst the rest of the series.

Asymmetrical enlargement of the lateral ventricles was noted more frequently in patients in the WHO's categories of infections and intoxications than in all the other patients submitted to pneumoencephalography (11/56 vs 27/274; p <0.05).

Enlargement of a single lateral ventricle (hemimacroventriculy) occurred more frequently in Yannet's postnatal category (13/59 vs 32/271; p <0.05) and less frequently

120

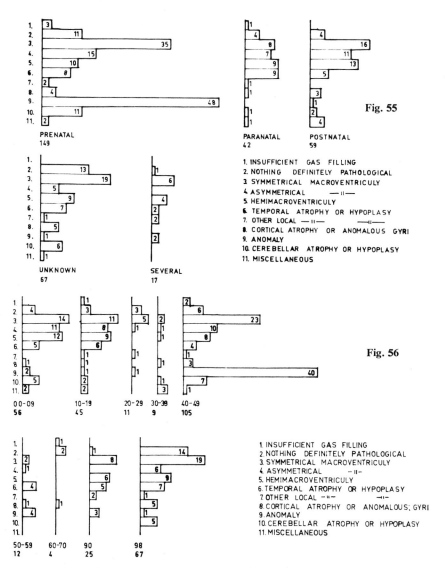

Fig. 55. Distribution of the main findings at pneumoencephalography throughout the aetiological categories of Yannet. The proportion of anomalies in the prenatal category is noticeably high.

Fig. 56. Distribution of the main findings at pneumoencephalography throughout the aetiological categories of the WHO. Anomalies occurred most frequently in the category of unknown prenatal influence, and normal findings most frequently in the category of other and unspecified causes. As with the skull X-ray findings (Figs. 52 and 53), there were marked similarities between the WHO's categories of trauma and physical agents, unknown prenatal influence and other and unspecified causes and Yannet's categories of perinatal, prenatal and unknown aetiological timepoint (*c.f.* Fig. 55).

00-09 = infections and intoxications (56 patients); 10-19 = trauma and physical agents; 20-29 = metabolic disorders; 30-39 = gross brain diseases; 40-49 = unknown prenatal influence; 50-59 = chromosome aberrations; 60-70 = prematurity and major psychiatric disorder; 90 = more than one probable cause; 98 = other and unspecified causes.

121

in his prenatal category (10/146 vs 35/184; p <0.01) than in the rest of the series. It was also found less frequently in the WHO's category of unknown prenatal influence (8/103 vs 37/227; p <0.05).

Dilatation of one or both temporal horns was noted more often in Yannet's perinatal category (9/41 vs 22/289; p <0.01), and less often both in his prenatal category (8/146 vs 23/184; p <0.05) and in the WHO's category of unknown prenatal influences (4/103 vs 27/227; p <0.05), than in the rest of the series.

Malformations of the brain were found more frequently in Yannet's prenatal category (48/146 vs 4/184; p <0.001) and in the WHO's category of unknown prenatal influence (40/103 vs 12/227; p <0.001) than in the rest of the series. They were found less frequently in Yannet's categories of perinatal aetiology (0/41 vs 52/289; p <0.01), postnatal aetiology (1/59 vs 51/271; p <0.01) and unknown aetiological timepoint (1/67 vs 51/263; p <0.001), and in the WHO's categories of infections and intoxications (2/56 vs 50/274; p <0.01), trauma and physical agents (1/44 vs 51/286; p <0.01) and other and unspecified causes (1/67 vs 51/263; p < 0.001).

There was no significant difference between the various aetiological categories in respect of the distribution of cases with symmetrical enlargement of the ventricles and those with cerebellar atrophy or dysplasia.

A number of statistically significant correlations were noted between individual pneumoencephalographic findings and particular aetiological categories as defined by Yannet and the WHO. These are listed below.

Amongst patients over the age of 20 years, symmetrical enlargement of the ventricles (macroventriculy), as defined by Nielsen et al. (1966a), was found more frequently in the WHO's category of trauma and physical agents than in the rest of the series (6/10 vs 22/92; p <0.05).

In patients aged 20 years or less, symmetrical macroventriculy (Evans' ratio 0.25 or more), without any difference in Evans' ratio and without displacement, was found less frequently in Yannet's perinatal category (14/32 vs 139/184; p <0.001) and in the WHO's category of trauma and physical agents (14/34 vs 139/182; p <0.001) than in the other categories. Bilateral enlargement of the ventricles (Evans' ratio 0.25 or more), with ratio difference (> 0.05) and without displacement, was less common in Yannet's prenatal category (10/92 vs 28/124; p <0.05), and more common in Yannet's perinatal category (12/32 vs 26/184; p <0.01), than in the rest of the series. It was also more common in the WHO's category of trauma and physical agents (14/34 vs 24/182; p <0.001).

Of the other smaller categories in Evans' (1942) classification of the size of the supratentorial ventricular space, slight (Evans' ratio 0.25 to 0.29) symmetrical macro-ventriculy without ratio difference and without displacement was found significantly more frequently in Yannet's category of unknown aetiological timepoint (13/40 vs 32/176; p <0.05) and in the WHO's category of other and unspecified causes (14/43 vs 31/173; p <0.05) than in the other patients aged 20 years or less. Extreme (Evans' ratio 0.40 or more) symmetrical macroventriculy, without ratio difference and without displacement, was found significantly more frequently in patients in Yannet's prenatal category than in the other patients aged 20 years or less (17/92 vs 10/124; p < 0.05).

Amongst Yannet's categories, the smallest mean width of the central part of the right lateral ventricle (right cella media) was found in the category of unknown aetiological timepoint (mean = 19.5 mm). In this respect, this category differed significantly from the categories of several aetiological timepoints (mean = 23.5 mm; p <0.01), postnatal timepoint (mean = 22.6 mm; p <0.01), and prenatal timepoint (mean = 21.8 mm; p <0.05). Amongst the WHO's categories, patients with other and unspecified forms of mental retardation were found to have the narrowest mean width of the right cella media (mean = 19.5 mm), The corresponding means in the following categories were significantly larger: gross brain diseases (mean = 24.4 mm; p <0.01), more than one probable cause (mean = 24.2 mm; p <0.01), infections and intoxications (mean = 22.5 mm; p <0.05) and unknown prenatal influence (mean = 21.7 mm; p <0.05).

Amongst the categories of Yannet, the mean width of the body of the left lateral ventricle (left cella media) was smallest in the category of unknown aetiological timepoint (mean = 20.4 mm), and was significantly smaller in this category than in those of postnatal timepoint (mean = 24.5 mm; p <0.01), perinatal timepoint (mean = 22.5 mm; p <0.05), and more than one aetiological timepoint (mean = 24.2 mm; p <0.05). Amongst the WHO's categories, the mean breadth of the left cella media was significantly smaller in the category of other and unspecified causes (mean = 20.5 mm) than in the categories of gross brain diseases (mean = 27.0 mm; p <0.01), infections and intoxications (mean = 23.9 mm; p <0.01) and trauma and physical agents (mean = 23.2 mm; p <0.05).

The mean length of the right septum caudate line (see page 24) was greatest in Yannet's postnatal category (mean = 16.7 mm). It was significantly longer in this category than in the categories of unknown (mean = 12.7 mm; p <0.001) and prenatal aetiological timepoints (mean = 13.9; p <0.05). Amongst the WHO's categories, the right septum caudate line was shortest in the category of other and unspecified causes (mean = 12.9 mm). It was significantly shorter in this category than in the categories of gross brain diseases (mean = 18.4 mm; p <0.01), infections and intoxications (mean = 16.3 mm; p <0.01) and trauma and physical agents (mean = 15.1 mm; p <0.05). Furthermore, the mean length of the right septum caudate line in the category of infections and intoxications was significantly greater than in the category of unknown prenatal influence (mean = 13.3 mm; p <0.05).

The mean length of the left septum caudate line was greater in the postnatal category than in all the other categories of Yannet (mean = 17.9 mm). It was significantly longer in this category than in the categories of unknown (mean = 13.6 mm; p <0.001) and of prenatal causative timepoint (mean = 14.2; p <0.01). Of the WHO's categories, that of gross brain diseases had the shortest mean length of the left septum caudate line (mean = 20.4 mm). There was a significant difference between the mean length in this category and that in the categories of other and unspecified causes (mean = 13.8 mm; p <0.01), unknown prenatal influence (mean = 13.5 mm; p <0.05), infections and intoxications (mean = 16.7 mm; p <0.05) and trauma and physical agents (mean = 16.4 mm; p <0.05). Furthermore, the mean length of the left septum caudate line in the category of other and unspecified causes was significantly shorter than the corresponding lengths in the categories of infections and intoxications (p <0.05) and of trauma and physical agents (p <0.05).

The mean size of the right frontal horn was smaller in the category of unknown causative timepoint than in other categories of Yannet (mean = 22.5 mm). It was significantly smaller in this category than in the category of more than one aetiological timepoint (mean = 27.0 mm; p <0.01) and in the postnatal category (mean = 26.2 mm; p <0.01). The mean size of the right frontal horn was significantly smaller in the WHO's category of other and unspecified causes (mean = 22.6 mm) than in the categories of infections and intoxications (mean = 25.9 mm; p <0.01), gross brain diseases (mean = 27.5 mm; p <0.01), more than one probable cause (mean = 27.8 mm; p <0.05) and trauma and physical agents (mean = 24.6 mm; p <0.05).

The mean size of the left frontal horn was found to be smaller in the category of unknown aetiological timepoint (mean = 23.6 mm) than in any of the other categories of Yannet. It was significantly smaller in this category than in those of postnatal (mean = 27.4 mm; p < 0.01) and more than one causative timepoint (mean = 27.8 mm; p <0.05). In addition, it was found to be significantly smaller in the prenatal category (mean = 24.7 mm) than in the postnatal category (mean = 27.4 mm; p <0.05). Using the WHO's classification, the size of the left frontal horn was significantly larger in patients with gross brain diseases (mean = 29.4 mm) than in those with other and unspecified forms of mental retardation (mean = 25.2 mm; p <0.01), chromosome abnormalities (mean = 22.3 mm; p < 0.05), and metabolic disorders (mean = 22.5 mm; p <0.05). It was also significantly larger in the category of other and unspecified causes than in the categories of more than one probable cause (mean = 28.9 mm; p < 0.05), infections and intoxications (mean = 26.7 mm; p <0.05), and trauma and physical agents (mean = 26.1 mm; p <0.05). The left frontal horn was smaller in the category of metabolic disorders than in the category of trauma and physical agents (p <0.05).

Using Yannet's classification, it was found that the right temporal horn was smallest in patients in the category of unknown causative timepoint (mean = 3.9 mm), and that there were significant differences between the mean size of the temporal horn in this category and that in the categories of more than one (mean = 7.3 mm; p <0.05) and postnatal (mean = 5.2 mm; p <0.05) aetiological timepoint. The temporal horn was significantly smaller in patients in the WHO's category of other and unspecified causes (mean = 4.1 mm) than in those in the category of more than one probable cause (mean = 7.7 mm; p <0.05). Moreover, the right temporal horn was significantly larger in patients with chromosome aberrations (mean = 5.2 mm) than in those with metabolic disorders (mean = 3.3 mm; p <0.05).

The left temporal horn was narrower in patients in the category of unknown causative timepoint than in any of the other categories of Yannet (mean = 5.2 mm). It was significantly narrower in this category than in the postnatal category (mean = 7.5 mm; p <0.05). Using the WHO's classification, patients in the category of trauma and physical agents tended to have left temporal horns of significantly greater size (mean = 8.0 mm) than patients in the categories of unknown prenatal influence (mean = 5.5 mm; p <0.05) and other and unspecified causes (mean = 5.4 mm; p <0.05). The mean size of the left temporal horn of patients in the category of metabolic disorders (mean = 3.7 mm) was significantly smaller than that of patients with gross brain diseases (mean = 6.0 mm; p < 0.05) and chromosome aberrations (mean = 6.6 mm; p < 0.05).

The right occipital horn tended to be particularly small in patients in Yannet's category of unknown causative timepoint (mean = 16.1 mm). There was a significant difference in this respect between these cases and those in the category of more than one causative timepoint (mean = 20.4 mm; p < 0.05). The right occipital horn of patients in the WHO's category of other and unspecified causes (mean = 16.3 mm) was significantly smaller than that of patients in the categories of more than one probable cause (mean = 21.6 mm; p < 0.05) and trauma and physical agents (mean = 19.0 mm; p < 0.05).

Using Yannet's classification, the left occipital horn was widest in patients in the postnatal aetiological category (mean = 22.7 mm). There was a significant difference between the mean width in this category and that in the categories of prenatal (mean = 18.1 mm; p < 0.01) and unknown (mean = 17.8 mm; p < 0.05) causative timepoint. Of the WHO's categories, that of other and unspecified causes had a significantly smaller mean width of the left occipital horn (mean = 18.1 mm) than the categories of gross brain diseases (mean = 26.1 mm; p < 0.01) and trauma and physical agents (mean = 22.4 mm; p < 0.05). The mean width of the left occipital horn was significantly smaller in the category of unknown prenatal influence (mean = 17.9 mm) than in the categories of trauma and physical agents (p < 0.05) and gross brain diseases (p < 0.05).

The mean width of the third ventricle was greatest in Yannet's postnatal category (mean = 8.8 mm). There was a significant difference between this category and those of unknown (mean = 7.1 mm; p < 0.01), prenatal (mean = 7.3 mm; p < 0.05) and perinatal (mean = 7.2 mm; p < 0.05) aetiological timepoint. The width of the third ventricle was significantly smaller in patients in the WHO's category of other and unspecified causes (mean = 7.1 mm) than in those in the categories of infections and intoxications (mean = 8.4 mm; p < 0.05) and gross brain diseases (mean = 9.3 mm; p < 0.05).

Malformations of the mid-line structures of the brain were examined only in those cases in which good visualisation was obtained on pneumoencephalography. They were found significantly more frequently in Yannet's prenatal category (30/127 vs 9/179; p < 0.001) and significantly less frequently in his perinatal (1/42 vs 38/264; p < 0.05), postnatal (2/55 vs 37/251; p < 0.05) and unknown aetiological timepoint (2/65 vs 37/241; p < 0.01) categories than in the rest of the series. Using the WHO's classification, mid-line abnormalities were found significantly more frequently in the category of unknown prenatal influence (24/89 vs 15/217; p < 0.001), and significantly less frequently in the category of other and unspecified causes (2/65 vs 37/241; p < 0.01) than in the other categories.

Lateral displacement of the cerebral mid-line structures was found more frequently in patients in the WHO's category of trauma and physical agents than in the other patients in the series (9/45 vs 22/283; p < 0.01).

Localised cortical atrophy or dysplasia was found more frequently in Yannet's postnatal category than elsewhere in the series (6/32 vs 10/142; p < 0.05).

Pathological findings in the infratentorial space on pneumoencephalography were found more frequently in the prenatal category (79/148 vs 73/186; p <0.01) and less frequently in that of unknown aetiological timepoint (23/66 vs 129/268; p <0.05) than in the rest of Yannet's categories. Using the WHO's classification, pathological infratentorial findings were significantly more common in the category of unknown prenatal influence (56/103 vs 96/231; p <0.05) and significantly less common in the category of other and unspecified causes (22/67 vs 130/267; p <0.05) than in the rest of the patients submitted to pneumoencephalography.

Infratentorial malformations on pneumoencephalography were noted significantly more often in Yannet's category of prenatal aetiology (34/149 vs 8/185; p <0.001) and significantly less often in his categories of postnatal aetiology (2/60 vs 40/274; p <0.05) and unknown aetiological timepoint (1/66 vs 41/268; p <0.01) than in the rest of the series. Infratentorial malformations were also found significantly more frequently in the WHO's category of unknown prenatal influence (26/103 vs 16/231; p <0.001) and significantly less frequently in the categories of infections and intoxications (1/57 vs 41/277; p <0.01) and of other and unspecified forms (2/66 vs 40/268; p <0.01) than in the rest of the series.

The vertical measurement of the fourth ventricle was smaller in Yannet's category of prenatal aetiology (mean = 13.0) than in his category of unknown causative timepoint (mean = 14.1 mm; p <0.05). Using the WHO's classification the vertical measurement of the fourth ventricle was smaller in the category of unknown prenatal influence (mean = 12.8 mm) than in the categories of other and unspecified aetiologies (mean = 14.2; p <0.01), infections and intoxications (mean = 14.3 mm; p <0.01) and gross brain diseases (mean = 15.0 mm; p <0.05). Furthermore, the mean vertical measurement of the fourth ventricle was significantly smaller in the category of chromosome aberrations (mean = 11.7 mm) than in the categories of other and unspecified causes (p < 0.05) and infections and intoxications (p < 0.05).

All other possible correlations between the findings on pneumoencephalography and the various aetiological categories as defined by Yannet or the WHO were without statistical significance.

CHAPTER 6

Discussion

Selection of Patients

Clearly, because of differences in the composition of the patient sample, the present study, which is concerned only with patients who were examined using neuroradiological techniques, cannot easily be compared with earlier investigations into the aetiology of mental retardation using conventional clinical methods (Larsen 1931, Penrose 1938, Halperin 1945, Thomas 1957, Hagne 1962, Pitt and Roboz 1965, Palo 1966, Covernton 1967, Dupont and Dreyer 1968). Furthermore, previous investigations using neuroradiological techniques also present difficulties of comparison, since, for the most part, they have either not given clear criteria for the selection of patients (Mäurer 1939, Levinson 1947, Casamajor *et al.* 1949, Anderson 1951, Charash and Dunning 1956, McLean and Manfredi 1962, Gaal 1963), or have used criteria very different from those used in the present study (Brett and Hoare 1969). However, judging from those studies which have presented clear criteria for the use of pneumoencephalography (Melchior 1961, Spitz *et al.* 1962, Gaal 1963, Dyggve and Melchior 1964), it seems that the criteria for the selection of patients in most previous neuroradiological studies may have been broadly similar, and some comparisons can be made.

Sex Distribution

The finding of a preponderance of males (58 per cent) in this series is in accordance with the findings of many other studies of the mentally retarded (*e.g.* Penrose 1938, Hagne 1962, Pitt and Roboz 1965, Palo 1966, Dupont and Dreyer 1968). The percentage of males (63 per cent) in the Finnish study of Palo (1966) agrees well with the figure in the present study, although it should be pointed out that the criteria for the selection of patients were quite different. Thus, the sex factor is unlikely to have had any significant effect on the distribution of the patients amongst the various aetiological categories in this study.

Age

The age range in this study (between 1 and 49 years) (Table IV) differs from that in many previous studies of mentally retarded patients (Melchior 1961, Hagne 1962, Koch, R. 1966, Covernton 1967), but is similar to that in several previous studies of institutionalised mental retardates (Pitt and Roboz 1965, Palo 1966, Dupont and Dreyer 1968). Because infants less than one year of age and adults aged over 49 years were not included in this series, disorders which manifest in patients outside this age range were not investigated.

Significance of Data Taken From Case Histories in the Elucidation of the Aetiology of Mental Retardation

Determination of Social Class

Although the proportion of patients from the lower social classes was significantly greater in this study than in the general population, it was not as great as in most previous studies of the mentally retarded (Penrose 1963*a*). This difference may be due to the fact that the majority of the patients in the present series were severely retarded, whereas low social class is known to be particularly associated with mild retardation.

Unmarried Mothers

The high proportion of children of unmarried mothers in this series suggests that the risk of having a mentally retarded child is greater when the mother is unmarried. The fact that infants of unmarried mothers are also known to be more at risk for congenital malformations (Klemmetti and Saxén 1970) points to some association between mental retardation and congenital malformations. This observation finds confirmation in the fact that, in more than 50 per cent of the cases in this series, the mental retardation was attributed to prenatal factors; furthermore, the proportion of macroscopic major malformations (16 per cent) was also significantly greater than in the general population (1.17 per cent, according to Klemetti and Saxén (1970)).

The reason why unmarried mothers are apparently more likely than married mothers to have children with congenital malformations is rather obscure. It may be that the unmarried mother takes less care of herself during pregnancy, and is therefore more susceptible to potentially damaging influences. It has also been suggested that attempted abortion is more frequent among unmarried mothers. On the other hand, against these suggestions is the surprising finding in this study that unmarried mothers seemed to be more immune to infections than married mothers. Another possibility is that genetic factors may play some rôle, in that the relative social instability of unmarried mothers may reflect some very minor degree of genetic maldevelopment or malfunction of the brain. However, with the changing attitude of society towards the unmarried mother and the increasing incidence of unmarried mothers in the higher social classes, it is unlikely that we shall be able to sort out this relationship in the future. It may be that in later series the differences between married and unmarried mothers will disappear.

Abnormalities of Pregnancy

Apart from the three patients in the WHO's category of more than one probable cause (Table XLII), the rest of the fifteen patients in whom toxaemia of pregnancy was thought to have been of primary aetiological significance were all cases in which no other possible aetiological factors were apparent, and in which the clinical picture was compatible with antenatal brain damage.

It is not possible to compare the prevalence of pregnancies complicated by such factors as infections, trauma and the use of drugs and poisonous substances during pregnancy in this series with that in the general population, since available data are unreliable. However, all the complications of pregnancy investigated in connection with the present study were complications which previous studies had suggested might be of aetiological significance for mental retardation. Thus, although few conclusions could be drawn from the present study, and complications during pregnancy were only considered to have been of aetiological significance in a limited number of cases (see page 27), such factors as toxaemia, infections, trauma and the use of drugs and ionizing radiation during pregnancy should all be regarded as potentially dangerous.

Delivery Without Skilled Assistance

Although significantly more common in this series than in the general population in 1952, births without trained assistance being at hand were not particularly associated with mental retardation due to birth injury. In fact, patients who had been born unattended were fairly evenly distributed throughout the various aetiological categories (including, for instance, the WHO's category of trauma and physical agents), and only in Yannet's category of unknown causative timepoint were they significantly more common than in the rest of the series.

Some of the children described in this series may have been placed at risk because of a lack of skilled assistance at the time of birth. However, nowadays less than 0.5 per cent of all deliveries take place outside hospital in Finland (Finland National Board of Health 1970).

Birthweight

The large number of patients whose birthweights were below 2500 g indicates a close association between low birthweight and mental retardation. It is difficult, however, to point to many clear associations between the presence of low birthweight and particular categories of mental retardation. The three patients who would fall into the WHO's category of prematurity without other cause of mental retardation had very low birthweights. There also seemed to be an association between low birthweight and the categories of metabolic disorders and mental retardation due to more than one probable cause. It is possible that some prenatal disturbance may already have affected the developing brain in such cases. On the other hand, it is not surprising that the mean birthweight of the patients with gross brain diseases was so high (4020 g). Although because of the small number of cases in this category it is not possible to draw any firm conclusions, this finding suggests that the growth of the brain in patients with mental retardation due to gross brain diseases may not be affected so early and to such a large extent as it is in patients with mental retardation due to prenatal disturbances.

All the other differences between the various aetiological categories of mental retardation in respect of birthweight, despite statistical significance (see pages 109 to 110), were small, and accordingly without clinical significance.

Abnormal Maturity

The high incidence of small-for-dates and pre-term infants in the categories of several aetiological timepoints and more than one probable cause is hardly surprising, since conditions of prenatal origin were commonly diagnosed in these categories, and abnormal maturity is of prenatal origin. Since abnormal maturity has a pre-

129

natal aetiology, it is also to be expected that small-for-dates, pre-term and post-term infants were comparatively rare in the postnatal categories and in the category of trauma and physical agents.

The most frequent form of abnormal maturity in this series was short gestation (37 cases or 11 per cent). Short gestation was once regarded as a significant cause of mental retardation, but, as the causes of short gestation have been clarified, the proportion of cases of mental retardation attributed directly to this has diminished considerably (Hagne 1962, Covernton 1967, Gupta and Virmani 1968, Roboz and Pitt 1970). In this series, short gestation itself was considered to be of primary aetiological significance in only three cases.

The finding of only 37 cases of short gestation is surprising in view of the fact that the majority of patients in this series were born many years ago, and suggests that the association between low birthweight due to short gestation and mental retardation may have been over-emphasised. Nevertheless, a number of studies have suggested that the incidence of handicapping conditions in low birthweight pre-term infants is particularly high (McDonald 1967, Drillien 1968a). It will be interesting to see whether a higher proportion of the relatively less severely retarded patients at the Rinnekoti will be found to have a history of low birthweight and short gestation.

Marked Asphyxia Immediately After Birth and Abnormalities in the Child's Condition During the Later Neonatal Period

The frequency of abnormalities in the child's condition immediately after birth (42 per cent) and of slight neonatal asphyxia (22 per cent) was high, but unfortunately no relevant control figures were available for comparison. Under these circumstances, all such perinatal factors must be regarded as potential causes of mental retardation (Malamud 1954, Wulf and Manzke 1965, Prechtl 1967, Roboz and Pitt 1968b, Windle 1968).

One problem in looking at the incidence of neonatal asphyxia in a population of such abnormal patients is that a neonate's behaviour may be influenced by some pre-existing brain abnormality; an anoxic episode may simply be a result of the pre-existing brain damage, and not cause any further damage. In this series, several patients reported to have experienced an anoxic episode in the neonatal period were also considered to have suffered prenatal brain damage. Although they were placed in the category of more than one probable cause, in view of the fact that babies are known to survive normally after severe episodes of neonatal asphyxia, it is probably wiser to ascribe the mental retardation in such cases to the pre-existing brain damage.

Epilepsy

The high frequency of epilepsy (62 per cent) in this series is partly due to the selection criteria used, in that all of the original 1000 patients who were still alive at the time of the study and had epilepsy (apart from a few isolated cases where severe heart disease made anaesthesia impossible) were included. The frequency of epilepsy throughout the Rinnekoti (approx. 30 per cent) is in line with the frequency reported in other studies (Hagne 1962, Dupont and Dreyer 1968, Gupta and Virmani 1968, Roboz and Pitt 1970).

Epilepsy was particularly common in Yannet's category of perinatal aetiology (86 per cent), and in the WHO's category of trauma at birth and physical agents (83 per cent). It was least common in Yannet's category of prenatal aetiology (50 per cent). Focal epilepsy was particularly associated with the category of trauma and physical agents (15, *i.e.* 40 per cent, of the 38 cases with epilepsy in this category had focal epilepsy). These figures cannot be compared with those in other investigations because of differences in the patient material.

It is unlikely that the specific causal factors of mental retardation, cerebral palsy and epilepsy will ever be positively identified, for these are clinical features of brain damage which are non-specific. The studies reported do suggest, however, that brain damage tends to be more extensive when cerebral palsy, mental retardation or epilepsy are complicated by other conditions. Epileptic fits themselves, especially if they are persistent, may produce brain damage and play a part in producing a progressive decline in the intellectual functioning of patients. Further apparent deterioration of intellectual functioning may be the result of the administration of heavy doses of anti-convulsant drugs. Further brain damage, as a result of epilepsy and intoxication as a result of the administration of anti-convulsive drugs, certainly occurred in a number of the epileptic patients in this study.

Significance of Physical Findings in the Aetiological Diagnosis of Mental Retardation
Height, Weight and Head Circumference

Longitudinal growth charts are not available for the patients in this series, as the case records contained insufficient detail. The measurements discussed here are those made in connection with this study.

The recording of small height, weight and head circumference measurements in the majority of patients is in accordance with the finding of many other studies that growth retardation is frequently associated with mental retardation (Mosier *et al.* 1965, Pryor and Thelander 1967). Only in a few cases (see extreme values in Figures 2-7) was growth within normal limits (*c.f.* the findings of Pozsonyi and Lobb (1967)). For this reason the data in the figures are presented in terms of extreme values rather than standard deviations.

Excess weight, especially in pre-pubertal girls, was noted only occasionally in some rare cases (Fig. 5). Some patients had abnormally large heads, as a result of, for example, hydrocephalus (Figs. 6 and 7). The frequency of head enlargement was similar for males and females.

In general, growth was most severely affected in the cases of prenatal aetiology. Height was least affected in Yannet's postnatal category, and weight and head circumference in Yannet's category of unknown aetiological timepoint and in the WHO's category of other and unspecified causes. It is hardly surprising that an early disturbance of the fetus is particularly likely to produce severe disturbance of growth.

A high proportion of the patients with enlarged heads were in Yannet's postnatal category. This finding is to be expected in view of the fact that the number of congenital hydrocephalics in this series was small.

Considered in isolation, and compared with those of normal children of the same ages, the head circumferences of many of the patients in Yannet's prenatal and postnatal categories were abnormally small. However, when considered in relation to stature as well as age, the head sizes of a number of these patients were effectively normal (see page 35). This relative method seems to be more natural, and can be recommended for assessing the head circumferences of mentally retarded patients.

Cephalic Index

No firm conclusions can be drawn from this study as to the value of cephalic index scores in the aetiological diagnosis of mental retardation, as the only associations found were with small aetiological subgroups. However, brachycephaly does seem to be especially associated with chromosome aberrations. This observation seems to be in line with that of Pryor and Thelander (1967) that children with Down's syndrome tend to have brachycephaly. However, the lowest limit for the cephalic index of brachycephaly in Pryor and Thelander's study (80.0) was not the same as that generally accepted in anthropology (Martin and Saller 1957) and adopted for this study (81.0).

Dyscrania

The finding of dyscrania or abnormalities in the size and form of the skull at physical examination is suggestive of a prenatal origin of mental retardation, since the size of the head is known to depend on the growth of the brain (see Bruijn 1963). Thus, the finding that dyscrania was more common in Yannet's prenatal category than in the rest of the series is not surprising.

Any comparison of the prevalence of dyscrania in this and other investigations is likely to be unrewarding, as the term 'dyscrania' is not used consistently. However, the association of dyscrania with mental retardation due to conditions of prenatal origin is apparent in a number of studies, for example in that of Pitt and Roboz (1965).

Sinistrality

It is generally accepted that left-handedness is more common in the mentally retarded than in normal school children. Though not as high as in some studies (*e.g.* Fischer-Williams 1969), the prevalence of left-handedness in this study (12.5 per cent) was high, and confirmed this view. However, it should be remembered that figures for the prevalence of left-handedness vary considerably from study to study (between 1 and 30 per cent), probably due to faulty research methods (Hécaen and Ajuriaguerra 1964).

The high prevalence of left-handedness amongst the mentally retarded may have some connection with the fact that the left hemisphere is more often affected than the right one during the early years (Taylor 1969). It has been suggested that the establishment of handedness represents a higher state of brain development; hence poor lateralisation with apparent sinistrality is commoner in very young children (Hécaen and Ajuriaguerra 1964).

The fact that handedness could not be determined in 19 per cent of this series is probably directly attributable to the selection of patients. A large proportion of them had paralysis of the limbs as well as severe mental retardation, so understandably hand preference was poorly established, and examination was difficult.

Major Malformations

Major malformations observed at physical examination are known to be strongly indicative of a prenatal aetiology for mental retardation.

Cutaneous Malformations

A number of cutaneous malformations, including those found in this series (see page 37), suggest a prenatal aetiology. Pigmentation disorder can also suggest a metabolic disorder as the cause of the mental retardation; for example, a patient whose face is sallow may have aspartylglucosaminuria. Adenoma sebaceum is part of the syndrome of tuberose sclerosis. Xeroderma pigmentosum is regarded as a manifestation of a systemic disorder which also affects the central nervous system (Hokkanen *et al.* 1969). The proportion of cases of phacomatosis in this series is similar to that reported in other series of low grade mentally retarded patients (Zaremba 1971), but is lower than that generally reported for the whole population (see Koch, G. 1966).

It is likely that more abnormal cutaneous findings are present in most populations of mentally retarded patients than has hitherto been reported, because mild abnormalities, for example pseudoxanthoma elasticum and congenital ichthyosis, may only be confirmed by microscopical study.

Neurological Disorders

The large number of neurological deficits found in this series of patients is largely a result of the selection criteria used; cerebral palsy and epilepsy, for example, were prominent indications for neuroradiological examinations (see Tables II and III).

Apart from upper motor neurone syndromes (which were particularly associated with the WHO's category of more than one probable cause and were relatively rare in the WHO's categories of unknown prenatal influence and other and unspecified causes) and cranial nerve syndromes (which were found particularly in Yannet's category of more than one aetiological timepoint), other neurological syndromes were fairly evenly distributed throughout the various aetiological categories.

Although there were no statistically significant differences between the various aetiological categories with regard to the distribution of the main forms of cerebral palsy, the differences in the distribution of the different forms of paresis (see page 115) were interesting. They suggested that postnatal lesions tend to be unilateral or asymmetrical, whereas prenatal lesions are more often bilateral and symmetrical.

The finding that cases of ataxia were significantly more common in Yannet's postnatal category suggests that the cerebellum may be more vulnerable to postnatal than to other aetiological factors.

In patients with dyskinesia, the findings were very varied, and because some of the patients were too severely retarded it was difficult to make a precise classification of the different varieties encountered. However, the percentage of patients exhibiting some form of dyskinesia in this series (38 per cent) is very similar to that reported in many other series of mentally retarded patients (*e.g.* 36 per cent—Fischer-Williams 1969). Because of the difficulties of classification, the distribution of cases of dyskinesia was not tested statistically.

Whereas Tuuteri *et al.* (1967) found that about 80 per cent of a representative sample of cerebral palsied patients coming from the community had spasticity, spastic forms accounted for only 55 per cent of the cases of cerebral palsy in the present mentally retarded series. On the other hand, dyskinesia was more common in the present series (22 per cent versus 8 per cent), as were mixed forms of cerebral palsy (20 per cent versus 12 per cent). Pure ataxic types were found with equal frequency in this series and in that of Tuuteri *et al.* Crothers and Paine (1959), on the other hand, reported figures for another more representative sample of cerebral palsied patients very similar to those in the present series (65 per cent spastic forms, 22 per cent dyskinetic forms, and 13 per cent mixed forms).

Although only 55 per cent of the cerebral palsied patients in this series had specifically spastic forms of cerebral palsy, if all the patients with spasticity are taken into consideration the percentage is higher (75 per cent), and more compatible with that found in more representative samples of patients with cerebral palsy.

Neurological signs indicative of a cerebellar lesion may have been more common in this series than has been reported, because in some cases they may have been masked by more severe extremital paresis.

Deafness and Blindness

The frequency of blindness (5 per cent) agrees well with that reported by Warburg (1966) in his study of institutionalised mentally retarded patients (5.5 per cent), but is significantly higher than in the general population of Finland (0.079 per cent, according to Vannas and Raivio 1963). The prevalence of congenital cataract in the general population is lower than that of blindness (Vannas and Raivio 1963), but in this series the opposite was the case, 20 cases (6 per cent) having congenital cataract, and 16 (5 per cent) being blind.

Deafness was also more common in this series (1 per cent) than in the general population of Finland (0.13 per cent; Lumio *et al.* 1966), and in close agreement with that reported in other series of mentally handicapped children (*e.g.* Koch, R. 1966).

Significance of EEG Findings in the Aetiological Diagnosis of Mental Retardation

Forty-seven (80 per cent) of the 59 patients in Yannet's postnatal category and 48 (86 per cent) of the 56 in the WHO's category of birth trauma and physical agents had markedly pathological EEG findings, whereas markedly pathological findings were recorded in only 34 (55 per cent) of the 62 cases in the WHO's category of other and unspecified causes. In this respect, the distribution of patients with markedly disturbed EEGs was similar to the distribution of patients with epilepsy and those with neurological deficits.

Diffuse slow wave abnormalities were found very frequently throughout the series, but were particularly common in the prenatal categories of Yannet and the WHO. The great prevalence of diffuse slow wave activity may be explained by the frequent use of phenotiazide, phenytoin and diazepam medication in these patients. It is well known that the first two of these drugs diminish the amount of EEG activity, and that diazepam produces β activity (Dumermuth 1965). On the other hand, β-activity has been noted in such metabolic disorders as Lowe's syndrome; however there were no cases of Lowe's syndrome in this series. The finding that localised EEG abnormalities were rarer in conditions of prenatal origin than in others supports the view that the phenomenon of β-activity may be particularly associated with mental retardation of prenatal aetiology.

Paroxysmal slow activity occurs in cases of cerebral mid-line tumours and other conditions leading to high intracranial pressure. The connection between paroxysmal slow activity and the WHO's category of unknown prenatal influence may be partly explained by handicapped CSF circulation. It should also be remembered that sleepiness may be a cause of paroxysmal slow activity.

Focal spikes and sharp waves were particularly common in the WHO's category of infections and intoxications (see page 116). Many cases in this category had conditions such as toxaemia of pregnancy and probable hypoglycaemia which are closely associated with perinatal affections with which focal spikes and sharp waves are known to be likely to occur.

Generalized regular EEG changes are known to have an idiopathic aetiology, and to be associated with petit mal epilepsy. Other generalized changes are considered to have an organic background, except for 14 and 6 Hz positive spikes, which are found quite frequently in the normal population (Eeg-Olofsson 1971). Generalized regular 3 Hz spikes and waves were found in only six cases in this series. Thus, as far as estimating the importance of generalized EEG changes in the aetiological diagnosis of mental retardation is concerned, they are of little value. The frequency of generalized EEG changes in the WHO's category of birth trauma and physical agents is not surprising, as such changes are often found in patients who have experienced cerebral damage around the time of birth (Dumermuth 1965).

The finding that in as many as 35 per cent of the 114 patients with focal EEG findings these were located in the temporal region is striking. Temporal focal changes are often found as the sequelae of severe neonatal hypoglycaemia, and are especially common after severe convulsions, when hypoxia, brain oedema and perhaps herniation may occur (Ounsted *et al.* 1966). As the majority of patients in the present series frequently suffer severe convulsions, the prevalence of focal EEG changes in the temporal region is probably explicable. There may also have been cases of neonatal hypoglycaemia in this series which it was not possible to diagnose at the time.

The finding of fluctuating localisation of focal EEG disturbances is partly dependent on the vigilance and the age of the patient, and is thus a phenomenon probably without specific clinical significance.

Focal EEG changes in other areas were so rare that further conclusions are not possible.

The higher incidence of focal EEG changes on the left side in patients in Yannet's postnatal category and in the WHO's category of trauma and physical agents is in accordance with the reported preponderance of left-sided lesions occurring in young children (Taylor 1969) and also with the finding that asymmetrical and unilateral spasticity are more likely to affect the right than the left side of the body.

Significance of Neuroradiological Methods in the Elucidation of the Aetiology of Mental Retardation

Skull X-Ray

In view of the high prevalence of congenital cranial deformities in Yannet's prenatal category (20 per cent) and in the WHO's category of unknown prenatal influence (24 per cent), congenital cranial deformity would seem to be a good indication of a prenatal aetiology of mental retardation. The demonstration of such deformities —they occurred in 10 per cent of this series—is one way in which skull x-ray can help in the elucidation of the aetiology of mental retardation.

The frequent finding of skull asymmetry indicative of unilateral intracranial lesions in Yannet's perinatal category (38 per cent) and in the WHO's category of birth trauma and physical agents (33 per cent) is in accordance with the observation that asymmetrical or unilateral neurological deficits and EEG changes were also associated with a perinatal and not with a prenatal aetiology. Signs of osseous asymmetry between the two sides of the skull may be aetiologically significant in mentally retarded patients just as they are in epileptics. Miribel *et al.* (1963) studied 100 cases of epilepsy, and found normal skulls in only 39. They reported 30 cases of hemiatrophy, 6 cases with one-sided bulging, and 25 cases which they described as borderline.

The frequent occurrence of normal radiological findings in the WHO's category of other and unspecified causes (32 per cent) and in Yannet's category of unknown aetiological timepoint (31 per cent) is in accordance with the rarity of epilepsy, neurological deficits and EEG abnormalities in these categories. Since they apply equally to both these 'unknown' categories, all the above findings suggest a close similarity between the WHO's category of other and unspecified causes and Yannet's category of unknown aetiological timepoint.

The relative preponderance of cases with asymmetry of the frontal sinuses in the postnatal categories is an indication that the aetiology of the mental retardation in patients with this finding is unlikely to be prenatal.

The large number of cases of persistent metopic fontanelle in the prenatal categories may also be of aetiological significance for mental retardation, although in general this finding is regarded as being asymptomatic (Lindgren 1954).

Cases of digital markings were fairly evenly distributed throughout the aetiological categories, so were of no significance as far as the elucidation of the aetiology of mental retardation is concerned.

Digital markings are seen more frequently in children and young adults than in older individuals (Pendergrass *et al.* 1957). According to Davidoff and Gass (1949) they occur in 45 per cent of adults, and are more prominent in persons with relatively thin cranial bones. Thus the prevalence of 16 per cent in the present series seems to be low in comparison with that in the general population; at the same time this low figure suggests that patients with thin cranial vaults were relatively rare. It is generally accepted that a thick cranial vault is in some way associated with such brain anomalies as atrophy and dysplasia, both of which manifest as macroventriculy on pneumoencephalography. Thus the low incidence of digital markings in the present series may be indirectly associated with the high incidence of cerebral atrophy and dysplasia.

The mean volume of the sella turcica in the category of gross brain diseases may have been particularly large because of the large number of cases of brain tumour in this category.

The other associations between the mean size of the cella turcica and the different aetiological categories of mental retardation (see page 119), for example that between a small mean volume and Yannet's prenatal category, were of very slight statistical significance so no definite conclusions can be drawn from them.

It seems that small skulls are frequently associated with severe mental retardation. In this series the prevalence of cases of microcephaly was high (skull volume below 5th percentile in 74 per cent) and that of macrocephaly was low (skull volume over 95th percentile in 4 per cent).

However, in the large American series of McLean and Manfredi (1962) only 15 per cent of the patients had small skulls and 5 per cent had large skulls. The difference between the findings of this study and those of McLean and Manfredi is probably attributable to the selection of patients; the present series included a higher proportion of severely mentally defective individuals. In any case, the interpretations of McLean and Manfredi cannot easily be compared with the results of this study, because they merely inspected the skull x-rays and did not measure the skull volume.

Although the criteria for judging 'normal' skull volumes are based on a British survey (Gordon 1966), the cranial volume measurements in this study seem to confirm what was suggested by the head circumference measurements, namely that mentally retarded patients tend to have small heads. Bearing in mind that skull volume depends on the growth of the brain, this observation suggests that the brains of microcephalic mentally retarded patients are affected very early. Hence it is not surprising to find that conditions of prenatal aetiology and small brain weights are also particularly common in the mentally retarded (Crome and Stern 1972).

As the results of this study show, skull x-ray examination can give important information about the intracranial space in the mentally retarded.

Echoencephalography

Echoencephalography was merely used as an aid in the selection of the patients for cerebral angiography and pneumoencephalography, so the results of this investigation were not expected to provide much information concerning the aetiology of mental retardation. Nevertheless, echoencephalography was an extremely useful aid in the diagnosis of macroventriculy in cases of hydrocephalus, and of hemi-macroventriculy or of dislocation of the cerebral mid-line in other cases.

The significance of additional spikes as the only abnormal finding on echoencephalography is not clear. In some cases they may suggest an extra cavity which would not fill with gas at pneumoencephalography (Sjögren 1965).

The patients in this series in whom echoencephalography revealed nothing definitely pathological did not have normal brains, as pathological findings in these patients were revealed by other neuroradiological methods.

As far as the aetiological diagnosis of mental retardation is concerned, the significance of echoencephalography alone is slight, but this method is to be recommended in screening patients who require examination by other neuroradiological techniques, to which it is a valuable supplement.

Cerebral Angiography

The high proportion of abnormal angiograms in Yannet's postnatal category (90 per cent) correlates with the increased prevalence of other neurological defects, such as epilepsy and cerebral palsy, and of abnormal findings on skull x-ray, amongst patients in this category.

Angiographic findings such as subdural haematoma (Fig. 23), arterial occlusion or 'moyamoya' disease (Fig. 24), venous occlusion (Fig. 25) and dysplasia of cerebral vessels (Fig. 34) can be regarded as pathognomonic of brain damage.

Vascular dysplasia is known to play an important rôle in the genesis of cerebral 'hemiatrophy' (Grüter and Hermann 1965). The results of this study have confirmed the importance of angiography as the only method by which certain cerebrovascular disorders, such as those listed above, can be identified during life.

In most instances, arterial and other cerebral aneurysms do not appear to be primary causes of mental retardation. However, arterial aneurysm may be of primary aetiological importance when rupture of the aneurysm in early childhood results in subarachnoid haemorrhage and produces severe brain damage. In such cases, an adequate neurological and angiographic study of the child is of great importance from the point of view of neurosurgery and other forms of treatment, and so indirectly influences the prognosis (Matson 1965).

Though cerebral angiography is an important diagnostic aid in cases of cerebral neoplasm (Figs. 28 and 30), both pneumoencephalography and brain scanning were usually also required before the diagnosis was made and treatment was initiated.

Because of the lack of comparable systematic studies of mentally retarded patints using cerebral angiography, no valid detailed comparison with other series is possible.

In his monograph on acute hemiplegia in childhood, Isler (1971) does not deal specifically with mental retardation. However, his series does include 33 mostly mildly retarded patients (Isler 1973, personal communication), and this appears to be one of the largest groups of mentally retarded patients investigated by cerebral angiography reported on to date. Isler's case reports include cases of arterio-venous aneurysm, venous aneurysm, microangioma, focal arteritis, spontaneous and fetal vascular occlusion, vasospasm, postictal hemiplegia, infectious-toxic encephalopathy, postvaccinal encephalopathy and 'moyamoya' disease, but none of cerebral neoplasm.

Although cerebral angiography alone is not sufficient to reveal the aetiology of mental retardation in the majority of cases, when the indications and contra-indications are carefully considered (see Table II) it is an extremely valuable supplement to other neuroradiological techniques.

Pneumoencephalography

The distribution of the main pneumoencephalographic findings amongst the various aetiological categories correlated well with the distribution of the main skull x-ray findings. For example, there was a relatively high proportion of normal pneumoencephalographic findings in Yannet's category of unknown aetiological timepoint (19 per cent) and in the WHO's category of other and unspecified causes (21 per cent), and a preponderance of malformations in Yannet's prenatal category (32 per cent) and in the WHO's category of unknown prenatal influence (38 per cent) (see Figs. 55 and 56).

The large numbers of cases of asymmetrical macroventriculy in the WHO's category of infections and intoxications, of hemimacroventriculy in Yannet's postnatal category, and of temporal horn dilatation in Yannet's perinatal category, suggest that asymmetrical and/or unilateral lesions tend to be of perinatal or postnatal origin. These findings are in line with the finding of an excess of focal neurological defects at physical examination in patients in the perinatal and postnatal aetiological categories. By contrast, in the prenatal categories asymmetrical and unilateral findings at pneumoencephalography were rare.

The relatively even distribution of cases of symmetrical macroventriculy and of cerebellar damage (except cerebellar malformations) throughout the various aetiological categories is in agreement with reports that several factors can cause symmetrical macroventriculy and that the cerebellum is vulnerable to a variety of different noxas.

Although symmetrical macroventriculy in patients over 20 years of age was associated with the WHO's category of trauma and physical agents, the same was not true in patients aged 20 years or less. Amongst these younger patients, symmetrical macroventriculy without any difference in Evans' ratio and without displacement was significantly rarer in the WHO's category of birth trauma and physical agents and in Yannet's perinatal category than in the rest of the series. This difference may be due to methodological differences. For example, the classification method of Nielsen *et al.* (1966*a*) used for patients aged over 20 years includes displacements with macroventriculies, and displacements are more likely to result from birth trauma and physical agents.

The finding that bilateral macroventriculy with ratio difference and without displacement (*i.e.* asymmetrical macroventriculy) was particularly associated with Yannet's perinatal category and also with the WHO's category of birth trauma and physical agents is in line with the clinical finding of an excess of patients with asymmetrical or unilateral neurological deficits in these two categories.

It would seem that the various single measurements reported on pages 48 to 52 (*i.e.* the width of the cella media, length of the nucleus caudatus septum line, and the widths of the frontal, temporal and occipital horns and of the third ventricle) have little significance as far as the aetiological diagnosis of mental retardation is concerned (pages 123 to 125).

The largest measurements were found mainly in Yannet's postnatal category and in the WHO's category of gross brain diseases, whereas the smallest measurements tended to be found in Yannet's category of unknown aetiological timepoint and in the WHO's category of other and unspecified causes. If the category of gross brain diseases was ignored, the largest measurements tended to be found in the WHO's categories of infections and intoxications, trauma and physical agents, and (slightly less often) more than one probable cause. These findings are in line with those concerning symptoms such as epilepsy, abnormal findings at neurological examination,

139

and abnormalities at electroencephalography, cerebral angiography and pneumo-encephalography.

Most of the differences between the right and the left sides were minimal and without great significance. Perhaps the temporal and occipital lobes are more vulnerable to damage as a result of noxious factors, for they showed lateral differences more often than other parts of the brain. This excess of cases of unilateral enlargement of the temporal and occipital horns correlates well with the finding that focal changes at EEG in this study were most common in the temporal and occipital areas. Also, the distribution of cases of right- and left-sided involvement throughout the various categories seems to correspond to the distribution of right- and left-sided focal EEG changes (*e.g.* although the left lateral ventricle was generally larger than the right one, there was an excess of right-sided enlargement of the temporal and occipital horns coupled with an excess of right-sided EEG changes in the category of more than one probable cause). These observations suggest that EEG really is important in the study of the aetiology of mental retardation (see Table XV). It is certainly worth measuring the occipital horns when there are focal findings on the EEG in the occipital and temporal regions.

It is generally said that there are great variations in the sizes of the occipital horns amongst the general population, and it is probable that quite large occipital horns may be found in normal patients. In the present study, however, the finding of enlargement of the occipital horns does seem to be of pathological significance.

The finding that malformations of the mid-line structures were particularly common in the prenatal categories of Yannet and the WHO is in accordance with the fact that these categories are particularly associated with congenital anomalies. The relatively high prevalence of lateral displacements of the mid-line structures in the WHO's category of trauma and physical agents correlates well with the excess of unilateral and asymmetrical clinical findings in this category.

The prevalence of the malformations listed in Table XXXII (*i.e.* agenesis of the septum pellucidum in seven cases or 2 per cent; communicating cavity in the septum pellucidum in seven cases or 2 per cent; non-communicating cavity in the septum pellucidum in eight cases or 2 per cent; agenesis of the corpus callosum in three cases or 1 per cent; cup-shaped corpus callosum and septum pellucidum in fourteen cases or 4 per cent) is strikingly greater than has been previously reported (for instance in boxers—Isherwood *et al.* 1966).

The large number of cases of insufficient cortical filling at pneumoencephal-ography may be a reflection of the known phenomenon that cortical gas filling in cases of macroventriculy is generally poor. However, it is not possible to say for certain whether or not some other factors, for instance some sequelae of arachnoiditis, may have been responsible. Since macroventriculy was the most frequent finding at pneumoencephalography in this series, the first mentioned explanation seems probable.

The excess of infratentorial pathological findings, of which many were definite malformations, in the prenatal categories of Yannet and the WHO may be due to the fact that cerebellar tissue is particularly vulnerable, and so may be affected in the very early stages of development.

The differences between the various aetiological categories in respect of the sizes of the third and fourth ventricles were striking. It was found that a small fourth ventricle was suggestive of a prenatal aetiology, whereas a large fourth ventricle was linked with an unknown aetiology. The first of these findings ties in well with the earlier observation that a narrow posterior cranial fossa seems to be particularly associated with a prenatal aetiology (Palo *et al.* 1970).

Some interesting observations can be made when the pneumoencephalographic findings described here are compared with those described in the literature. The prevalence of pathological findings on pneumoencephalography in the present series (about 90 per cent), though in agreement with the findings of Gaal (1963), was higher than that in many other earlier studies (*e.g.* Casamajor *et al.* 1949, Anderson 1951, Charash and Dunning 1956). On the other hand, previous studies using the fractional technique (Malamud and Garoutte 1954, Vesterdal *et al.* 1954, Salomonsen *et al.* 1957, Hagberg *et al.* 1959, Melchior 1961, Bruijn 1963, Brett and Hoare 1969) have revealed abnormalities in the supratentorial ventricular space which are, in many respects, similar to those noted in the present study, although other findings, such as those relating to the temporal horns and the infratentorial space, were not recorded carefully in these studies.

Brain tumour was found in only one of Anderson's (1951) 240 patients and in one per cent (3/338) of the present series. These figures are significantly smaller than those reported in some neuropathological studies, for example that of Christensen *et al.* 1964). This difference is not unexpected, however, for macroscopic studies such as the neuroradiological investigations used in this study were not combined with microscopic investigations which can reveal otherwise unsuspected tumours and small areas of dysplasia.

The differences between this and other studies with regard to the prevalence of pathological findings at pneumoencephalography are, of course, attributable to several factors. In addition to differences in the criteria used for selecting the patients, differences in pneumoencephalographic techniques can be important causes of discrepancies between results. As is illustrated in Tables XXIX and XXXVI, there were a number of pathological findings in the temporal areas and also in the infratentorial space in this series, which earlier studies—which have provided information chiefly about the supratentorial ventricular space—have failed to show. It is known that the size of the supratentorial ventricular space does not correlate very closely with the presence or absence of intellectual impairment in the human (Nielsen *et al.* 1966*a*).

Complications arising in connection with pneumoencephalography in this series were rare (Iivanainen *et al.* 1970*a*). In one case a severe but transient complication did arise due to the unexpected behaviour of the anaesthetic gas mixture used as a contrast medium (Collan and Iivanainen 1969), but over-all the experience of this study suggests that pneumoencephalography is a safe and worthwhile method of investigating mentally retarded patients.

Brain Scanning With Radioisotopes

Brain scanning with radioisotopes helped in the diagnosis of brain tumour (*e.g,* astrocytoma—Fig. 30). Thus, it was one of a chain of neurological examinations as a result of which it was possible to carry out successful surgical and x-ray therapy. Brain scanning should therefore be considered as a recognised procedure for diagnosing abnormalities of the brain in mentally retarded patients, as well as in patients of normal intelligence. It is indicated in the screening of patients suspected of having brain tumours.

Cerebral haemodynamics were not undertaken in the present series.

Comments on the Aetiological Classification of Mental Retardation

Malamud (1954), in a study of 543 mentally retarded patients, reported a frequency of congenital malformations as high as 74 per cent. Gross and Kaltenbäck (1962) found brain malformations in over one third of 631 mentally retarded patients, while Christensen *et al.* (1964) diagnosed cortical dysplasia in 65 per cent of 175 mental retardates at autopsy. In another autopsy study, Freytag and Lindenberg (1967) reported that 50 per cent of their patients had cerebral lesions attributable to prenatal factors. Thus, the proportion of cases in this series in which the mental retardation was considered to have a prenatal aetiology (about 50 per cent) was in accordance with the results of most important neuropathological studies. Yannet (1945) also believed that more than one half of all mentally retarded patients had suffered some form of prenatal brain damage.

On the other hand, in several other series of living institutionalised patients (*e.g.* Pitt and Roboz 1965, Palo 1966) the proportion considered to have a prenatal aetiology has been much smaller, and more in line with the aetiological classification of the present series before the detailed neuroradiological investigations were carried out. Thus, one of the results of the present study has been to produce clinical and neuroradiological findings which are more in agreement with previous pathological findings. This has not been the case in the past, when, as shown by the above examples, although pathological findings have often suggested much prenatal damage, clinical studies have not been able to demonstrate this.

In the study of Dupont and Dreyer (1968), cases with a prenatal aetiology were particularly rare. Only about 13 per cent of their 900 institutionalised patients in Denmark were placed in the prenatal category, whereas 550 (61 per cent) were placed in the category of unknown causes without neurological signs. The marked discrepancy between these findings and those of the present study suggests marked differences in the criteria used for selecting patients and/or the methods of investigation.

In comparison with the remainder of the present series of 1000 patients, the group of 338 patients investigated here contained fewer cases of Down's syndrome or hereditary mental retardation, and more cases of mental retardation of uncertain cause accompanied by neurological signs (see Tables XXXVIII, XXXIX, XLIII and Tables XLIV, XLV and XLVI). These differences are attributable to the criteria used for selection into the present series. It is possible that the use of neuroradiological methods might have revealed more abnormal brain findings amongst the 662 patients not reported on here, in which case the number of these patients classified as having no neurological signs would be reduced. However, such a large scale study is impracticable, and we shall have to rely on autopsy findings for information as to whether any of these patients do have undetected brain abnormalities.

142

Birth Injuries

Birth injuries had previously been over-diagnosed amongst the patients in this series, because of a tendency to assume that birth injury had occurred whenever a child was found to be in a poor condition immediately after birth and during the neonatal period. In fact, it is easy to understand how already abnormal brains affected prenatally are more vulnerable to stresses at birth than are normal healthy brains. Hence, babies with prenatal brain damage are likely to be in a poor condition immediately after birth. The belief that birth trauma was the primary cause of the poor condition of these patients would seem to have been based on erroneous arguments, especially in those cases where the delivery was without complications. The primary cause in such cases is prenatal, although often unknown, and birth injury is at most of secondary importance as far as the development of mental retardation is concerned (Fig. 33).

On the other hand, of course, it must be remembered that there are cases of so-called normal delivery in which a perinatal injury has been sustained and has gone unrecognised or at least unrecorded.

Although it is often difficult to separate the two mechanisms, it is generally believed that hypoxic injury at birth is more common than mechanical injury (Penrose 1963a). In the present study, however, the numbers of cases of mechanical birth injury and of hypoxic birth injury were the same (see Table XXXIX). This can be explained by the fact that cases of mechanical birth injury, being particularly likely to suffer from epileptic and focal neurological sequelae, more frequently met the criteria for inclusion in this study.

The presence in some cases of a unilateral lesion of the cerebral hemisphere may have been due to a unilateral insufficiency of cerebral circulation in the fetus, caused by, for example, unilateral compression of the carotid artery.

The proportion of cases in which birth injury was the primary cause of the mental retardation may have been even smaller than is reported here, because in the majority of cases it was not possible to obtain microscopic pictures of the brain. On the other hand, it should be remembered that some well-known causes of brain damage in the perinatal period, for example hypoglycaemia, probably occurred more frequently than it would appear from the available case records.

Changes in the Aetiological Classification as a Result of the Present Study

One considerable change resulting from the present investigations was a reduction in the number of cases in Heber's category of 'unknown or presumed psychological cause, with the functional reaction alone manifest' (category VIII—see page 3) from 12 to 1 per cent. In other words, the examinations and investigations carried out revealed neurological deficits such as epilepsy, cerebral palsy and pathological findings at pneumoencephalography in a number of additional patients, who could no longer, therefore, be classified in this category of mental retardation due to uncertain cause without neurological signs. If a more specific diagnosis could not be made, these cases were transferred to Heber's category VII ('of uncertain cause with the structural reactions manifest').

143

The increase in the number of cases diagnosed as being due to infections was the result of finding on skull x-ray and on pneumoencephalography, and also on fundoscopy, of changes typical of infectious diseases such as toxoplasmosis. There was no significant change in the number of cases attributed to intoxication.

Toxaemia of pregnancy, which was listed as a possible cause of mental retardation in the WHO's classification of 1968, was regarded as an aetiological factor in this series in certain cases where no other cause could be found and where the clinical picture was compatible with antenatal hypoxic brain damage. Some authors, for example Pitt and Roboz (1965), do not accept toxaemia of pregnancy as a primary cause of mental retardation, because in many cases they have been able to distinguish other likely primary causes. On the other hand, there are several follow-up studies which support the view accepted here, *i.e.* that pre-eclampsia is of aetiological importance (*e.g.* Scholz *et al.* 1967). So long as the primary causes of toxaemia are not known and no other factors closely associated with mental retardation and with toxaemia are discovered, it seems reasonable to regard toxaemia as the aetiological factor responsible for the mental retardation in cases where no other causes can be found.

Some cases of metabolic diseases, such as Prader-Willi syndrome, myotonic dystrophy and aspartylglucosaminuria, were diagnosed for the first time during the present investigations. The last mentioned condition was defined by Palo and Mattson (1970). There were no cases of phenylketonuria in this series, but this is known to be a rare disease in Finland (Palo 1967). The finding of only one case of neonatal hypoglycaemia can be attributed to the fact that at the time of the birth of many of the patients in this series few diagnostic methods were available, and also to the fact that so many of the patients were born at home where few cases of neonatal hypoglycaemia would have been noticed or recorded. Thus, there may have been many more unrecognised cases. If they showed any neurological deficits, it is probable that such cases would have been classified in the category of other and unspecified causes of mental retardation.

In some cases, brain neoplasm (astrocytoma), xeroderma pigmentosum, telangiectatic ataxia of Louis Bar, and spino-cerebellar degeneration with encephalopathy were also diagnosed for the first time as a result of the present series of investigations. In addition, some other cases in the category of gross brain diseases were found to have been wrongly diagnosed.

The decrease in the number of cases in which major psychiatric disorders were considered to be of aetiological significance for the mental retardation was the result of finding previously unrecognised defects, such as temporal lobe atrophy, at pneumoencephalography (see Fig. 50). In such cases, the psychotic disturbance was not regarded as primary from the aetiological point of view.

Other Observations on the Aetiological Classification of the Patients in This Series

The category of more than one aetiological timepoint seems to be necessary in Yannet's classification, for in a significant proportion of the patients in this series both prenatal and perinatal factors were thought to have been of aetiological significance. However, it is clear that in such cases the primary cause is the prenatal one.

144

When the categories of Yannet and the WHO are compared, it is notable that the composition of Yannet's category of unknown aetiological timepoint and that of the WHO's category of other and unspecified forms are similar, in that the findings and symptoms characteristic of patients in these two categories are often, though not always, the same. In the same way, Yannet's perinatal category is similar to the WHO's category of trauma and physical agents. Both these categories include cases with occlusive cerebro-vascular disorders such as 'moyamoya' disease (Fig. 24). Such cases are included in the category of birth trauma and physical agents, even though vascular occlusions have an obscure aetiology and may to some extent be caused by genetic factors.

The proportion of cases in Yannet's category of more than one aetiological timepoint is naturally smaller than that in the WHO's category of more than one probable cause, because several causes may operate at the same timepoint (see Table XLII).

An attempt to classify the aetiology of the mental retardation was made in every case in this series, although in twenty per cent (*i.e.* those in Yannet's category of unknown aetiological timepoint and the WHO's category of other and unspecified causes) the definite cause was unknown. In all these cases abnormalities were found on neurological examination and as a result of the neuroradiological investigations (including pneumoencephalography), but the aetiology of the mental retardation could not be specified with certainty. It is possible that some patients with genetically determined forms of mental defect were included in these 'unknown' groups; however, it was not the object of the present study to analyse the operation of genetic factors, and only immediate relatives were considered so far as hereditary disease was concerned.

Conclusions

It must be remembered that the population investigated here is a very selected one, and is not representative of the whole population of mentally retarded patients (see Chapter 2). Thus no definite conclusions can be drawn as to the distribution of different aetiological forms of mental deficit throughout the whole mentally retarded population. The principal aim of the present volume is to describe the neurological findings and their significance for the aetiological diagnosis of mental retardation. It is for this reason that special attention has been paid to the changes in the aetiological diagnoses which were made necessary by the findings of the detailed neurological examinations and neuroradiological investigations.

The view of Hagne (1962) that it should be possible to make a fairly accurate aetiological diagnosis in about 90 per cent of patients suffering from mental retardation would seem to be correct. This view is supported by the finding that a similar percentage of the patients in the present series showed pathological changes on pneumoencephalography. On the other hand, the view of Dupont (1968) that it is only possible to make an aetiological diagnosis in a about 43 per cent of mentally retarded patients in hospitals seems to be too modest. It may be correct, however, in circumstances in which detailed neurological and neuroradiological studies are not made.

A study of the aetiology of mental retardation based on the same principles as the one described here is to be recommended for all mentally retarded patients, wherever the indications for such investigations are present. The same care should be taken in investigating and prescribing treatment for the mentally retarded as is taken with patients of normal intelligence. As Richards wrote in 1963 'the diagnosis in patients suffering from mental retardation should be as complete as possible, and every available modern technique of investigation, such as chromatography and cytogenetic studies should be used.' The author would agree with Richards' recommendation while proposing that the words 'neuroradiological studies' should be added. It is also to be recommended that such investigations should be performed as early as possible, to ensure that they are of the greatest possible benefit to the patient himself.

The present study has shown that knowledge of the pathological changes which take place in the brains of mentally retarded patients can be helpful in the choice of suitable treatment (*e.g.* Fig. 30), and also for individual rehabilitation. A greater understanding of the causes of mental retardation can also help the parents and relatives who, if the doctor is able to provide definite information as to the probable cause of their child's retardation, are more likely to have confidence in him and less likely to feel it necessary to spend time and money going from doctor to doctor or from quack to quack in search of an answer. Detailed information can also help to free some parents from a feeling of self-recrimination, by convincing them that they are in no way responsible for their child's retardation.

These are just some of the ways in which this and other studies which provide detailed information concerning the aetiology of mental retardation can be of use both for those involved in the work of preventing mental retardation and for society as a whole.

Appendices

APPENDIX TABLE I

Main findings in the seventy patients placed in the WHO's (1968) aetiological category of unknown prenatal influence who had cerebral defects which could account for the mental retardation.

Case No.	Clinical findings	Neuroradiological findings
001	Toe anomaly. Right hemiparesis.	Hypoplastic left middle cerebral artery. Non-defined angiopathy. Moderate left hemimacroventriculy.
002 (Fig. 40)	Epilepsy. Autism.	Asymmetrical microventriculy. Ependymal fusion involving the upper part of the right cella media. Large calcar avis and thick corpus callosum.
020	Low height (below 2.5 percentile). Asymmetrical hyperbrachycephalic skull (skull index 104). Accelerated joint reflexes of the lower extremities.	Asymmetrical severe macroventriculy.
021	Malformed left lower extremity. Anisocoria. Atactic gait. Dyspigmentation of skin. Squint.	Basilar impression. Mild asymmetrical macroventriculy. Cerebellar atrophy or dysplasia. Enlarged sulci in left parietal cortex.
032	Micrognathia. Right simian crease. Hypertelorism. Thinning hair. Highly arched palate. Malformed ears. Bilateral congenital ptosis.	Platybasia. Severe asymmetrical macroventriculy.
039	Low weight (below 2.5 percentile). Small head circumference (below 2nd percentile). Slender build, with bird-like appearance. Tapering ears. Pectus carinatum. Micrognathia. Arachnodactylia. Optic atrophy. Spastic tetraplegia. Epilepsy.	Mild asymmetrical macroventriculy. Moderate cortical dysplasia or atrophy, most prominent in the right fronto-parietal region.
043	Small height, weight and head circumference. Low forehead-hair limit. Micrognathia. Malformed ears. Clinodactyly. Marmoreal skin. Spastic tetraplegia. Epilepsy. Optic atrophy. Squint.	Cisterna magna reaching unusually far into the cranium. Occipital horns situated far apart and directed cranially.
052	Small head circumference. Large malformed ears. Marmoreal skin. Dyspigmentation of skin. Deformed breast. Highly arched palate. Epilepsy. Spastic diplegia.	Moderate left hemimacroventriculy. Enlargement of both fissurae Sylvii.

Case No.	Clinical findings	Neuroradiological findings
056	Low height. Micrognathia. Bilateral epicanthus. Spastic tetraplegia. Right-sided Horner's syndrome. Squint.	Dysplasia and aplasia of cerebral vessels. Microventriculy in association with large defects of cortical brain tissue.
113	Low height and weight. Malformed low-set ears. Oblique palpebral fissure. Abnormal teeth. Cleft palate. Pectus excavatum. Optic atrophy. Epilepsy.	Deformed ventricular system with mild macroventriculy. Large collateral trigones. Saccular formation near to the angle between the right caudate nucleus and corpus callosum.
114	Low height and weight. Dyspigmentation of skin. Pectus excavatum. Spastic diplegia. Epilepsy. Signs indicative of cerebellar lesion.	Moderate right hemimacroventriculy. Dysplastic parietal lobes. Cerebellar dysplasia.
157	Small height, weight and head circumference. Deformed breast. Tapering fingers. Highly arched palate. Micrognathia.	Asymmetrical moderate macroventriculy, with agenesis of the septum pellucidum and an extra cavity in the right fronto-parietal region of the cortex.
160	Asymmetrical face. Dyspigmentation of the skin. Malformed left ear. Operated cheilognathouranoschisis. Abnormal teeth.	Metopic frontal suture. Small narrow ventricles and a broad septum pellucidum.
189	Epilepsy.	Left acute subdural haematoma shown at cerebral angiography. Autopsy: macrencephaly with small ventricles. Brain weight 1750 g.
204 (Fig. 34)	Small height, weight and head circumference. Short neck. Undescended testes. Forehead sloping backwards. Epilepsy. Spastic tetraplegia.	Large deformed ventricles, with a large communicating hole through left frontal lobe, and a widespread tissue defect in right side of cortex. Very large cisterna magna. Brain stem small and poorly developed. Dysplasia and aplasia of cerebral vessels.
221	Small head circumference. Malformed ears and tongue. Marmoreal skin. Thoracic kyphosis. Abnormal teeth. Highly arched palate.	Moderate macroventriculy. Marked cortical dysplasia or atrophy.
227	Deformed low-set ears. Dyspigmentation of skin. Asymmetrical pectus excavatum. Small penis. Highly arched palate. Undescended testes. Muscular hypotonia.	Agenesis of the corpus callosum. Cortical atrophy or dysplasia in the right parietal region.
260 (Fig. 35)	Small height, weight, and head circumference. Ear and toe deformities. High palate. Flatfoot. Spastic diplegia. Epilepsy. Squint. Optic atrophy.	Partial agenesis of the corpus callosum. Marked cortical dysplasia or atrophy.
261	Low height. Micrognathia. Lip deformity. Bilateral exophthalmus. Highly arched palate.	Small frontal part of skull. Moderate cortical dysplasia or atrophy.

Case No.	Clinical findings	Neuroradiological findings
284	Low height and weight. Sharp nose. Marmoreal skin. Bilateral congenital cataract. Squint.	Mild macroventriculy. Mild left-sided cortical atrophy or dysplasia. Cerebellar dysplasia or atrophy.
286	Undescended testes.	Mild macroventriculy. Broad septum pellucidum. Narrow cortical sulci.
294	Ape-like appearance. Thoracic kyphosis. Keratoconus. Epilepsy. Spastic paraplegia.	Mild macroventriculy.
295	Low height. Malformed ears. Pectus excavatum. Simian crease. High palate. Epilepsy.	Moderate asymmetrical macroventriculy shown on pneumoencephalography. Heterotopia of gyri revealed at autopsy.
298	Small height and weight. Grey-coloured hair. Hollow eyes. Spastic tetraplegia. Epilepsy.	Basilar impression. Mild macroventriculy. Enlargement of the left temporal horn. Bilateral parietal cortical atrophy or dysplasia. Hypoplastic cerebellum.
299	Low height and weight. Hypertelorism. Low nasal bridge. Highly arched palate.	Microventriculy. Ependymal fusion involving left cella media.
300 (Fig. 33)	Small height and weight. Pectus excavatum. Bushy eyebrows. Highly arched palate. Squint. Epilepsy. Optic atrophy. Spastic tetraplegia.	Large defects in the tissue of the cerebral cortex. Dysplasia and aplasia of cerebral vessels. An avascular cyst-like large finding in the area of the distal arches of both middle cerebral arteries.
302	Low height and weight. Malformed ears. Bilateral clinodactyly. Simian crease.	Mild macroventriculy.
311	Small head circumference. Pectus excavatum. Flatfoot. Micrognathia. Epilepsy. Spastic left hemiparesis.	Asymmetrical moderate macroventriculy, with enlargement of both temporal horns. Large recessus suprapinealis.
313	Flatfoot. Epilepsy.	Microventriculy. Dysplastic cerebellum.
336	Thoracic kyphosis. Highly arched palate. Cutaneous striae. Signs of bilateral upper motor neurone lesion.	Microventriculy. Moderate cortical dysplasia or atrophy.
345	Small head circumference. Large deformed ears. Undescended testes. Squint. Spastic diplegia. Epilepsy.	Severe macroventriculy. Trigemina primitiva. Microgyria revealed at autopsy.
354	Low height and weight. Micrognathia. Undescended testes. Marmoreal skin. Spastic paraplegia.	Agenesis of the septum pellucidum. An extra cavity in the posterior interhemispheric space. Enlargement of both temporal horns.
355	Small height, weight, and head circumference. Syndactyly of fingers. Pectus excavatum. Malformed ears and toes. Thoraco-lumbar kyphoscoliosis. Flatfoot. Spastic diplegia.	Dysplastic cerebellum.
381	Short neck. Prominent chin. Undescended testes. Flatfoot.	Mild macroventriculy. Cerebellar dysplasia.

Case No.	Clinical findings	Neuroradiological findings
388 (Fig. 36)	Low height and weight. Marmoreal skin. Low snout-like palate and mouth. Bilateral anophthalmia. Flat-foot. Muscular hypotonia.	Small orbitae. Agenesis of the septum pellucidum. Moderate macroventriculy with mis-shapen and abnormally medially situated temporal horns.
397	Small height and head circumference. Triangle-shaped face. Hypertelorism. Maxillar prognathia. Bilateral clinodactyly. Pectus excavatum. Thoracic scoliosis. Asymmetrical head. Forehead prominent. Epilepsy.	Mild macroventriculy with enlargement of both temporal horns.
408	Small height and head circumference. Highly arched palate. Flat foot. Epilepsy. Spastic triplegia. Squint.	Moderate macroventriculy, with asymmetrical enlargement of the temporal horns. Cup-shaped corpus callosum. Narrow posterior fossa. Cortical dysplasia or atrophy.
412	Low height. Malformed ears. Submucous cleft palate. Uvula difida. Small penis. Epilepsy. Accelerated achilles reflex.	Cyst of the septum pellucidum.
413	Toe abnormality. Right simian crease. Paresis of left oculo-motor nerve	Deviation of the left striothalamic vein. Narrow posterior fossa. Small lateral ventricles.
435	Right side of the body poorly developed. Right spastic hemiparesis. Epilepsy. Aphasia.	Hypoplasia of the left middle cerebral artery and the left hemisphere. Severe left hemimacroventriculy.
443	Epilepsy. Severe dolichocephaly.	Mild macroventriculy with enlargement of the left temporal horn and with ventricular bands.
450	Small height, weight, and head circumference. Short neck. Pterygium colli. Ear deformity. Broad nasal bridge. Marmoreal skin. Pectus excavatum. Asymmetrical sternum. Low forehead-hair limit. Syndactyly of fingers. Epilepsy. Squint. Thoracic kyphosis. Flatfoot.	Metopic frontal suture. Deformed lateral ventricles. Enlargement of the left temporal horn. Moderate general cortical dysplasia or atrophy.
473 (Fig. 37)	Small height and head circumference. Micrognathia. Spastic diplegia.	Pericallosal arch in abnormally posterior position. Mild asymmetrical macroventriculy. Short frontal horns. An extra cavity in upper parts of both cellae mediae
475	Large head circumference (over 98th percentile). Thoracic venous markings unusually clear.	Metopic frontal suture. Mild asymmetrical macroventriculy. Cerebellar dysplasia or atrophy.
481	Small height, weight, and head circumference. Sandal gap. Undescended testes. Bilateral congenital cataract and micro-ophthalmia. Accelerated quadriceps reflexes.	Moderate left hemimacroventriculy.

Case No.	Clinical findings	Neuroradiological findings
489	Small head circumference. Highly arched palate. Squint.	Microventriculy. Cerebellar dysplasia.
494	Hypertelorism. Thoracic scoliosis.	Small sella turcica. Microventriculy. Broad septum pellucidum.
497	Low height and weight. Asymmetrical head. Thoracic scoliosis. Highly arched palate. Spastic tetraplegia.	Asymmetrical, moderately large, deformed common lateral ventricle, with extra communicating cavity into left frontal lobe and with displacement to the left.
519 (Fig. 31)	Small head circumference. Dyspigmentation of skin. Restlessness. Hypacusis.	Microventriculy. Narrow posterior fossa.
525	Low height and weight. Micrognathia. Epilepsy.	Tapering skull. Broad septum pellucidum. Moderate macroventriculy. Moderate general cortical dysplasia or atrophy.
549	Highly arched palate. Squint. Spastic diplegia. Epilepsy.	Tapering skull. Agenesis of the corpus callosum. Hypoplasia of the right hemisphere. Cortical dysplasia in region of sylvian fissures on both sides.
555 (Fig. 39)	Low height. Pectus excavatum. Flatfoot. Hyperextensible joints. Squint. Epilepsy. Cerebellar syndrome.	Severe hypoplasia of cerebellar vermis. Pericallosal arch prominent and tightened, and striothalamic vein displaced laterally, suggesting moderate macroventriculy. The veins in the posterior fossa poorly developed. Transverse sinus in abnormally low position.
567	Low height and weight. Pectus excavatum. Malformed ears. Asymmetrical face.	Asymmetrical skull. Moderate asymmetrical macroventriculy with enlargement of both temporal horns. Hypoplasia of the right hemisphere.
573	Low height and weight. Large head circumference. Right microophthalmia. Squint. Nystagmus. Cochlear degeneration.	Moderate asymmetrical macroventriculy with large temporal horns. Mild cortical dysplasia or atrophy in the fronto-parietal region of both hemispheres.
574 (Fig. 32)	Low height and weight. Hare lip and cleft palate. Short neck. Malformed ears. Micrognathia. Marmoreal skin. Tapering fingers. Abnormality of teeth. Spastic paraplegia.	Platybasia. Basilar impression. Microventriculy with large temporal horns. Poorly-developed brain stem.
617	Low weight and small head circumference. Thoracic scoliosis. Systolic heart murmur. Positive protecting reflex. Spastic diplegia. Athetosis. Epilepsy.	Mild macroventriculy. Cup-shaped corpus callosum. Cerebellar dysplasia or atrophy.
649	Small height, weight, and head circumference. Asymmetrical mammary glands and feet. Bilateral keratoconus. Squint. Athetosis. Epilepsy. Primary amenorrhea.	Severe left hemimacroventriculy.

Case No.	Clinical findings	Neuroradiological findings
668	Cutaneous striae. Signs of bilateral upper motor neurone lesion. Left extrapyramidal syndrome. Epilepsy.	Cavity of the septum pellucidum. Large temporal horns.
697	Small head circumference. Dyspigmentation of skin. Squint. Optic atrophy. Spastic diplegia. Epilepsy.	Agenesis of the septum pellucidum. Moderately enlarged and deformed ventricles, with an extra communicating cavity in the frontal lobe on both sides. Cerebellar dysplasia.
721	Small height, weight, and head circumference. Highly arched palate. Optic atrophy. Spastic triplegia.	Right cella media moderately enlarged. Both occipital and temporal horns severely enlarged. A communicating cavity in the septum pellucidum. Cerebellar dysplasia. Aplasia of cerebral vessels.
738	Small height, weight, and head circumference. Pectus excavatum. Severe myopia. Flatfoot. Spastic diplegia. Epilepsy.	Agenesis of the septum pellucidum. Moderate asymmetrical macroventriculy. Hypoplasia of brain stem and cerebellum.
752	Small height and head circumference. Epicanthus. Thoracic kyphosis. Bilateral ptosis. Paresis of left oculomotor nerve. Accelerated reflexes in lower extremities. Epilepsy.	Severe asymmetrical macroventriculy, with considerable enlargement of the right occipital horn.
763	Small head circumference. Hypertelorism. Dyspigmentation of skin. Systolic heart murmur.	Microventriculy. Cerebellar dysplasia or atrophy.
803	Pectus excavatum. Systolic heart murmur. Highly arched palate.	Enlarged deformed temporal horns.
836	Low weight. Asymmetrical ears. Squint. Spastic right hemiparesis.	Mild macroventriculy, with large temporal horns. Cup-shaped corpus callosum.
862	Small height, weight, and head circumference. Forehead sloping backwards. Asymmetrical deformed chest. Highly arched palate. Spastic tetraplegia. Thoracic kyphoscoliosis. Epilepsy.	Metopic frontal suture. Mild right hemimacroventriculy. A small prominence on the lateral surface of left temporal horn. Agenesis of the cerebellum.
865	Large head circumference. Systolic heart murmur. Micro-ophthalmia. Tapering skull.	Mild macroventriculy. Cerebellar dysplasia or atrophy.
932	Low height and weight. Short neck. Prognathia. Umbilical and inguinal hernias. Spastic diplegia. Epilepsy.	Metopic frontal suture, hypertrophic lambdoid suture. Hypoplastic atlas. Enlargement of left temporal horn. Small brain stem. Narrow cortical sulci. Autopsy examination revealed cortical dysplasia and a ruptured aneurysm of left middle cerebral artery.
943	Low height and weight. Asymmetrical chest. Squint. Spastic tetraplegia. Epilepsy.	Malformed atlas. Right temporo-parietal cranial exostosis. Moderate left hemimacroventriculy.

Case No.	Clinical findings	Neuroradiological findings
999	Low height and weight. Low fore-head-hair limit. Dyspigmentation of skin. Syndactyly of fingers. Eyebrows over nasal root. Highly arched palate. Squint. Flatfoot. Hyperextensible joints. Spastic tetraplegia.	Flattened posterior part of skull. Metopic frontal suture. Moderate asymmetrical macroventriculy. Marked cortical dysplasia or atrophy. Cerebellar dysplasia.

APPENDIX TABLE II

Main findings in the twenty patients who were placed in the WHO's category of unknown prenatal influence but in whom there were insufficient cerebral findings to account for the mental retardation

Case No.	Clinical findings	Neuroradiological findings
068	Flatfoot. Diabetes insipidus.	Mild macroventriculy. Cavity in the septum pellucidum.
172	Small height, weight and head circumference. In external appearance like his brother, patient No. 173. Epilepsy.	Cerebellar dysplasia. Pneumoencephalo-graphic appearances similar to those in patient No. 173.
173	Small height, weight and head circumference. Albinismus. Squint. Acrocyanosis. Marmoreal skin. Epilepsy.	Cerebellar dysplasia.
180	Small height and head circumference. Narrow head. Hypotelorism. Thick subcutis. Epilepsy.	Metopic frontal suture. Narrow posterior fossa. No intraventricular gas filling. Deviation of left middle cerebral artery.
218	Low height. Epilepsy. Spastic para-paresis.	Cerebellar dysplasia.
222	Low height. Mild micrognathia. Pectus carinatum. Highly arched palate. Hypoplastic external genitals. Abnormal teeth. Transient optic oedema. Muscular hypotonia. Flatfoot. Syndrome of benign intracranial hyper-tension.	Cerebellar tonsilla below foramen occipitale magnum. No intraventricular gas filling. Transverse sinus lowly situated, suggesting small infratentorial space.
289	Low height and weight. Broad face. Micrognathia. Pectus excavatum. Broad palate. Front teeth directed outwards. Squint. Spastic paraplegia.	Metopic frontal suture. Cerebellar dysplasia.
323	Low height. Bushy eyebrows over nasal root. Cleft palate. Toe syn-dactyly and anomaly. Micrognathia. Situs inversus colonis. Signs of bilateral upper motor neurone lesion.	Asymmetrical normal-sized ventricles. Large recessus suprapinealis.

Case No.	Clinical findings	Neuroradiological findings
396 (Fig. 38)	Taybi-Rubinstein syndrome. Optic atrophy. Spastic paraplegia.	Asymmetry of the circle of Willis. Small cerebral ventricles. Thick corpus callosum. Cerebellar dysplasia.
410	Low height and weight. Abnormal ears. Bushy eyebrows. Long eyelashes. Hairy coat on back. Highly arched palate. Dystonic dyskinesia.	Cavity of septum pellucidum.
411	Small head circumference. Highly arched palate. Operated choanal atresia.	Narrow posterior fossa.
436	Low height and weight. Anhidrotic ectodermal dysplasia of skin. Total alopecia. Dyspigmentation of the skin. Bilateral ear anomaly. Toe syndactyly. Nose beaked. Nostrils and external openings of ears small. Pectus carinatum. Cleft palate. Nystagmus.	Mild macroventriculy.
463	Small head circumference. Bilateral ear anomaly. Epicanthus. Systolic heart murmur.	Small asymmetrical ventricles. Cerebellar dysplasia.
517	Low height and weight. Short neck. Epicanthus. Bilateral palpebral ptosis. Thoracic kyphosis. Finger syndactyly. Six fingers and six toes on each side. Epiglottis with three parts. Sandal gap. Undescended testes. Squint.	Egg-shaped skull. Craniosynostosis. Large temporal horns.
734	Low weight. Large head circumference. Abnormal low-set ears. Upper front teeth prominent. Lumbar scoliosis. Right hemiparesis.	Cerebellar dysplasia. Thick skull.
780	Local alopecia on scalp. Epicanthus. Highly arched palate.	Large sella turcica. Cerebellar dysplasia.
813	Cleft palate. Epilepsy.	Mild macroventriculy. Mild cortical dysplasia or atrophy in right fronto-temporal area.
855	Toe and finger anomaly. Abnormal low-set ears. Short broad neck. Flat-foot. Cutaneous striae. Right Horner's syndrome. Squint. Nystagmus. Spastic triplegia. Cerebellar syndrome. Arnold-Chiari syndrome.	Cerebellar tonsilla situated about 12 mm below foramen occipitale magnum. No intraventricular gas filling. Mildly enlarged sulci in parietal cortex.
871	Micrognathia. Highly arched palate. Upper front teeth pointing outwards. Epilepsy.	Thick skull. No definite abnormalities on pneumoencephalography.
891	Low height and weight. Bilateral congenital cataract. Nystagmus.	No definite abnormality on pneumo-encephalography.

Main findings in the sixty-seven patients classified in the WHO's category of other and unspecified forms of mental retardation

Case No.	Clinical and EEG findings	Neuroradiological findings
000	Mental retardation of fluctuating progressive course. Accelerated joint reflexes.	Severe asymmetrical macroventriculy. Moderate cortical atrophy.
018	Epilepsy. Spastic tetraplegia.	Severe symmetrical macroventriculy.
045	Fits of restlessness. Squint. Focal EEG changes in left temporal area.	Mild macroventriculy with suspected left-sided temporal expansion (carotid angiography and pneumoencephalography). Normal findings on brain scanning with radioisotopes.
063	Epilepsy. Paraparesis.	Mild macroventriculy.
073	Low height and weight. Progressive course. Epilepsy. Spastic diplegia.	Normal findings on pneumoencephalography.
076	Low height. Epilepsy.	Moderate left hemimacroventriculy.
103	Small height and head circumference. Epilepsy. Muscular hypotonia. Slight truncal ataxia.	Cerebellar atrophy or dysplasia.
115	Low height. Epilepsy. Autism. Focal EEG changes in the left frontal area.	Severe asymmetrical macroventriculy shown at pneumoencephalography and left carotid angiography.
130	Epilepsy. Continuous paroxysmal activity of 1-2 Hz on EEG.	Normal findings on pneumoencephalography.
168	Fits of restlessness.	Enlargement of left temporal horn. Cyst of the septum pellucidum.
182	Small weight, height and head circumference. Epilepsy. Accelerated quadriceps reflexes.	Normal findings on pneumoencephalography.
197	Dysphasia. Diffuse generalised changes on EEG.	Mild macroventriculy. Cerebellar atrophy.
217	Small head. Focal EEG changes of 3-4 Hz in both temporal areas.	Moderate left hemimacroventriculy. Cerebellar atrophy or dysplasia.
240	Accelerated achilles reflexes.	Mild macroventriculy, with severe enlargement of both temporal horns.
259	Epilepsy. Squint.	Large sella turcica. Small ventricles. Mild cortical atrophy in left parietal area. Mild cerebellar atrophy.
262	Low height. Epilepsy. Restlessness.	Enlargement of both temporal horns. Mild cortical atrophy.
265	Large head. Epilepsy. Beta-alaninuria.	Mild macroventriculy, with enlargement of both temporal horns.
269	Small head. Epilepsy.	Mild macroventriculy with enlargement of both temporal horns.

Case No.	Clinical findings	Neuroradiological findings
276	Low weight. Epilepsy. Pectus excavatum. Epicanthus. Diffuse EEG changes of 3-4 Hz with paroxysmal episodes dominating on the right side.	Normal findings on pneumoencephalgraphy.
280 (Fig. 50)	Autism. Dyspigmentation of skin. Expressive dysphasia. Diffuse EEG changes dominating on the right side.	Enlargement of left temporal horn. Cerebellar atrophy.
282	Low height and weight. Epilepsy. Diffuse EEG changes with slow waves in frontal areas.	Enlargement of left temporal horn.
305	Male with feminine features. Diffuse EEG changes.	Moderate macroventriculy.
315	Epilepsy. Paroxysmal 5 Hz EEG activity.	Moderate left hemimacroventriculy.
320	Small height. Cutaneous striae. Epilepsy.	Large suprapineal recess. Small cerebellum.
322	Focal 4-6 Hz EEG changes in right temporal area.	Mild cortical atrophy. Normal findings on right carotid angiography.
326	Low height. Spastic diplegia. Athetosis.	Cerebellar atrophy or dysplasia.
330	Epilepsy. Spastic paraplegia.	Moderate left hemimacroventriculy.
334 (Fig. 48)	Epilepsy. Atactic gait.	Severe left hemimacroventriculy. Enlargement of both temporal horns. Cerebellar atrophy or dysplasia.
340	Epilepsy. Paraplegia (after poliomyelitis).	Normal findings on pneumoencephalography.
350	Epilepsy.	Moderate macroventriculy, with enlargement of left temporal horn. Cerebellar dysplasia.
362	Psychotic episodes. Non-defined dyskinesia. Diffuse EEG changes with slow waves in parietal areas. Symptoms of benign intracranial hypertension.	Small ventricles.
370	Small height, weight, and head circumference. Optic atrophy. Epilepsy. Spastic tetraplegia.	Moderate macroventriculy.
392	Small height and head circumference. Dysphasia.	Mild left hemimacroventriculy.
432	Small height, weight, and head circumference. Epilepsy. Spastic diplegia.	Normal findings on pneumoencephalography.
448	Epilepsy. Squint.	Moderate cortical atrophy.
476	Low weight. Epilepsy. Focal EEG changes on the right side.	Asymmetrical normal-sized ventricles. Normal findings on right carotid angiography.

Case No.	Clinical and EEG findings	Neuroradiological findings
478	Epilepsy. Diffuse EEG changes with slow subcortical epileptic activity.	Mild macroventriculy.
505	Polydactyly with deformed thumb of right hand.	Mild right hemimacroventriculy.
542	Small height and head circumference. Asymmetrical face.	Large suprapineal recess. Small brain stem.
571	Small height, weight, and head circumference.	Moderate asymmetrical macroventriculy.
604	Low height. Epilepsy. Diffuse EEG changes, with 2-4-6 Hz activity in left temporo-basal area.	Mild macroventriculy, with enlargement of the left temporal horn. Cerebellar atrophy. Moderate cortical atrophy.
606	Deformity of left pupil. Bilateral dysmetria. Diffuse EEG changes.	Enlargement of the left temporal horn. Cerebellar atrophy.
634	Small height. Large head circumference. Optic atrophy.	Severe asymmetrical macroventriculy. Marked cortical frontal atrophy.
636	Low height and weight. Spastic diplegia. Optic atrophy.	Severe asymmetrical macroventriculy.
673	Low height and weight. Spastic paraplegia.	Mild macroventriculy.
688	Epilepsy. Diffuse EEG changes, with deep paroxysmal activity of middle frequency.	Normal findings on pneumoencephalography.
715	Low height. Epilepsy. Cystine and lysine present in urine. Accelerated quadriceps reflexes. Diffuse EEG changes with paroxysmal activity, spikes dominating on the left side.	Normal findings at cerebral angiography and pneumoencephalography.
759	Low height and weight. Epilepsy. Spastic diplegia.	Severe macroventriculy and cortical atrophy.
767	Small height, weight, and head circumference. Epilepsy. Atrophy of tongue. Severe EEG changes with background activity of 2-4 Hz.	Marked cortical atrophy.
782	Low height and weight. Epilepsy. Spastic diplegia.	Enlargement of both temporal horns.
793 (Fig. 49)	Epilepsy. Diffuse EEG changes.	Mild macroventriculy with extra communicating cavity in the right occipito-parietal region.
797	Epilepsy. Cerebellar syndrome. Signs of bilateral upper motor neurone lesion.	Severe asymmetrical macroventriculy. Poorly-developed brain stem.
823	Epilepsy. Signs of extrapyramidal and cerebellar lesions.	Asymmetrical normal-sized ventricles. Cerebellar atrophy.
833	Low height. Epilepsy. Non-defined dyskinesia. Amblyopia.	Mild left hemimacroventriculy.

Case No.	Clinical and EEG findings	Neuroradiological findings
835 (Fig. 51)	Low weight. Epilepsy. Spastic diplegia.	Moderate left hemimacroventriculy. Atrophy of the brain stem and cerebellum. Moderate cortical atrophy.
839	Low height. Epilepsy. Squint.	Normal findings on pneumoencephalography.
840	Large head. Epilepsy. Focal EEG changes on the right side.	Moderate left hemimacroventriculy. Extremely large cisterna magna.
845	Right spastic hemiparesis.	Enlargement of left temporal horn. Cerebellar atrophy.
850	Low height. Spastic diplegia.	Mild macroventriculy, with enlargement of the left temporal horn. Cerebellar atrophy. Mild cortical atrophy.
870	Small height, weight, and head circumference. Epilepsy. Spastic diplegia.	Moderate macroventriculy. Small brain stem and cerebellum.
877	Epilepsy. Amaurosis. Squint. Diffuse EEG changes with paroxysmal left-dominating theta spikes.	Mild symmetrical macroventriculy.
882	Epilepsy. Spastic tetraplegia.	Moderate macroventriculy. Cerebellar atrophy. Enlargement of both fissurae Sylvii.
886	Low height and weight. Epilepsy. Diffuse EEG changes with focal abnormalities in left temporo-parietal area.	Mild cortical atrophy.
949	Low height and weight. Epilepsy. Spastic paraplegia. Ataxia.	Cerebellar atrophy or dysplasia.
963	Low height. Epilepsy. Diffuse EEG changes	Normal findings on pneumoencephalography.
965	Epilepsy. Diffuse EEG changes.	Asymmetrical normal-sized ventricles. Cerebellar atrophy. Mild cortical atrophy.
998	Small height and head circumference. Epilepsy. Psychotic periods. Cerebellar dysarthria.	Cerebellar atrophy or dysplasia.

APPENDIX TABLE IV

Variables of clinical history and physical examination

Sex	Height	Reactions of pupillae
Age	Weight	Size of pupillae
Intelligence quotient	Head circumference	Cataract
Social class	Cephalic index	State of back
Marital status of parents	Handedness	State of joints
Family history of mental retardation	Skull anomaly	Muscular atrophy
Previous abortions and still-births of mother	Eye anomaly	Muscular tone
	Lip-palate deformity	Function of cranial nerves
	Heart anomaly	Spasticity
Maternal age	Foot deformity	Dyskinesia
Abnormalities during pregnancy	Epicanthus	Fine motor function
	Ear anomaly	Ataxia
Poison or medicine during pregnancy	Chin anomaly	Romberg's test
	Tongue anomaly	Reflexes
Birth order	Simian crease	Pain sensibility
Place of delivery	Clinodactyly	Syndrome of cranial nerve lesion
Mode of delivery	Finger anomaly	
Birthweight	Toe anomaly	Syndrome of upper motor neurone lesion
Maturity of newborn	Chest deformity	
Number of infants resulting from same pregnancy	Hernias	Syndrome of extrapyramidal lesion
	Kryptorchidism	
Condition of child immediately after birth	Sandal gap	Syndrome of cerebellar lesion
	Nasal deformity	Other neurological syndrome
Condition of child later in the neonatal period	Abnormality of genitals	Ability to speak
	Abnormality of skin	Ability to walk
Age of child when mental retardation was diagnosed	Seeing ability	Ability to sit
	Hearing ability	Ability to dress
Type of onset of mental retardation	Eye grounds	Ability to undress
	Ptosis of upper eyelid	Ability to feed self
Epilepsy	Squint	Bowel and bladder control
	Nystagmus	

(A) Normal lateral carotid arteriogram, according to Fischer.

(B) Normal antero-posterior carotid arteriogram, according to Fischer.

C1 to C5:   internal carotid artery

    C1 = terminal portion
    C2 = superior horizontal portion of the siphon
    C3 = anterior vertical portion of the siphon
    C4 = inferior horizontal portion of the siphon
    C5 = infrasinusal portion of the internal carotid

M1 to M5:   middle cerebral artery or sylvian artery

    M1 = first segment
    M2 = second segment
    M4 = posterior parietal artery
    M5 = artery of the angular gyrus
    ATP = posterior temporal artery

A1 to A5:   anterior cerebral artery

    A1 = first segment
    A2 = second segment
    A3 = third segment
    AFP = artery to the frontal pole
    A4 = pericallosal artery
    A5 = calloso-marginal artery

ACP: posterior communicating and posterior cerebral arteries

AchA: anterior choroidal artery

(C) Normal position of deep veins (lateral view).

(D) Normal position of deep veins (antero-posterior view).

(E) Normal position of deep veins (antero-posterior half-axial view).

    Ɔ: foramen of Monro
    VS: septal vein
    VTS: thalamo-striate vein
    VCI: internal cerebral vein of Galen
    VB: basal vein of Rosenthal
    GVG: great vein of Galen
    SLI: inferior longitudinal sinus
    SD: straight sinus

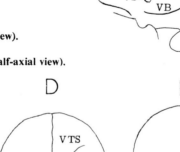

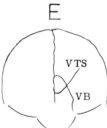

(Re-drawn with permission from Bonnal, J., Legré, J. (1958) *L'Angiographie Cérébrale*. Paris: Masson.)

References

Abrams, H. L. (1961) *Angiography, Vol. 1*. Boston: Little Brown.

Akesson, H. O. (1961) *Epidemiology and Genetics of Mental Deficiency in a Southern Swedish Population*. Thesis, University of Uppsala.

Anderson, F. M. (1951) 'Pneumoencephalography in children. A review of 400 cases.' *Bulletin of the Los Angeles Neurological Society*, **16**, 125.

Angrisani, D., Fina, G., Serra, C. (1961) 'Studio elettroencephalographico sull'idioza amaurotica tipo Vogt-Spielmeyer.' *Ospedale Psichiatrico*, **29**, 247.

Autio, S. (1972) '*Aspartylglycosaminuria. Analysis of Thirty-four Cases*. Journal of Mental Deficiency Research Monograph Series, No. 1. London: National Society for Mentally Handicapped Children.

Bäckström-Järvinen, L. (1964) 'Heights and weights of Finnish children and young adults.' *Annales Paediatriae Fenniae*, **10**, Suppl. 23.

Bagh, K. van, Hortling, H. (1958) 'Blodfynd vid juvenil amaurotisk idioti.' *Nordisk Medicin*, **38**, 1072.

Bartalos, M., Baramki, T. A. (1967) *Medical Cytogenetics*. Baltimore: Williams & Wilkins.

Beley, A., Sevestre, P., Lecuyer, R. M. J., Leroy, C. (1959) 'Contribution à l'E.E.G. des mongoliens.' *Revue Neurologique*, **101**, 457.

Benda, C. E. (1960) 'Die Oligophrenien (Entwicklungsstörungen und Schwachsinnszustände).' *in* Gruhle, H. W., Jung, R., Mayer-Gross, W., Müller, M. (Eds.) *Psychiatrie der Gegenwart. Forschung und Praxis. Band II*. Berlin: Springer. p. 869.

Berg, J. M., Smith, G. F. (1971) 'Behaviour and intelligence in males with XYY sex chromosomes.' *in* Primrose, D. A. A. (Ed.) *Proceedings of the 2nd International Congress of the International Association for the Scientific Study of Mental Deficiency*. Warsaw: Polish Medical Publishers. p. 135.

Berger, H. (1929) 'Über das Elektroenkephalogramm des Menschen.' *Archiv für Psychiatrie und Nervenkrankheiten*, **87**, 527.

Bickel, H. (1968) 'Inborn errors of metabolism associated with brain damage. Early detection and prevention of their manifestations.' *in Brain Damage by Inborn Errors of Metabolism. Symposium Organised by the Interdisciplinary Society of Biological Psychiatry, Amsterdam, 1967*. Haarlem: deErven F. Bohn.

Birch, H. G. (1968) 'Health and the education of socially disadvantaged children.' *Developmental Medicine and Child Neurology*, **10**, 580.

—— Richardson, S. A., Baird, D., Horobin, H., Illsley, R. (1970) *Mental Subnormality in the Community: a Clinical and Epidemiologic Study*. Baltimore: Williams and Wilkins.

Blau, M., Bender, M. A. (1962) 'Radiomercury (Hg^{203}) labeled Neohydrin. A new agent for brain tumor localization.' *Journal of Nuclear Medicine*, **3**, 83.

Blaw, M. E., Torres, F. (1967) 'Treatment for pseudoretardation associated with epilepsy.' *Modern Treatment*, **4**, 799.

Bourneville, D. M. (1880) 'Sclérose tubéreuse des circonvolutions cérébrales; idiotie et épilepsie hémiplégique.' *Archives de Neurologie*, **1**, 81.

Brain, (Lord), Walton, J. N. (1969) *Brain's Diseases of the Nervous System, 7th Edn*. London: Oxford University Press.

Brandt, S., de la Garde, M., Rosendal, T. (1955) 'The technique of pneumo-encephalography in children.' *Acta Paediatrica* (*Uppsala*), **44**, Suppl. 103, 61.

—— Brünner, S., Westergaard-Nielsen, V. (1961) 'Arteriographic studies in children with cerebral palsy.' *Acta Paediatrica* (*Uppsala*), **50**, 586.

Bredmose, G. V., Christensen, E. (1955) 'Value of brain microscopy for clinic of various forms of mental deficiency.' *Acta Psychiatrica et Neurologica Scandinavica*, **30**, 91.

Brett, E. M., Hoare, R. D. (1969) 'An assessment of the value and limitations of air encephalography in children with mental retardation and with epilepsy.' *Brain*, **92**, 731.

Bruijn, G. W. (1959) 'Pneumoencephalography in the diagnosis of cerebral atrophy.' *Thesis*, Utrecht.

—— (1963) 'Die neuroradiologische Einschätzung des Ventrikelsystems und seine Beziehungen zum Gehirn und Schädel im Säuglings- und Kindesalter.' *in* Müller, D. (Ed.) *Neuroradiologische Diagnostik und Symptomatik der Hirnentwicklung im Kindesalter*. Berlin: VEB Volk und Gesundheit. p. 429.

Campbell, J. A. (1966) 'Roentgen aspects of cranial configurations.' *Radiologic Clinics of North America*, **4**, 11.

Carr, D. H. (1965) 'Chromosome studies in spontaneous abortions.' *Obstetrics and Gynecology*, **26**, 308.

Carter, C. H. (Ed.) (1965) *Medical Aspects of Mental Retardation*. Springfield, Ill.: C. C Thomas.

—— (1966) *Handbook of Mental Retardation Syndromes*. Springfield, Ill.: C. C Thomas.

Casamajor, L., Laidlaw, R. W., Kozinn, P. J. (1949) 'Validity of pneumoencephalographic diagnosis: a study of five hundred pneumoencephalograms in children.' *Journal of the American Medical Association*, **140**, 1329.

—— —— —— (1951) 'The technique of pneumoencephalography in children: comparative results with air and oxygen injection.' *Journal of Pediatrics*, **38**, 463.

Chapelle, A. de la (1962) 'Cytogenetical and clinical observations in female gonadal dysgenesis.' *Acta Endocrinologica (Copenhagen)*, **40**, Suppl. 65.

—— (1963) 'Sex chromosome abnormalities among the mentally defective in Finland.' *Journal of Mental Deficiency Research*, **7**, 129.

—— Wennström, J., Hortling, H., Ockey, C. H. (1966) 'Isochromosome-X in man. Part I.' *Hereditas (Lund)*, **54**, 260.

Charash, L. I., Dunning, H. S. (1956) 'An appraisal of pneumoencephalography in mental retardation and epilepsy.' *Pediatrics*, **18**, 716.

Chatrian, G. E., White, L. E., Daly, D. (1963) 'Electroencephalographic patterns resembling those of sleep in certain comatose states after injuries to the head.' *Electroencephalography and Clinical Neurophysiology*, **15**, 272.

Chicago Conference (1966) 'Standardization in Human cytogenetics.' *in Birth Defects: Original Article Series, II*, 2. New York: The National Foundation.

Christensen, E., Melchior, J., Bredmose, G. V. (1964) 'A survey of neuropathological findings in 175 mentally retarded patients.' *in* Øster, J., Sletved, H. (Eds.) *International Copenhagen Conference on the Scientific Study of Mental Retardation.* Copenhagen: Statens Andssvage Forsorg. p. 427.

Cobb, W., Hill, D. (1950) 'Electroencephalogram in subacute progressive encephalitis.' *Brain*, **73**, 392.

Collan, R., Iivanainen, M. (1969) 'Cardiac arrest caused by rapid elimination of nitrous oxide from cerebral ventricles after encephalography.' *Canadian Anaesthetists Society Journal*, **16**, 519.

Covernton, J. S. (1967) 'A report on the activities of the diagnostic clinic of the intellectually retarded services in the Mental Health Dept. of South Australia.' *Medical Journal of Australia*, **i**, 1245.

Crome, L. (1960) 'The brain and mental retardation.' *British Medical Journal*, **1**, 897.

—— Stern, J. (1970) *The Pathology of Mental Retardation, 2nd edn.* Edinburgh: Churchill/Livingstone.

Crothers, B., Paine, R. (1959) *The Natural History of Cerebral Palsy.* Cambridge, Mass.: Harvard University Press.

Cummins, H., Midlo, C. (1943) *Finger Prints, Palms and Soles.* Philadelphia: Blakiston. (Reprinted: (1961) New York: Dover Publications.)

Dandy, W. E. (1918) 'Ventriculography following the injection of air into the cerebral ventricles.' *Annals of Surgery*, **68**, 5.

Dannenbaum, P. (1926) 'Beiträge zur Encephalographie im Kindesalter.' *Zeitschrift für Kinderheilkunde*, **42**, 578.

Davidoff, L. M., Gass, H. (1949) 'Convolutional markings in the skull roentgenograms of patients with headache.' *American Journal of Roentgenology*, **61**, 317.

Decker, K., Backmund, H. (1970) *Pädiatrische Neuroradiologie.* Stuttgart: Thieme.

DeLang, F. H., Wagner, H. N. (1969) *Atlas of Nuclear Medicine, Vol. 1. Brain.* Philadelphia: W. B. Saunders.

Dent, C. E., Harris, H. (1956) 'Hereditary forms of rickets and osteomalacia.' *Journal of Bone and Joint Surgery*, **38B**, 211.

Di Chiro, G. (1961*a*) *An Atlas of Detailed Normal Pneumoencephalographic Anatomy.* Springfield, Ill.: C. C Thomas.

—— (1961*b*) 'RISA encephalography and conventional neuroradiological methods.' *Acta Radiologica (Stockholm)*, **55**, Suppl. 201.

—— Nelson, K. B. (1962) 'The volume of the sella turcica.' *American Journal of Roentgenology*, **87**, 989.

Diethelm, L., Strnad, F. (1963) 'Röntgendiagnostik des Schädels I-II.' *in* Olsson, O., Strnad, F., Vieten, H., Zuppinger, A. (Eds.) *Handbuch der Medizinischen Radiologie.* Berlin: Springer.

Dorst, J. P. (1964) 'Functional craniology: an aid in interpreting roentgenograms of the skull.' *Radiologic Clinics of North America*, **2**, 347.

Drillien, C. M. (1968*a*) 'Causes of handicap in the low weight infant.' *in* Jonxis, J. H. P., Visser, H. K. A., Troelstra, J. A. (Eds.) *Nutricia Symposium on Aspects of Praematurity and Dysmaturity.* Leiden: H. E. Stenfert Kroese. p. 287.

—— (1968*b*) 'Studies in mental handicap. II. Some obstetric factors of possible aetiological importance.' *Archives of Disease in Childhood*, **43**, 283.

Dumermuth, G. (1965) *Elektroencephalographie im Kindesalter. Einführung und Atlas.* Stuttgart: Thieme.

Dupont, A. (1968) 'Nye synspunkter med hensyn til aetiologi, behandling og forskning ved åndssvaghed.' *Nordisk Medicin*, **80**, 973.

—— Dreyer, K. (1968) 'Mentally retarded patients classified according to AAMD system.' *Danish Medical Bulletin*, **15**, 18.

Eastham, R. D., Jancar, J. (1968) *Clinical Pathology in Mental Retardation.* Bristol: John Wright.
Eeg-Olofsson, O. (1971) 'The development of the electroencephalogram in normal children from the age of 1 through 15 years. 14 and 6 Hz positive spike phenomenon.' *Neuropädiatrie*, **2**, 405.
Eley, R. C., Vogt, E. C. (1932) 'Encephalography in children; further observations in children with fixed lesions of the brain.' *American Journal of Roentgenology*, **27**, 686.
Emery, J. L. (1967) 'The examination of the normal and hydrocephalic infant brain using ultrasound.' *Developmental Medicine and Child Neurology*, Suppl. 13, 87.
Engeset, A., Skraastad, E. (1964) 'Methods of measurement in encephalography.' *Neurology (Minneapolis)*, **14**, 381.
Epstein, J. A., Epstein, B. S. (1967) 'Deformities of the skull surfaces in infancy and childhood.' *Journal of Pediatrics*, **70**, 636.
Dyggve, H. V., Melchior, J. C. (1964) 'Pneumoencephalography and mental retardation.' *in* Øster, J., Sletved, H. (Eds.) *International Copenhagen Conference on the Scientific Study of Mental Retardation.* Copenhagen: Statens Andssvage Forsorg. Vol. 2, p. 854.
Evans, W. A. (1942) 'An encephalographic ratio for estimating ventricular enlargement and cerebral atrophy.' *Archives of Neurology and Psychiatry*, **47**, 931.
Finland, Central Medical Board (1955) *The Official Statistics of Finland. XI. Health and Medical Care, 1939-1952.* Helsinki.
Finland, Central Statistical Office (1954) *Statistical Yearbook of Finland. New Series, 49th year, 1953.* Helsinki.
Finland, National Board of Health (1970) *The Official Statistics of Finland. XI: 70, 71. Public Health and Medical Care 1967-1968.* Helsinki.
Fischer-Williams, M. (1969) 'The neurological aspects of "mental" subnormality. Part I.' *Journal of Mental Subnormality*, **15**, 21.
Følling, A. (1934) 'Über Ausscheidung von Phenylbrenztraubensäure in den Harn als Stoffwechselanomalie in Verbindung mit Imbezillität.' *Hoppe-Seylers Zeitschrift für physiologischer Chemie*, **227**, 169.
Freytag, E., Lindenberg, E. (1967) 'Neuropathologic findings in patients of a hospital for the mentally deficient. A survey of 359 cases.' *Johns Hopkins Medical Journal*, **121**, 379.
Gaal I. (1963) 'Die Beduetung der pneumoencephalographischen Untersuchungen bei Kindern mit psychischen Entwicklungsstörungen.' *in* Stur, O. (Ed.) *Proceedings of the Second International Congress on Mental Retardation.* Basel: Karger. p. 226.
Gastaut, H., Roger, J., Soulayrol, R., Tassinari, C. A., Régis, H., Dravet, C., Bernard, R., Pinsard, N., Saint-Jean, M. (1966) 'Childhood epileptic encephalopathy with diffuse slow spike-waves (otherwise known as "petit mal" variant) or Lennox syndrome.' *Epilepsia*, **7**, 139.
Gelof, M. (1963) 'Comparisons of systems of classification relating degree of retardation to measured intelligence.' *American Journal of Mental Deficiency*, **68**, 297.
Gibbs, E. L., Gibbs, F. A. (1962) 'Extreme spindles: correlation of electroencephalographic sleep pattern with mental retardation.' *Science*, **138**, 1106.
—— Rich, C. L., Fois, A., Gibbs, F. A. (1960) 'Electroencephalographic study of mentally retarded persons.' *American Journal of Mental Deficiency*, **65**, 236.
Gibbs, F. A., Gibbs, E. L. (1965) 'The electroencephalogram in mental retardation.' *in* Carter, C. H. (Ed.) *Medical Aspects of Mental Retardation.* Springfield, Ill.: C. C. Thomas. p. 112.
Gordon, I. R. S. (1966) 'Measurement of cranial capacity in children.' *British Journal of Radiology*, **39**, 377.
Gross, A., Kaltenbäck, E. (1962) 'Die perinatale Hirnschädigung als ätiologischer Faktor der psychischen Entwicklungsstörungen im Kindesalter.' *in* Jacob, H. (Ed.) *Proceedings of the Fourth International Congress for Neuropathology. Vol. 3.* Stuttgart: Thieme. p. 24.
—— Rett, A., Seitelberger, F. (1964) 'Ergebnisse vergleichender klinischer und anatomischer Untersuchungen an zerebralgeschädigten Kindern.' *in* Øster, J., Sletved, H. (Ed.) *International Copenhagen Conference on the Scientific Study of Mental Retardation.* Copenhagen: Statens Andssvage Forsorg. Vol. 1. p. 451.
Grüter, W., Hermann, E. (1965) 'Zur Genese der Hemiatrophia cerebri.' *Radiologe*, **5**, 441.
Gupta, P. C., Virmani, V. (1968) 'Analysis of 200 cases of mental retardation.' *Neurology of India*, **16**, 77.
Hagberg. B., Hamfelt, A., Holmdahl, M. H., Lodin, H. (1959) 'Pneumoencephalography in early infancy; risks, clinical indications and technical considerations.' *Acta Paediatrica (Uppsala)*, **48**, Suppl. 117, 61.
—— Kollberg, H., Sourander, P., Akesson, H. O. (1969) 'Infantile globoid cell leukodystrophy (Krabbe's disease). A clinical and genetic study of 32 Swedish cases 1953-1967.' *Neuropädiatrie*, **1**, 74.
Hagne, I. (1962) 'Mental retardation.' *Nordisk Medicin*, **67**, 801.
Halonen, H., Halonen, V., Donner, M., Iivanainen, M., Vuolio, M., Mäkinen, M. (1973) 'Occlusive disease of intracranial main arteries with collateral networks in children.' *Neuropädiatrie*, **4**, 187.
Halperin, S. L. (1945) 'A clinico-genetical study of mental defect.' *American Journal of Mental Deficiency*, **50**, 8.

Hambert, G., Frey, T. S. (1964) 'The electroencephalogram in the Klinefelter syndrome.' *Acta Psychiatrica Scandinavica*, **40**, 28.
Heber, R. (1959) 'A manual on terminology and classification in mental retardation.' *American Journal of Mental Deficiency*, **64**, monograph suppl., no. 2.
—— (1961) 'A manual on terminology and classification in mental retardation.' *American Journal of Mental Deficiency*, **66**, monograph suppl. (2nd edn.)
Hécaen, H., Ajuriaguerra, J. de (1964) *Left-Handedness: Manual Superiority and Cerebral Dominance.* New York: Grune & Stratton.
Hedenström, I. V. and Schorsch, G. (1966) 'Photosensibilität im Eeg bei Epileptikern und bei Oligophrenien mit seltenen Anfällen.' *Archiv für Psychiatrie und Nervenkrankheiten*, **208**, 147.
Helsinki, Institute of Midwifery (1952) *Yearbook of the Institute of Midwifery.* Helsinki.
Hirai, T., Izawa, S. (1964) 'An electroencephalographic study of mongolism—with special reference to its E.E.G. development and intermediate fast wave.' *Psychiatria et Neurologica Japonica*, **66**, 18.
Hokkanen, E., Iivanainen, M., Waltimo, O. (1969) 'Zu den neurologischen Manifestationen des Xeroderma pigmentosum.' *Deutsche Zeitschrift für Nervenheilkunde*, **196**, 206.
Huntley, C. J. (1967) 'Treatment of pseudoretardation from non-neurologic causes.' *Modern Treatment*, **4**, 747.
Iivanainen, M., Collan, R. (1968) 'Pneumoenkefalografian vaikutus likvorin tavallisimpiin laboratoriokokeisiin.' *Duodecim (Helsinki)*, **84**, 836.
—— Kostiainen, E. (1971) 'Changes in the electrophoretic pattern of the lumbar cerebrospinal fluid during fractional gas encephalography.' *Acta Neurologica Scandinavica*, **47**, 91.
—— Collan, R., Donner, M. (1970a) 'Adverse effects of pneumoencephalography performed under general anaesthesia in children.' *Annals of Clinical Research*, **2**, 71.
—— Gripenberg, U., Hongell, K. (1970b) 'Neurological aspects of mental retardation associated with chromosome aberrations.' *Acta Paediatrica Scandinavica*, **59**, Suppl. 206, 100.
Illig, R., Dumermuth, G., Prader, A. (1963) 'Das oculo-cerebro-renale Syndrom. Klinische, metabolische und electroencephalographische Befunde bei 3 fällen.' *Helvetica Paediatrica Acta*, **18**, 173.
Isherwood, I., Mawdsley, C., Ferguson, F. R. (1966) 'Pneumoencephalographic changes in boxers.' *Acta Radiologica (Diagnosis)*, **5**, 654.
Isler, W. (1971) *Acute Hemiplegias and Hemisyndromes in Childhood.* Clinics in Developmental Medicine, Nos. 41/42. London: S.I.M.P. with Heinemann Medical.
Jacobsen, P. A., Dupont, A. (1971) 'Chromosomes in severely mentally retarded patients with congenital malformations.' *in* Primrose, D. A. A. (Ed.) *Proceedings of the 2nd International Congress of the International Association for the Scientific Study of Mental Deficiency.* Warsaw: Polish Medical Publishers, p. 195.
Jedrysek, E., Rosenblatt, J. S., Wortis, J. (1968) 'Social class influences on intellectual development.' *in* Richards, B. W. (Ed.) *Proceedings of the 1st Congress of the International Association for the Scientific Study of Mental Deficiency.* Reigate, Surrey: Michael Jackson. p. 256.
Jeppsson, S. (1961) 'Echoencephalography. IV. The midline echo; an evaluation of its usefulness for diagnosing intracranial expansivities and an investigation into its sources.' *Acta Chirurgica Scandinavica*, **121**, Suppl. 272.
Kallio, N., Mäki, N. (1934) 'Suomen koulunuorison vasenkätisyydestä.' *Suomen Kasvatusopillisen Yhdistyksen Aikakauskirja*, **71**, 77.
Kantero, R.-L. (1971) Unpublished data from the Finnish Centre for Study in Child Growth and Development, University of Helsinki.
Klemetti, A. (1966) 'Relationship of selected environmental factors to pregnancy outcome and congenital malformations.' *Annales Paediatriae Fenniae*, Suppl. 26.
—— Saxén, L. (1967) 'Prospective versus retrospective approach in the search for environmental causes of malformations.' *American Journal of Public Health*, **57**, 2071.
—— —— (1970) *The Finnish Register of Congenital Malformations. Organization and Six Years of Experience.* Bulletin No. 9 of the Health Services Research Council of the National Board of Health in Finland.
Knudsen, P. A. (1958) 'Ventriklernes størrelseforhold i anatomisk normale hjerner fra voksne mennesker.' *Thesis*, Copenhagen.
Koch. G. (1966) 'Phakomatosen.' *in* Becker, P. E. (Ed.) *Humangenetik, Band V/I.* Stuttgart: Georg Thieme. p. 34.
Koch, R. (1966) 'Mental retardation: an important public health problem.' *Journal of the American Physiotherapy Association*, **46**, 745.
Kruse, F., Schaetz, G., (1935) 'Autoptisch kontrollierte Encephalogramme.' *in Abhandlung der Kinderheilkunde, Heft* 37. Berlin: Karger.
Laitinen, L. (1956) 'Craniosynostosis. Premature fusion of the cranial sutures.' *Annales Paediatriae Fenniae.* **2**, Suppl. 6.
Lajtha, A. (Ed.) (1972) *Handbook of Neurochemistry, Volume VII: Pathological Chemistry of the Nervous System.* London and New York: Plenum Press.
Lamy, M., Frezal, J., Rey, J., Larsen, C. (1962) 'Etudes metaboliques du syndrome de Lowe.' *Revue Francaise d'Etudes Cliniques et Biologiques*, **7**, 271.

Langdon Down, J. (1886) 'Observations on an ethnic classification of idiots.' *Clinical Lectures and Reports of the London Hospital*, **3**, 259.

Larsen, E. J. (1931) 'A neurologic study on 1000 mental defectives.' *Acta Psychiatrica et Neurologica Scandinavica*, **6**, 37.

Lejeune, J., Gautier, M., Turpin, R. (1959) 'Etudes des chromosomes somatiques de neuf enfants mongoliens.' *Comptes Rendus Hebdomadaires des Séances de l'Academie des Sciences*, **248**, 1721.

Leksell, L. (1955/56) 'Echoencephalography. I. Detection of intracranial complications following head injury.' *Acta Chirurgica Scandinavica*, **110**, 301.

Lelong, M., Satgé, P. (1962) 'Etiologia de las encefalopatias crónicas infantiles. Ensayo de clasificación cronológica.' *Revista Cubana de Pediatria*, **34**, 95.

Levinson, A. (1947) 'Pneumoencephalography in mentally deficient children.' *American Journal of Mental Deficiency*, **52**, 1.

Liesmaa, M. (1972) 'Congenital cataract and ectopia lentis. An anlaysis of 152 patients treated in 1943-1967.' *Acta Ophthalmologica*, **50**, Suppl. 112.

Lindgren, E. (1954) 'Röntgenologie.' *in* Olivecrona, H., Tönnis, W. (Eds.) *Handbuch der Neurochirurgie*. Berlin: Springer.

Little, W. J. (1861) 'On the influence of abnormal parturition, difficult labours, premature birth, and asphyxia neonatorum, on the mental and physical condition of the child, especially in relation to deformities.' *Transactions of the Obstetrical and Gynaecological Society of London*, **3**, 293.

Lodin, H. (1968) 'Size and development of the cerebral ventricular system in childhood.' *Acta Radiologica (Diagnosis)*, **7**, 385.

Löfgren, L. (1937) 'Über die Anthropologie der Bewohner von Uusimaa.' *Annales Academiae Scientiarum Fennicae,A*, **47**, (4).

Lorber, J., Zachary, R. B. (1968) 'Primary congenital hydrocephalus. Long-term results of controlled therapeutic trial.' *Archives of Disease in Childhood*, **43**, 516.

Lumio, J. S., Piirainen, H., Paljakka, P. (1966) 'Marriages between the deaf and hereditary deafness in Finland.' *Acta Oto-Laryngologica*, **62**, 265.

McAfee, J. G., Fueger, C. F., Stern, H. S., Wagner, H. N., Migita, T. (1964) 'Tc^{99m} pertechnetate for brain scanning.' *Journal of Nuclear Medicine* **5**, 811.

McDonald, A. (1967) *Children of Very Low Birth Weight. A Survey of 1128 Children with a Birth Weight of 4lb (1800g) or Less. Research Monograph No. 1.* London: Spastics Society with Heinemann Medical.

MacGillivray, R. C. (1967) 'Cutis verticis gyrata and mental retardation.' *Scottish Medical Journal*, **12**, 450.

MacKinnon, I. L., Kennedy, J. A., Davies, J. V. (1956) 'Estimation of skull capacity from roentgenologic measurements.' *American Journal of Roentgenology*, **76**, 303.

McLean, W. T., Manfredi, H. M. (1962) 'Roentgen skull abnormalities in mental deficiency.' *American Journal of Diseases of Children*, **103**, 140.

Mader, A. (1923) 'Encephalographische Erfahrungen im Säuglingsalter.' *Medizinische Klinik*, **19**, 1427.

Malamud, N. (1954) 'Recent trends in classification of neuropathological findings in mental deficiency.' *American Journal of Mental Deficiency*, **58**, 438.

—— Garoutte, B. (1954) 'Pneumoencephalography in children with mental defect and/or cerebral palsy.' *American Journal of Diseases of Children*, **87**, 16.

—— Itabashi, H. H., Castor, J., Messinger, H. B. (1964) 'An etiologic and diagnostic study of cerebral palsy. A preliminary report.' *Journal of Pediatrics*, **65**, 270.

Martin, R., Saller, K. (1957) *Lehrbuch der Anthropologie, Band I, dritte Auflage.* Stuttgart: Georg Fischer.

Matson, D. D. (1965) 'Intracranial aneurysms in childhood.' *Journal of Neurosurgery*, **23**, 578.

Mäurer, H. (1939) 'Über encephalographische Befunde bei Schwachsinnigen (unter besonderer berücksichtigung des erblichen Schwachsinns).' *Medizinische Welt*, **13**, 699.

Melchior, J. C. (1961) 'Pneumoencephalography in atrophic brain lesions in infancy and childhood.' *Acta Paediatrica (Uppsala)*, **50**, Suppl. 127.

Meyer, J.-E. (1949) 'Zur Ätiologie und Pathogenese des fetalen und frühkindlichen Cerebralschadens.' *Zeitschrift für Kinderheilkunde*, **67**, 123.

Miribel, J., Nieto, M., Favel, P. (1963) 'The value of simple radiography of the skull in epilepsy.' *Epilepsia*, **4**, 261.

Moniz, E. (1927) 'L'encéphalographie artérielle, son importance dans la localisation des tumeurs cérébrales.' *Revue Neurologique*, **2**, 72.

Moorhead, P. S., Nowell, R. C., Mellman, W. J., Battins, D. M., Hungerford, D. A. (1960) 'Chromosome preparations of leucocytes cultured from human peripheral blood.' *Experimental Cell Research*, **20**, 613.

Mosier, H. D., Grossman, H. J., Dingman, H. F. (1965) 'Physical growth in mental defectives.' *Pediatrics*, **36**, 465.

Nelson, T. R. (1955) 'A clinical study of pre-eclampsia. Part I.' *Journal of Obstetrics and Gynaecology of the British Empire*, **62**, 48.

Nielsen, R., Petersen, O., Thygesen, P., Willanger, R. (1966a) 'Encephalographic ventricular atrophy. Relationships between size of ventricular system and intellectual impairment.' *Acta Radiologica (Diagnosis)*, **4**, 240.

—— —— —— —— (1966b) 'Encephalographic cortical atrophy. Relationships to ventricular atrophy and intellectual impairment.' *Acta Radiologica (Diagnosis)*, **4**, 437.

Nieman, E. A. (1961) 'The electroencephalogram in congenital hypothyroidism: a study of 10 cases.' *Journal of Neurology, Neurosurgery and Psychiatry*, **24**, 50.

O'Connor, N., Tizard, J. (1956) *The Social Problems of Mental Deficiency*. London: Pergamon.

O'Gorman, G. (1967) *The Nature of Childhood Autism*. London: Butterworth.

Øster, J. (1968) *Det Andsvage Barn. 2nd edn.* Copenhagen: Munksgaard.

Ounsted, C., Lindsay, J., Norman, R. (1966) *Biological Factors in Temporal Lobe Epilepsy*. Clinics in Developmental Medicine, No. 22. London: Spastics Society with Heinemann Medical.

Paine, R. S., Oppé, T. E. (1966) *Neurological Examination of Children*. Clinics in Developmental Medicine, Nos. 20/21. London: Spastics Society with Heinemann Medical.

Palo, J. (1966) 'Eräiden aineenvaihduntahäiriöiden esiintyminen keskushermoston kehitysvauriotapauksissa. Tutkimus 2177 suomalaisesta vajaamielisestä henkilöstä.' *Thesis*, Helsinki.

—— (1967) 'Prevalence of phenylketonuria and some other metabolic disorders among mentally retarded patients in Finland.' *Acta Neurologica Scandinavica*, **43**, 573.

—— Iivanainen, M. (1971) 'The cutis verticis gyrata and mental retardation syndrome in a 4-year-old boy.' *Acta Paediatrica Scandinavica*, **60**, 346.

—— Mattson, K. (1970) 'Eleven new cases of aspartylglucosaminuria.' *Journal of Mental Deficiency Research*, **14**, 168.

—— Lydecken, K., Kivalo, E. (1966) 'Etiological aspects of mental deficiency in autopsied patients.' *American Journal of Mental Deficiency*, **71**, 401.

—— Iivanainen, N., Blomqvist, K., Pesonen, S. (1970) 'Aetiological aspects of the cutis verticis gyrata and mental retardation syndrome.' *Journal of Mental Deficiency Research*, **14**, 33.

—— Savolainen, H., Iivanainen, M. (1973) 'Free aminoacids and carbohydrates in the cerebrospinal fluid of 305 mentally retarded patients: a screening study.' *Journal of Mental Deficiency Research*, **17**, 139.

Pendergrass, E. P., Schaeffer, J. P., Hodes, P. J. (1957) *The Head and Neck in Roentgen Diagnosis, Vol. 1., 2nd edn.* Oxford: Blackwell.

Penrose, L. S. (1938) *A Clinical and Genetic Study of 1280 Cases of Mental Defect*. M.R.C. Special Report Series, No. 229. London: H.M.S.O.

—— (1963a) *The Biology of Mental Defect. 3rd edn.* London: Sidgwick and Jackson.

—— (1963b) 'Finger-prints, palms and chromosomes.' *Nature*, **197**, 933.

—— Loesch, D. (1971) 'Classification of normal and abnormal dermatoglyphics.' *in* Primrose, D. A. A. (Ed.) *Proceedings of the 2nd Congress of the International Association for the Scientific Study of Mental Deficiency*. Warsaw: Polish Medical Publishers. p. 355.

Pitt, D., Roboz, P. (1965) 'A survey of 782 cases of mental deficiency.' *Journal of Mental Deficiency Research*, **9**, 4.

Polani, P. E. (1967) 'Chromosome anomalies and the brain.' *Guy's Hospital Reports*, **116**, 865.

Pozsonyi, J., Lobb, H. (1967) 'Growth in mentally retarded children.' *Journal of Pediatrics*, **71**, 865.

Prechtl, H. F. R. (1967) 'Neurological sequelae of prenatal and perinatal complications.' *British Medical Journal*, **4**, 763.

Pryor, H. B., Thelander, H. E. (1967) 'Growth deviations in handicapped children. An anthropometric study.' *Clinical Pediatrics*, **6**, 501.

Rauhala, U. (1966) '*Suomalaisen yhteiskunnan sosiaalinen kerrostuneisuus*. Porvoo—Helsinki: WSOY.

Richards, B. W. (1963) 'Mental retardation: methods of diagnosis and some recently described syndromes.' *Canadian Medical Association Journal*, **89**, 1024.

Robertson, E. G. (1957) *Pneumoencephalography*. Springfield, Ill.: C. C Thomas.

Roboz, P., Pitt, D. (1968a) 'Studies on 782 cases of mental deficiency. Part I.' *Australian Paediatric Journal*, **4**, 79.

—— —— (1968b) 'Studies on 782 cases of mental deficiency. Part II.' *Australian Paediatric Journal*, **4**, 260.

—— —— (1969a) 'Studies on 782 cases of mental deficiency. Part III.' *Australian Paediatric Journal*, **5**, 38.

—— —— (1969b) 'Studies on 782 cases of mental deficiency. Part IV.' *Australian Paediatric Journal*, **5**, 137.

—— —— (1970) 'Studies on 782 cases of mental deficiency, Part V.' *Australian Paediatric Journal*, **6**, 185.

Rose, D. E., Rittmanic P. A. (1968) 'Evoked response tests with mentally retarded.' *Archives of Otolaryngology*, **88**, 495.

Salomonsen, L., Eek, S., Skatvedt, M. (1957) 'Pneumoencephalographic findings in cerebral palsy, epilepsy and oligophrenia.' *Annnales Paediatriae Fenniae*, **3**, 602.

Saxén, L., Härö, S. (1964) 'Vastasyntyneiden epämuodostumat Suomessa.' *Duodecim (Helsinki)*, **80**, 257.

Schmidt, H. (1966) 'Main principles in disturbed development of the skull. Radiological investigations.' *Acta Radiologica (Diagnosis)*, **5**, 68.

Scholz, B., Eggers, H., Külz, J., Wagner, K.-D., Kyank, H. (1967) 'Zur körperlich-psychischen Entwicklung von kindern gestosekranker Mütter.' *Geburtshilfe und Frauenheilkunde*, **27**, 749.

Schuleman, I. H. (1953) 'Review of encephalograms done over a five year period.' *Diseases of the Nervous System*, **14**, 355.

Seppäläinen, A.-M. (1969) 'Objektiv hörselundersökning hos utvecklingsstörda.' *Nordisk Medicin*, **82**, 1171.

—— Kivalo, E. (1967) 'EEG findings and epilepsy in Down's syndrome.' *Journal of Mental Deficiency Research*, **11**, 116.

Sjögren, I. (1965) 'Echo-ventriculography in infantile hydrocephalus. A preliminary report.' *Acta Neurologica Scandinavica*, **41**, Suppl. 13, 13.

Sjögren, I., Bergström, K., Lodin, H. (1968) 'Echoencephalography in infants and children: comparison with cerebral pneumography in measuring ventricular size.' *Acta Radiologica (Diagnosis)*, **7**, Suppl. 278.

Smith, H. V., Crothers, B. (1950) 'Subdural fluid as a consequence of pneumoencephalography.' *Pediatrics*, **5**, 375.

Spitz, E. B., Adamson, W. C., Noe, W. L. (1962) 'Criteria for pneumoencephalography in differential diagnostic study of mental subnormality.' *American Journal of Mental Deficiency*, **66**, 561.

Spitzer, R., Quilliam, R. L. (1958) 'Observations in congenital anomalies in teeth and skull in two groups of mental defectives (A comparative study).' *British Journal of Radiology*, **31**, 596.

Stadler, H. (1961) 'The EEG in phenylketonuria.' *Annales Paediatrici*, **197**, 429.

Stein, Z., Susser, M. (1963) 'The social distribution of mental retardation.' *American Journal of Mental Deficiency*, **57**, 811.

Suzuki, J., Takaku, A. (1969) 'Cerebrovascular "moyamoya" disease. Disease showing abnormal net-like vessels in base of brain.' *Archives of Neurology*, **20**, 288.

Szulman, A. E. (1965) 'Chromosomal aberrations in spontaneous human abortions.' *New England Journal of Medicine*, **272**, 811.

Takkunen, R.-L., Telkkä, A. (1964) 'Finnische anthropometrische Tabellen für Vaterschafts-Untersuchungen.' *Annales Academiae Scientiarum Fennicae*, A5, 105.

Taveras, J. M. (1969) 'Multiple progressive intracranial arterial occlusions: a syndrome of children and young adults.' *American Journal of Roentgenology*, **106**, 235.

Taylor, D. C. (1969) 'Differential rates of cerebral maturation between sexes and between hemispheres. Evidence from epilepsy.' *Lancet*, **2**, 140.

Telkkä, A. (1952) 'Anthropologische Untersuchung von Bewohnern der Landschaft Häme.' *Annales Academiae Scientiarum Fennicae*, A5, 30.

Terplan, K. L., Sandberg, A. A., Aceto, T. (1966) 'Structural anomalies in the cerebellum in association with trisomy.' *Journal of the American Medical Association*, **197**, 557.

Thomas, D. H. H. (1957) 'A survey of mental deficiency problems in the United States of America.' *Journal of Mental Deficiency Research*, **1**, 33.

Till, K., Hoare, R. D. (1962) 'Cerebral angiography in investigation of acute hemiplegia in childhood.' *in* Bax, M., Mitchell, R. (Eds.) *Acute Hemiplegia in Childhood*. Clinics in Developmental Medicine, No. 6. London: National Spastics Society with Heinemann. p. 69.

Tizard, J. (1970) 'The role of social institutions in the causation, prevention and alleviation of mental retardation.' *in* Haywood, H. C. (Ed.) *Social-Cultural Aspects of Mental Retardation*. New York: Appleton Century Crofts. p. 281.

Tredgold, A. F. (1908) *A Textbook of Mental Deficiency*. London: Ballière, Tindall & Cox.

Truffi, G. (1929) 'Intorno alla cutis verticis gyrata.' *Archivio Italiano di Dermatologia, Venereologia e Sessuologia*, **4**, 451.

Tuuteri, L., Donner, M., Eklund, J., Leisti, L., Rinne, A.-L., Strandström, G., Ylppö, L. (1967) 'Incidence of cerebral palsy in Finland.' *Annales Paediatriae Fenniae*, **13**, 41.

Uchida, I. A., Soltan, H. C. (1963) 'Evaluation of dermatoglyphics in medical genetics.' *Pediatric Clinics of North America*, **10**, 409.

University of Helsinki (1952) *Statistics of the Living Births from the Departments I and II of Obstetrics*.

Vannas, S., Raivio, T. (1963) 'Sokeuden syistä Suomessa.' *Duodecim (Helsinki)*, **79**, 850.

Vesterdal, J., Foght-Nielsen, K. E., Thomsen, G. (1954) 'Pneumo-encephalography in a pediatric department; review of 214 cases with special reference to brain atrophy.' *Acta Paediatrica (Uppsala)*, **43**, 120.

Walton, J. N. (Ed.) (1970) *Disorders of Voluntary Muscle*, 2nd edn. Edinburgh: Churchill Livingstone.

Warburg, M. (1963) 'Diseases of the eye among mental defectives.' *Acta Ophthalmologica*, **41**, 157.

—— (1966) 'Behovet for oftalmologisk service på en institution for åndssvage.' *Ugeskrift for Laeger*, **128**, 427.

Weintraub, W. (1953) 'Etude des variations de la capacité des ventricules cérébraux.' *Encéphale*, **42**, 521.

West, K. A. (1967) 'Correlations between ultrasonic and roentgenologic findings in infantile hydrocephalus.' *Acta Paediatrica Scandinavica*, **56**, 27.

Wildenskov, H. O. (1934) *Investigations into the Causes of Mental Deficiency*. Copenhagen: Munksgaard.

Windle, W. F. (1968) 'Brain damage at birth.' *Journal of the American Medical Association*, **206**, 1967.

World Health Organization (1948, 1968) *The International Classification of Diseases*. Geneva: W.H.O.

Wulf, H., Manzke, H. (1965) 'Zur Prognose der Asphyxia neonatorum. (Katamnesen von 107 asphyktisch geborenen Kindern.)' *Zeitschrift für Geburthilfe und Frauenheilkunde*, **164**, 300.

Yakovlev, P. I. (1960) 'Anatomy of the human brain and the problem of mental retardation.' *in* Bowman, P. W., Mautner, H. V. (Eds.) *Mental Retardation. Proceedings of the 1st International Conference*. New York: Grune & Stratton. p. 1.

Yannet, H. (1945) 'Diagnostic classification of patients with mental deficiency.' *American Journal of Diseases of Children*, **70**, 83.

—— (1956) 'Mental deficiency.' *Advances in Pediatrics*, **8**, 217.

Zapella, M. (1964) 'Postural reactions in 100 children with cerebral palsy and mental handicap.' *Developmental Medicine and Child Neurology*, **6**, 475.

Zaremba, J. (1971) 'Phacomatoses among children with low-grade mental retardation.' *in* Primrose, D. A. A. (Ed.) *Proceedings of the 2nd Congress of the International Association for the Scientific Study of Mental Deficiency*. Warsaw: Polish Medical Publishers, p. 361.

Name Index

CORRIGENDA

Page 3, line 27. For 'minor variations' read 'oligophrenia simplex'.

Page 6, line 11. For 'Eastman and Jancar 1968' read 'Eastham and Jancar 1968'

Page 30, line 3. For 'Saxén and Klemetti 1970' read 'Klemetti and Saxén 1970'.

Page 40, Table XIV. For 'prevalence' read 'frequency'.

Page 41, line 1. For 'prevalence' read 'frequency'.